Narrative of the Life of Frederick Douglass

Narrative of the Life of Frederick Douglass

An American Slave.

Written by Himself.

And Selected Essays and Speeches

FREDERICK DOUGLASS

Introduction and Notes by
Dale Edwyna Smith

Barnes & Noble

NEW YORK

SIGNATURE EDITIONS

BARNES & NOBLE

NEW YORK

387 Park Avenue South
New York, NY 10016

Introduction, Annotations, and Further Reading
© 2012 by Sterling Publishing Co., Inc.

This 2012 edition published by Sterling Publishing Co., Inc.

ISBN 978-1-4351-3664-9 (print format)
ISBN 978-1-4351-4118-6 (ebook)

For information about custom editions, special sales,
and premium and corporate purchases,
please contact Sterling Special Sales at 800-805-5489 or
specialsales@sterlingpublishing.com

Manufactured in the United States of America

4 6 8 10 9 7 5 3

www.sterlingpublishing.com

CONTENTS

THE LIFE AND TIMES OF FREDERICK DOUGLASS

1818   Douglass gave 1818 as the approximate year of his birth, remarking that slaves knew as much about their date of birth as did horses. He was born in Maryland.

1825   Douglass' mother, with whom he had rarely been permitted to spend time, dies.

1826   Douglass' owner Sophia Auld begins to teach him to read; the lessons are stopped abruptly by her husband, who feels that literacy makes blacks unfit for slavery.

1829   David Walker's *Appeal,* a forceful critique of American slavery, is published by its free black author.

1829   Douglass apprentices on the Baltimore docks to learn the trade of caulking ships; taking advantage of the urban environment, he begins to plan escapes.

1831   Literate slave preacher Nat Turner leads slaves in a rebellion in Southampton County, Virginia, prompting the Virginia legislature to debate whether to end slavery in the state.

1833   Douglass is sent to spend one year with slave-breaker Edward Covey.

1836   The escape plan of Douglass and four other slaves is revealed before it can be implemented; Douglass had used his ability to read and write to forge passes for his companions.

1837   In Baltimore, Douglass meets Anna Murray, a free black woman, who will later become his wife.

1838   Perhaps with assistance from his future wife, who may have helped with forged papers and disguises, Douglass escapes from slavery and runs away to the free state of New York; in freedom, he names himself anew, and from that point on is known to history as "Frederick Douglass."

1839   Douglass begins to attend anti-slavery meetings and meets *Liberator* editor William Lloyd Garrison; it is Garrison who begins to urge Douglass to use his gift of language to speak publicly against slavery.

1841   Douglass speaks publicly for the first time against slavery at an anti-slavery convention in Nantucket, Massachusetts.

1844   Douglass meets fellow former slave abolitionist Sojourner Truth at the Northampton Association of Education and Industry, a utopian community in Northampton, Massachusetts.

1845   *Narrative of the Life of Frederick Douglass, An American Slave* is published; because publication of his life story makes Douglass' fugitive status public, he and his wife move to England, where he continues to lecture against slavery.

1846   British abolitionists raise funds and pay Douglass' former owner, making Douglass legally free.

1847   Douglass and his wife return to the United States.

1847   Douglass establishes *The North Star,* an anti-slavery newspaper.

1848   Douglass attends the first US women's suffrage convention, in Seneca Falls, New York, and supports *The Declaration of Sentiments*' demand for women's suffrage.

1850   The Compromise of 1850 authorizes a strict fugitive slave law.

1851   Douglass ends his alliance with William Lloyd Garrison because of a disagreement over anti-slavery philosophy.

1852   Douglass delivers his oration "What to the Slave is the Fourth of July?" in Rochester, New York; he delivers this masterful critique of slavery using political, economic, cultural, and religious examples of the hypocrisy of celebrating "independence."

1853   *The Heroic Slave,* Douglass' only known work of fiction, is published.

1855   *My Bondage and My Freedom,* an updated version of the *Narrative,* is published; this edition includes Douglass' scathing "Letter to his Old Master."

1857   The Supreme Court rules that the slave Dred Scott is not a citizen and does not have standing to sue for his freedom based on his residence in free territory; the Court states that the founding fathers had never intended the rights and privileges set forth in the Constitution to apply to Africans or their descendants.

1859   Douglass begins publishing *Douglass' Monthly.*

1860   Douglass' daughter Annie dies.

        Douglass announces his support for Republican Party presidential candidate Abraham Lincoln.

1861   After the Civil War begins, Douglass becomes an advisor to President Lincoln.

1863   After the Emancipation Proclamation authorizes formation of free black Union regiments, Douglass becomes a recruiter for the Massachusetts 54th Colored Infantry, in which two of his sons serve.

1865   Douglass joins the battle for black suffrage rights.

        On December 6, the Thirteenth Amendment is ratified.

1868   On July 9, the Fourteenth Amendment is ratified.

1870   On February 3, the Fifteenth Amendment is ratified.

        Douglass becomes editor of the *New National Era* newspaper.

1874   Douglass is appointed president of the Freedman's Savings and Trust Company, a bank providing financial services to freed slaves.

1876   Douglass delivers an oration in honor of the installation of the Freedmen's Monument in Washington, DC; his addressing those assembled as "fellow citizens" underscores the success of the long struggle of slaves for freedom.

1877   President Rutherford B. Hayes appoints Douglass US Marshal for the District of Columbia.

1881   President James A. Garfield appoints Douglass recorder of deeds for the District of Columbia.

        Douglass publishes *Life and Times of Frederick Douglass, Written by Himself,* the last of his three autobiographies.

1882   Douglass' wife, Anna, dies.

1884   Douglass marries his secretary, Helen Pitts, a white woman who had been active in the women's rights movement.

1889   President Benjamin Harrison appoints Douglass US Minister Resident and Consul-General to Haiti.

1892   Douglass publishes a revised edition of *Life and Times of Frederick Douglass, Written by Himself.*

1894   Douglass publishes an anti-lynching pamphlet, *The Lessons of the Hour.*

1895   Frederick Douglass dies on February 20.

INTRODUCTION

NARRATIVE OF THE LIFE OF FREDERICK DOUGLASS, AN AMERICAN SLAVE (1845) is a cautionary tale that reminds readers in the starkest terms of the origins of the United States, a nation that, while supposedly committed to individual liberty, constructed a political and economic foundation in part dependent on chattel slavery, a system in which people were legally defined as property. Douglass' story reveals the successful transformation of a slave into a free person, as well as the education of a citizen. His life symbolized the possibility of transcending literal and figurative slavery and embracing the full potential of the American experiment. Even in his 1841 debut as an anti-slavery speaker, Douglass was well on his way to becoming what fellow black abolitionist James McCune Smith described as "a Representative American man."[1] The first of three autobiographies, Frederick Douglass' *Narrative* provided graphic descriptions of the inner workings of American slavery and became an invaluable weapon in the growing abolitionist movement to end slavery.

Douglass estimated the year of his birth as about 1818, although he admitted that "slaves know as little of their ages as horses know of theirs." A white man who may have been Douglass' owner was thought to be his father, but Douglass reported definite and specific biographical information about his mother, Harriet Bailey, and his maternal grandparents, Isaac and Betty Bailey. In the *Narrative*, Douglass reminds the reader of the law that defined a slave woman's offspring as slaves, exempting white fathers from personal or legal responsibility while increasing their slave holdings. The labyrinthine genealogies that resulted frequently led to the selling of slave siblings to forestall abuse of the black slave by free white siblings or the slave owner's wife. Other than his mother's name, Douglass knew very little about her, because their owner separated them when Douglass was an infant, and his mother died when he was about seven years old. This early, wrenching removal of his only known parent disrupted Douglass' relationship with his two sisters and one brother. Although Douglass' story—and that of the majority of escaped slave memoirs—chronicles the evolution of slave to free manhood, the inclusion of specific details about female members of his family ironically provides invaluable insights into definitions of femininity and womanhood for black women within slave communities.

When he was seven or eight years old, Douglass was moved from rural Talbot County, Maryland, to Baltimore, where he was greeted by his new mistress, Mrs. Auld, a kind woman who initiated Douglass' formal education by teaching him to read. When her husband found out, he ordered her to stop at once as:

Learning will *spoil* the best nigger in the world . . . He would at once become unmanageable, and of no value to his master . . . It would make him discontented and unhappy.

Douglass overheard this damning harangue, which he reported revealed the secret of the white slave power and the key to his own freedom. In the *Narrative,* he credited both the kindness of his mistress and the intransigent opposition of his master for inspiring him to learn to read at all costs. The shrewd strategy Douglass employed to gain access to books was to develop the friendship of white boys his age, some of whom he bribed with bread he had been given at home. By the age of twelve, he had begun to study texts that included philosophies and debates about slavery and freedom. It was in this way that Douglass discovered the word *abolition,* a word whispered even in print.

But Douglass' education was two-pronged: part came from literacy and books, the rest from the variety and constant revelation of new things available in an urban setting. Working with Irish dock workers, Douglass was told that if he ran away to the north, he would be free; and he began to form a plan based on expanding his education from reading to writing. Again, Douglass enlisted unknowing white boys by playing on their vanity, first claiming to be able to write better than they. This was supplemented by secretly practicing penmanship in his young master's school copybooks. However, Douglass' long-range plan to run away was diverted when he was moved back to the country. About fourteen years old at the time, Douglass lamented his failure to run away before being taken from the city, which provided an easier escape route than from a rural farm. But Douglass' time in the city—and doubtless, the knowledge he harbored that he could read and write—had indeed unfitted him for the life of a slave.

The adolescent Douglass emanated a sense of self that his owner found unacceptable and set about to "break." The graphic description of the adolescent Douglass being "broken" is interwoven in a pattern of beatings as chastisement or "correction" of slaves throughout the *Narrative*. Edward Covey, a poor white farmer with a local reputation as an effective "nigger-breaker," was given the task of breaking Frederick Douglass, who arrived at Covey's on January 1, 1833. Douglass lived at Covey's farm for one year and received his first beating within the first week, then almost a beating every week for the next six months. Douglass recounted that he considered himself broken by Covey, though a spark of hope remained and kept him from killing Covey, or himself. After one of his many beatings, Douglass walked the seven miles back to his owner's farm to ask for his protection; his owner told him that he had been hired to Covey for one year and must return to him.

Douglass marked this event as a reclaiming of his "manhood," which he also associated with a renewed "determination to be free." He wrote in the *Narrative*:

> I did not hesitate to let it be known of me, that the white man who expected to succeed in whipping, must also succeed in killing me.

Douglass was a slave for another four years after the incident at Covey's, and although he engaged in a number of fights, he was never whipped again. The *Narrative* delineates how the crucible of slavery produced an individual slave driven by an incontrovertible belief in human liberty despite also fracturing and fragmenting the slave community. Continuous disruptions of the family or kin bond were accomplished by selling off slaves and a deliberate effort at psychological and physical abuse was caused by frequent whippings based on an arbitrary, and therefore unknowable, catalog of offenses; thus, the administration of the whippings was always a shock.

In January 1834, Douglass was moved to the house of William Freeland, about three miles away, where he soon assembled a group of slaves and taught them reading and writing under the guise of a Sunday School at the home of a free man of color. (As with a number of the people who helped him along the way, Douglass did not reveal the man's identity in order to protect him from retaliation for aiding and abetting a slave to run away; or in effect, for stealing slave property.) Despite Douglass' description of a loyal community of slaves at Freeland's, when Freeland renewed the contract for his hire for another year (1835), Douglass began to plan his escape; even a good master was not acceptable. Having conceived an escape route by water through the Chesapeake Bay, Douglass created written passes for himself and his comrades. His anxiety increased as the date of departure approached; he knew that if he did not at least attempt to escape, he would be admitting, as he wrote in the *Narrative*, that he was "fit only to be [a] slave[s]." But the plan was betrayed, and blame for the escape plan was pinned on Douglass.

Douglass continued to be tormented by his desire for freedom, although torn by the realization that escaping slavery would mean leaving loved ones behind. But somehow Douglass reconciled those losses, and on September 3, 1838, made it to the free state of New York using means he did not divulge. He was apologetic but realistic when he wrote that there were details he must not reveal, even if such information contained critical details about the institution of slavery. Those details, he knew, would provide damaging intelligence that could be used by the slave owners. Finally a free man, Douglass was nevertheless lonely and isolated, unable to trust anyone white or black, lest he find himself returned to slavery. Befriended by a man in the anti-slavery movement, Douglass was shortly reunited with his future wife, a free woman of color, Anna Murray.[2] The two married, and made arrangements to settle in New Bedford, Massachusetts, where Douglass could practice his skill as a ship caulker. Although his mother had named him "Frederick Augustus Washington" and he briefly went by the names Frederick Bailey, Stanley, and Frederick Johnson, it was in New Bedford that the name Douglass was chosen for him, based on a character in a book by the owner of the house he first stayed in.

Freedom set well with the new Mr. Frederick Douglass. He discovered a free community of color, some of whose members were also escaped slaves. He experienced racial discrimination when looking for work, but ultimately found work as a laborer. Douglass happily admitted that the "new, dirty, and hard work" was a pleasure because he was at last his own master. Shortly after that, Douglass came across the abolitionist newspaper *The Liberator*, edited by William Lloyd Garrison. The newspaper's discussion of anti-slavery principles ignited a passion in Douglass, although initially he hesitated to speak at convention meetings because he felt what he wanted to say was better said by others. In August 1841, Douglass was finally persuaded to speak for the anti-slavery cause, and it gave him a new level of freedom. He went on a round of speaking tours to generate support for the abolitionist movement, often accompanied by Garrison, whose preface to the *Narrative* described Douglass as a boon to the cause of "universal liberty" and "the land of his birth." This effusive praise came in response to Douglass' debut speech at an 1841 Massachusetts anti-slavery convention, where Garrison was inspired by Douglass' "wit, . . . strength of reasoning, and fluency of language." A fugitive from the peculiar justice of slave law, Douglass' very presence at the convention condemned not only slavery, but also the disturbing alliance of "corrupt . . . law, government, and churches that sustained the system."[3] Garrison suggested that the Maryland brand of slavery Douglass survived was less cruel than slavery in the Deep South, but he never let audiences forget the punishment inflicted on Douglass, mind and body.

Douglass' trenchant and persuasive analysis of the dilemma of a nation purportedly based on individual liberties but supported by chattel slavery created some doubt that either Douglass had not written the works that bore his name or was not what he claimed to be and had never been a slave.[4]

> At last the apprehended trouble came. People doubted if I had ever been a slave. They said I did not talk like a slave, look like a slave, nor act like a slave, and that they believed I had never been south of Mason and Dixon's line.[5]

To convince white audiences otherwise, Douglass had sometimes been encouraged to include "a *little* of the plantation manner of speech" because it was "not best that you seem too learned."

The *Narrative* contains a critique of American Christianity, with its vocal celebrities of the pulpit who defended slavery, owned slaves, or both. For Douglass, such hypocrisy chafed, and he challenged a society that seemed oblivious to the contradiction: While the South made consistent use of the Bible to support the moral validity of slavery, the North remained silent on the subject in the name of "peace." Suspecting he had offended some by his indictment of certain Christians, Douglass added an appendix to later editions of the *Narrative*, stating that he was not "an opponent of all religion"—only of "slaveholding religion"—and drew attention to the "widest possible difference" he discerned between "the Christianity of this land, and the Christianity of Christ." In fact, Douglass saw "no reason, but the most deceitful one, for calling the religion of this land Christianity" at all.

> We have man-stealers for ministers, women-whippers for missionaries, and cradle-plunderers for church members . . . He who sells my sister, for purposes of prostitution, stands forth as the pious advocate of purity. He who proclaims it a religious duty to read the Bible denies me the right of learning to read the name of the God who made me . . . We see the thief preaching against theft, and the adulterer against adultery. We have men sold to build churches . . .

The political philosophy of Frederick Douglass contributed to an evolving debate on American citizenship in the nineteenth century with Douglass supporting women's suffrage and the franchise for freed slaves after the Civil War, when he became an enthusiastic supporter of the Republican Party. His early ideas regarding equality in the body politic were not so much inchoate as lacking in clear historical contextual support; for example, Douglass' early vigorous support for the anti-slavery views of Garrison (i.e., the Constitution was a pro-slavery document and US citizens should refrain from voting because to do so would, in some manner, also support the continuation of the institution of slavery) cooled as Douglass came to believe that,

> . . . to abstain from voting, was to refuse to exercise a legitimate and powerful means for abolishing slavery; and that the Constitution of the United States not only contained no guarantees in favor of slavery, but . . . is . . . an anti-slavery instrument, demanding the abolition of slavery as a condition of its own existence . . . [6]

In 1851, Douglass broke with Garrison.

Although Douglass' *Narrative* is unique in some respects, it belongs to the genre within American history and literature as the "slave narrative"—a genre consisting of memoirs written by escaped slaves, which were often used as tools by the anti-slavery movement. Illustrative of the variety of forms of resistance to slavery by slaves themselves, the narratives have been referred to as "the first distinctively American literary genre."[7] Like Douglass' *Narrative*, the authenticity of slave memoirs was often vouchsafed by a preface or introduction by a known white abolitionist. Douglass was not the only former slave whose literacy and rhetorical skills made him an object of suspicion. Thus, the slave narrative provided evidence not only of the barbarity of slavery, but of the humanity of the slave; however, because the majority of such narratives were written by men, the triumph realized was one of reclaimed masculinity over and above humanity in general. The antebellum era is unique in that it produced slave narratives, which stand as an ironic monument both to American slavery as an institution and to the indomitable will of slaves who refused to surrender to that institution and used the forbidden tool of literacy to expand the parameters of American freedom.

Frederick Douglass was among a handful of escaped slaves who not only wrote narratives, but continued to write in freedom and to critique a society that condoned legally imposed social inequality. This edition includes eleven speeches and essays that Douglass produced after the *Narrative* was published, providing a window to his intellectual and political evolution between 1845 and 1876. The materials present a basic description of what American slavery was, especially from the perspective of the slave, and encompass a variety of critiques on slavery, including Douglass' 1852 exegesis of the Constitution ("What to the Slave is the Fourth of July?") and his 1876 oration at the dedication of Freedmen's Monument, during which he applied the scornful epithet "white man's President" to Abraham Lincoln, the man many viewed as the Great Emancipator. According to Douglass, Lincoln had been,

> . . . entirely devoted to the welfare of white men. He was ready and willing at any time . . . to deny, postpone and sacrifice the rights of humanity in the colored people to promote the welfare of the white people of this country. . . . He was ready to execute all the supposed constitutional guarantees of the United States Constitution in favor of the slave system. . . . He was willing to pursue, recapture, and send back the fugitive slave to his master, and to suppress a slave rising for liberty. . . . The race to which we belong were not the special objects of his consideration . . .

Although Douglass had broken with his mentor, William Lloyd Garrison, on just these points regarding the intent or ability of the Constitution to protect and defend the institution of slavery, in later years, it is clear he had second thoughts.

Frederick Douglass refused to accept that his place in life was as a slave, and he worked to change that condition first for himself and then for others. But Douglass' story is not only concerned with race-based slavery, so it is instructive that it not be limited to racialized critique; rather, the *Narrative* and Douglass' other writings are "American . . . for Americans, in the fullest sense of the idea."[8] Indeed, the *Narrative* has been compared to Benjamin Franklin's *Autobiography* (first published in its entirety in English in 1868), among others, as a requisite text on the evolution of American racial, cultural, and political identity. The *Narrative* eloquently analyzes the evolution of American chattel slavery and that of one man's movement from chattel to citizen.

Dale Edwyna Smith received her Ph.D. in the History of American Civilization from Harvard University. She has taught at St. Louis University, Washington University, College of the Holy Cross, Suffolk University, Tufts University, and is currently teaching at Bunker Hill Community College in Boston. She is the author of *The Slaves of Liberty: Freedom in Amite County, Mississippi, 1820–1868* and numerous articles and reviews.

PREFACE

IN THE MONTH OF AUGUST, 1841, I ATTENDED AN ANTI-SLAVERY convention in Nantucket, at which it was my happiness to become acquainted with FREDERICK DOUGLASS, the writer of the following Narrative.[1] He was a stranger to nearly every member of that body; but, having recently made his escape from the southern prison-house of bondage, and feeling his curiosity excited to ascertain the principles and measures of the abolitionists—of whom he had heard a somewhat vague description while he was a slave—he was induced to give his attendance, on the occasion alluded to, though at that time a resident in New Bedford.

Fortunate, most fortunate occurrence! Fortunate for the millions of his manacled brethren, yet panting for deliverance from their awful thraldom! Fortunate for the cause of Negro emancipation, and of universal liberty! Fortunate for the land of his birth, which he has already done so much to save and bless! Fortunate for a large circle of friends and acquaintances, whose sympathy and affection he has strongly secured by the many sufferings he has endured, by his virtuous traits of character, by his ever-abiding remembrance—fortunate for the multitudes, in various parts of our republic, whose minds he has enlightened on the subject of slavery, and who have been melted to tears by his pathos, or roused to virtuous indignation by his stirring eloquence against the enslavers of men! Fortunate for himself, as it at once brought him into the field of public usefulness, "gave the world assurance of a MAN," quickened the slumbering energies of his soul, and consecrated him to the great work of breaking the rod of the oppressor, and letting the oppressed go free!

I shall never forget his first speech at the convention—the extraordinary emotion it excited in my own mind—the powerful impression it created upon a crowded auditory, completely taken by surprise—the applause which followed from the beginning to the end of his felicitous remarks. I think I never hated slavery so intensely as at that moment; certainly, my perception of the enormous outrage which is inflicted by it, on the godlike nature of its victims, was rendered far more clear than ever. There stood one, in physical proportion and stature commanding and exact—in intellect richly endowed—in natural eloquence a prodigy—in soul manifestly "created but a little lower than the angels"—yet a slave, ay, a fugitive slave—trembling for his safety, hardly daring to believe that on the American soil, a single white person could be found who would befriend him at all hazards, for the love of God and humanity! Capable of high attainments as an intellectual and moral being—needing nothing but a comparatively small amount of cultivation to make him an ornament to society and a blessing to his race—by the law of the land, by the voice of the people, by the terms of the slave code, he was only a piece of property, a beast of burden, a chattel personal, nevertheless!

A beloved friend from New Bedford prevailed on Mr. DOUGLASS to address the convention: He came forward to the platform with a hesitancy and embarrassment, necessarily the attendants of a sensitive mind in such a novel position. After apologizing for his ignorance, and reminding the audience that slavery was a poor school for the human intellect and heart, he proceeded to narrate some of the facts in his own history as a slave, and in the course of his speech gave utterance to many noble thoughts and thrilling reflections. As soon as he had taken his seat, filled with hope and admiration, I rose, and declared that PATRICK HENRY, of revolutionary fame, never made a speech more eloquent in the cause of liberty, than the one we had just listened to from the lips of that hunted fugitive. So I believed at that time—such is my belief now. I reminded the audience of the peril which surrounded this self-emancipated young man at the North—even in Massachusetts, on the soil of the Pilgrim Fathers, among the descendants of revolutionary sires; and I appealed to them, whether they would ever allow him to be carried back into slavery—law or no law, constitution or no constitution. The response was unanimous and in thunder-tones—"NO!" "Will you succor and protect him as a brother-man—a resident of the old Bay States?" "YES!" shouted the whole mass, with an energy so startling, that the ruthless tyrants south of Mason and Dixon's line might almost have heard the mighty burst of feeling, and recognized it as the pledge of an invincible determination, on the part of those who gave it, never to betray him that wanders, but to hide the outcast, and firmly to abide the consequences.

It was at once deeply impressed upon my mind, that, if Mr. DOUG-LASS could be persuaded to consecrate his time and talents to the promotion of the anti-slavery enterprise, a powerful impetus would be given to it, and a stunning blow at the same time inflicted on northern prejudice against a colored complexion. I therefore endeavored to instill hope and courage into his mind, in order that he might dare to engage in a vocation so anomalous and responsible for a person in his situation; and I was seconded in this effort by warm-hearted friends, especially by the late General Agent of the Massachusetts Anti-Slavery Society, Mr. JOHN A. COLLINS, whose judgment in this instance entirely coincided with my own. At first, he could give no encouragement; with unfeigned diffidence, he expressed his conviction that he was not adequate to the performance of so great a task; the path marked out was wholly an untrodden one; he was sincerely apprehensive that he should do more harm than good. After much deliberation, however, he consented to make a trial; and ever since that period, he has acted as a lecturing agent, under the auspices either of the American or the Massachusetts Anti-Slavery Society. In labors he has been most abundant; and his success in combating prejudice, in gaining proselytes, in agitating the public mind, has far surpassed the most sanguine expectations that were raised at the commencement of his brilliant career. He has borne himself with gentleness and meekness, yet with true manliness of character. As a public speaker, he excels in pathos, wit, comparison, imitation, strength of reasoning, and fluency of language. There is in him that union of head and heart, which is indispensable to an enlightenment of the heads and a winning of the hearts of others. May his strength continue to be equal to his day! May he continue to "grow in grace, and in the knowledge of God," that he may be increasingly serviceable in the cause of bleeding humanity, whether at home or abroad!

It is certainly a very remarkable fact, that one of the most efficient advocates of the slave population, now before the public, is a fugitive slave, in the person of FREDERICK DOUGLASS; and that the free colored population of the United States are as ably represented by one of their own number, in the person of CHARLES LENOX REMOND, whose eloquent appeals have extorted the highest applause of multitudes on both sides of the Atlantic. Let the calumniators of the colored race despise themselves for their baseness and illiberality of spirit, and henceforth cease to talk of the natural inferiority of those who require nothing but time and opportunity to attain to the highest point of human excellence.

It may, perhaps, be fairly questioned, whether any other portion of the population of the earth could have endured the privations, sufferings and horrors of slavery, without having become more degraded in the scale of humanity than the slaves of African descent. Nothing has been left undone to cripple their intellects, darken their minds, debase their moral nature, obliterate all traces of their relationship to mankind; and yet how wonderfully they have sustained the mighty load of a most frightful bondage, under which they have been groaning for centuries! To illustrate the effect of slavery on the white man—to show that he has no powers of endurance, in such a condition, superior to those of his black brother—DANIEL O'CONNELL, the distinguished advocate of universal emancipation, and the mightiest champion of prostrate but not conquered Ireland, relates the following anecdote in a speech delivered by him in the Conciliation Hall, Dublin, before the Loyal National Repeal Association, March 31, 1845. "No matter," said Mr. O'CONNELL, "under what specious term it may disguise itself, slavery is still hideous. *It has a natural, an inevitable tendency to brutalize every noble faculty of man.* An American sailor, who was cast away on the shore of Africa, where he was kept in slavery for three years, was, at the expiration of that period, found to be imbruted and stultified—he had lost all reasoning power; and having forgotten his native language, could only utter some savage gibberish between Arabic and English, which nobody could understand, and which even he himself found difficulty in pronouncing. So much for the humanizing influence of THE DOMESTIC INSTITUTION!" Admitting this to have been an extraordinary case of mental deterioration, it proves at least that the white slave can sink as low in the scale of humanity as the black one.

Mr. DOUGLASS has very properly chosen to write his own Narrative, in his own style, and according to the best of his ability, rather than to employ some one else. It is, therefore, entirely his own production; and, considering how long and dark was the career he had to run as a slave—how few have been his opportunities to improve his mind since he broke his iron fetters—it is, in my judgment, highly creditable to his head and heart. He who can peruse it without a tearful eye, a heaving breast, an afflicted spirit—without being filled with an unutterable abhorrence of slavery and all its abettors, and animated with a determination to seek the immediate overthrow of that execrable system—without trembling for the fate of this country in the hands of a righteous God, who is ever on the side of the oppressed, and whose arm is not shortened that it cannot save—must have a flinty heart, and be qualified to act the part of a trafficker "in slaves and the souls of men." I am confident that it is essentially true in all its statements; that nothing has been set down in malice, nothing exaggerated, nothing drawn from the imagination; that it comes short of the reality, rather than overstates a single fact in regard to SLAVERY AS IT IS. The experience of FREDERICK DOUGLASS, as a slave, was not a peculiar one; his lot was not especially a hard one; his case may be regarded as a very fair specimen of the treatment of slaves in Maryland, in which State it is conceded that they are better fed and less cruelly treated than in Georgia, Alabama, or Louisiana. Many have suffered incomparably more, while very few on the plantations have suffered less, than himself. Yet how deplorable was his situation! What terrible chastisements were inflicted upon his person! What still more shocking outrages were perpetrated upon his mind! With all his noble powers and sublime aspirations, how like a brute was he treated, even by those professing to have the same mind in them that was in Christ Jesus! To what dreadful

liabilities was he continually subjected! How destitute of friendly coun-
sel and aid, even in his greatest extremities! How heavy was the
midnight of woe which shrouded in blackness the last ray of hope, and
filled the future with terror and gloom! What longings after freedom
took possession of his breast, and how his misery augmented, in proportion as he grew reflective and intelligent—thus demonstrating that
a happy slave is an extinct man! How he thought, reasoned, felt, under
the lash of the driver, with the chains upon his limbs! What perils he
encountered in his endeavors to escape from his horrible doom! And
how signal have been his deliverance and preservation in the midst of
a nation of pitiless enemies!

This Narrative contains many affecting incidents, many passages
of great eloquence and power; but I think the most thrilling one of
them all is the description DOUGLASS gives of his feelings, as he stood
soliloquizing respecting his fate, and the chances of his one day being
a freeman, on the banks of the Chesapeake Bay—viewing the reced-
ing vessels as they flew with their white wings before the breeze, and
apostrophizing them as animated by the living spirit of freedom. Who
can read that passage, and be insensible to its pathos and sublimity?
Compressed into it is a whole Alexandrian library of thought, feeling, and sentiment—all that can, all that need be urged, in the form
of expostulation, entreaty, rebuke, against that crime of crimes—
making man the property of his fellow-man! O, how accursed is that
system, which entombs the godlike mind of man, defaces the divine
image, reduces those who by creation were crowned with glory and
honor to a level with four-footed beasts, and exalts the dealer in
human flesh above all that is called God! Why should its existence be
prolonged one hour? Is it not evil, only evil, and that continually?
What does its presence imply but the absence of all fear of God, all
regard for man, on the part of the people of the United States?
Heaven speed its eternal overthrow!

So profoundly ignorant of the nature of slavery are many persons,
that they are stubbornly incredulous whenever they read or listen to
any recital of the cruelties which are daily inflicted on its victims. They
do not deny that the slaves are held as property, but that terrible fact
seems to convey to their minds no idea of injustice, exposure to outrage,

or savage barbarity. Tell them of cruel scourgings, of mutilations and brandings, of scenes of pollution and blood, of the banishment of all light and knowledge, and they affect to be greatly indignant at such enormous exaggerations, such wholesale misstatements, such abominable libels on the character of the southern planters! As if all these direful outrages were not the natural results of slavery! As if it were less cruel to reduce a human being to the condition of a thing, than to give him a severe flagellation, or to deprive him of necessary food and clothing! As if whips, chains, thumb-screws, paddles, bloodhounds, overseers, drivers, patrols, were not all indispensable to keep the slaves down, and to give protection to their ruthless oppressors! As if, when the marriage institution is abolished, concubinage, adultery, and incest, must not necessarily abound; when all the rights of humanity are annihilated, any barrier remains to protect the victim from the fury of the spoiler; when absolute power is assumed over life and liberty, it will not be wielded with destructive sway! Skeptics of this character abound in society. In some few instances, their incredulity arises from a want of reflection; but, generally, it indicates a hatred of the light, a desire to shield slavery from the assaults of its foes, a contempt of the colored race, whether bond or free. Such will try to discredit the shocking tales of slaveholding cruelty which are recorded in this truthful Narrative; but they will labor in vain. Mr. DOUGLASS has frankly disclosed the place of his birth, the names of those who claimed ownership in his body and soul, and the names also of those who committed the crimes which he has alleged against them. His statements, therefore, may easily be disproved, if they are untrue.

In the course of his Narrative, he relates two instances of murderous cruelty—in one of which a planter deliberately shot a slave belonging to a neighboring plantation, who had unintentionally gotten within his lordly domain in quest of fish; and in the other, an overseer blew out the brains of a slave who had fled to a stream of water to escape a bloody scourging. Mr. DOUGLASS states that in neither of these instances was any thing done by way of legal arrest or judicial investigation. The Baltimore American, of March 17, 1845, relates a similar case of atrocity, perpetrated with similar impunity—as follows: "*Shooting a Slave.* We learn, upon the authority of a letter from

Charles county, Maryland, received by a gentleman of this city, that a young man, named Matthews, a nephew of General Matthews, and whose father, it is believed, holds an office at Washington, killed one of the slaves upon his father's farm by shooting him. The letter states that young Matthews had been left in charge of the farm; that he gave an order to the servant, which was disobeyed, when he proceeded to the house, *obtained a gun, and, returning, shot the servant.* He immediately, the letter continues, fled to his father's residence, where he still remains unmolested." Let it never be forgotten, that no slaveholder or overseer can be convicted of any outrage perpetrated on the person of a slave, however diabolical it may be, on the testimony of colored witnesses, whether bond or free. By the slave code, they are adjudged to be as incompetent to testify against a white man, as though they were indeed a part of the brute creation. Hence, there is no legal protection in fact, whatever there may be in form, for the slave population; and any amount of cruelty may be inflicted on them with impunity. Is it possible for the human mind to conceive of a more horrible state of society?

The effect of a religious profession on the conduct of southern masters is vividly described in the following Narrative, and shown to be any thing but salutary. In the nature of the case, it must be in the highest degree pernicious. The testimony of Mr. Douglass, on this point, is sustained by a cloud of witnesses, whose veracity is unimpeachable. "A slaveholder's profession of Christianity is a palpable imposture. He is a felon of the highest grade. He is a man-stealer. It is of no importance what you put in the other scale."

Reader! Are you with the man-stealers in sympathy and purpose, or on the side of their down-trodden victims? If with the former, then are you the foe of God and man. If with the latter, what are you prepared to do and dare in their behalf? Be faithful, be vigilant, be untiring in your efforts to break every yoke, and let the oppressed go free. Come what may—cost what it may—inscribe on the banner which you unfurl to the breeze, as your religious and political motto—"No Compromise with Slavery! No Union with Slaveholders!"

WM. LLOYD GARRISON[2]
Boston, May 1, 1845

LETTER FROM WENDELL PHILLIPS, ESQ.

Boston, April 22, 1845

My Dear Friend:

You remember the old fable of "The Man and the Lion," where the lion complained that he should not be so misrepresented "when the lions wrote history."

I am glad the time has come when the "lions write history." We have been left long enough to gather the character of slavery from the involuntary evidence of the masters. One might, indeed, rest sufficiently satisfied with what, it is evident, must be, in general, the results of such a relation, without seeking farther to find whether they have followed in every instance. Indeed, those who stare at the half-peck of corn a week, and love to count the lashes on the slave's back, are seldom the "stuff" out of which reformers and abolitionists are to be made. I remember that, in 1838, many were waiting for the results of the West India experiment, before they could come into our ranks. Those "results" have come long ago; but, alas! few of that number have come with them, as converts. A man must be disposed to judge of emancipation by other tests than whether it has increased the produce of sugar—and to hate slavery for other reasons than because it starves men and whips women—before he is ready to lay the first stone of his anti-slavery life.

I was glad to learn, in your story, how early the most neglected of God's children waken to a sense of their rights, and of the injustice done them. Experience is a keen teacher; and long before you had mastered your A B C, or knew where the "white sails" of the Chesapeake were bound, you began, I see, to gauge the wretchedness of the slave, not by his hunger and want, not by his lashes and toil, but by the cruel and blighting death which gathers over his soul.

In connection with this, there is one circumstance which makes your recollections peculiarly valuable, and renders your early insight the more remarkable. You come from that part of the country where we are told slavery appears with its fairest features. Let us hear, then, what it is at its best estate—gaze on its bright side, if it has one; and then imagination may task her powers to add dark lines to the picture, as she travels southward to that (for the colored man) Valley of the Shadow of Death, where the Mississippi sweeps along.

Again, we have known you long, and can put the most entire confidence in your truth, candor, and sincerity. Every one who has heard you speak has felt, and, I am confident, every one who reads your book will feel, persuaded that you give them a fair specimen of the whole truth. No one-sided portrait—no wholesale complaints—but strict justice done, whenever individual kindliness has neutralized, for a moment, the deadly system with which it was strangely allied. You have been with us, too, some years, and can fairly compare the twilight of rights, which your race enjoy at the North, with that "noon of night" under which they labor south of Mason and Dixon's line. Tell us whether, after all, the half-free colored man of Massachusetts is worse off than the pampered slave of the rice swamps!

In reading your life, no one can say that we have unfairly picked out some rare specimens of cruelty. We know that the bitter drops, which even you have drained from the cup, are no incidental aggravations, no individual ills, but such as must mingle always and necessarily in the lot of every slave. They are the essential ingredients, not the occasional results, of the system.

After all, I shall read your book with trembling for you. Some years ago, when you were beginning to tell me your real name and birthplace, you may remember I stopped you, and preferred to remain ignorant of all. With the exception of a vague description, so I continued, till the other day, when you read me your memoirs. I hardly knew, at the time, whether to thank you or not for the sight of them, when I reflected that it was still dangerous, in Massachusetts, for honest men to tell their names! They say the fathers, in 1776, signed the Declaration of Independence with the halter about their necks. You, too, publish your declaration of freedom with danger compassing you around. In all the broad lands which the Constitution of the United States overshadows, there is no single spot—however narrow or desolate—where a fugitive slave can plant himself and say, "I am safe." The whole armory of Northern Law has no shield for you. I am free to say that, in your place, I should throw the MS into the fire.

You, perhaps, may tell your story in safety, endeared as you are to so many warm hearts by rare gifts, and a still rarer devotion of them to the service of others. But it will be owing only to your labors, and the fearless efforts of those who, trampling the laws and Constitution of the country under their feet, are determined that they will "hide the outcast," and that their hearths shall be, spite of the law, an asylum for the oppressed, if, some time or other, the humblest may stand in our streets, and bear witness in safety against the cruelties of which he has been the victim.

Yet it is sad to think, that these very throbbing hearts which welcome your story, and form your best safeguard in telling it, are all beating contrary to the "statute in such case made and provided." Go on, my dear friend, till you, and those who, like you, have been saved, so as by fire, from the dark prisonhouse, shall stereotype these free, illegal pulses into statutes; and New England, cutting loose from a blood-stained Union, shall glory in being the house of refuge for the oppressed—till we no longer merely "hide the outcast," or make a merit of standing idly by while he is hunted in our midst; but, consecrating anew the soil of the Pilgrims as an asylum for the oppressed, proclaim our welcome to the slave so loudly, that the tones shall reach every hut in the Carolinas, and make the broken-hearted bondman leap up at the thought of old Massachusetts.

God speed the day!
Till then, and ever,
Yours truly,
Wendell Phillips

Narrative of the Life of Frederick Douglass

CHAPTER I

I was born in Tuckahoe, near Hillsborough, and about twelve miles from Easton, in Talbot county, Maryland. I have no accurate knowledge of my age,[1] never having seen any authentic record containing it. By far the larger part of the slaves know as little of their ages as horses know of theirs, and it is the wish of most masters within my knowledge to keep their slaves thus ignorant. I do not remember to have ever met a slave who could tell of his birthday. They seldom come nearer to it than planting-time, harvest-time, cherry-time, spring-time, or fall-time. A want of information concerning my own was a source of unhappiness to me even during childhood. The white children could tell their ages. I could not tell why I ought to be deprived of the same privilege. I was not allowed to make any inquiries of my master concerning it. He deemed all such inquiries on the part of a slave improper and impertinent, and evidence of a restless spirit. The nearest estimate I can give makes me now between twenty-seven and twenty-eight years of age. I come to this, from hearing my master say, some time during 1835, I was about seventeen years old.

My mother was named Harriet Bailey. She was the daughter of Isaac and Betsey Bailey, both colored, and quite dark. My mother was of a darker complexion than either my grandmother or grandfather.

My father was a white man. He was admitted to be such by all I ever heard speak of my parentage. The opinion was also whispered that my master was my father; but of the correctness of this opinion, I know nothing; the means of knowing was withheld from me. My mother and

I were separated when I was but an infant—before I knew her as my mother. It is a common custom, in the part of Maryland from which I ran away, to part children from their mothers at a very early age. Frequently, before the child has reached its twelfth month, its mother is taken from it, and hired out on some farm a considerable distance off, and the child is placed under the care of an old woman, too old for field labor. For what this separation is done, I do not know, unless it be to hinder the development of the child's affection toward its mother, and to blunt and destroy the natural affection of the mother for the child. This is the inevitable result.

I never saw my mother, to know her as such, more than four or five times in my life; and each of these times was very short in duration, and at night. She was hired by a Mr. Stewart, who lived about twelve miles from my home. She made her journeys to see me in the night, traveling the whole distance on foot, after the performance of her day's work. She was a field hand, and a whipping is the penalty of not being in the field at sunrise, unless a slave has special permission from his or her master to the contrary—a permission which they seldom get, and one that gives to him that gives it the proud name of being a kind master. I do not recollect of ever seeing my mother by the light of day. She was with me in the night. She would lie down with me, and get me to sleep, but long before I waked she was gone. Very little communication ever took place between us. Death soon ended what little we could have while she lived, and with it her hardships and suffering. She died when I was about seven years old, on one of my master's farms, near Lee's Mill. I was not allowed to be present during her illness, at her death, or burial. She was gone long before I knew any thing about it. Never having enjoyed, to any considerable extent, her soothing presence, her tender and watchful care, I received the tidings of her death with much the same emotions I should have probably felt at the death of a stranger.

Called thus suddenly away, she left me without the slightest intimation of who my father was. The whisper that my master was my father, may or may not be true; and, true or false, it is of but little consequence to my purpose whilst the fact remains, in all its glaring odiousness, that slaveholders have ordained, and by law established, that the children of slave women shall in all cases follow the condition of their mothers;[2] and this is done too obviously to administer to their own lusts, and make a gratification of their wicked desires profitable as well as pleasurable; for by this cunning arrangement, the slaveholder, in cases not a few, sustains to his slaves the double relation of master and father.

I know of such cases; and it is worthy of remark that such slaves invariably suffer greater hardships, and have more to contend with, than others. They are, in the first place, a constant offence to their mistress. She is ever disposed to find fault with them; they can seldom do any thing to please her; she is never better pleased than when she sees them under the lash, especially when she suspects her husband of showing to his mulatto children favors which he withholds from his black slaves. The master is frequently compelled to sell this class of his slaves, out of deference to the feelings of his white wife; and, cruel as the deed may strike any one to be, for a man to sell his own children to human flesh-mongers, it is often the dictate of humanity for him to do so; for, unless he does this, he must not only whip them himself, but must stand by and see one white son tie up his brother, of but few shades darker complexion than himself, and ply the gory lash to his naked back; and if he lisp one word of disapproval, it is set down to his parental partiality, and only makes a bad matter worse, both for himself and the slave whom he would protect and defend.

Every year brings with it multitudes of this class of slaves. It was doubtless in consequence of a knowledge of this fact, that one great statesman of the South predicted the downfall of slavery by the inevitable laws of population. Whether this prophecy is ever fulfilled or not, it is nevertheless plain that a very different-looking class of people are springing up at the South, and are now held in slavery, from those originally brought to this country from Africa; and if their increase will do no other good, it will do away the force of the argument, that God cursed Ham, and therefore American slavery is right. If the lineal descendants of Ham are alone to be scripturally enslaved, it is certain that slavery at the South must soon become unscriptural; for thousands are ushered into the world, annually, who, like myself, owe their existence to white fathers, and those fathers most frequently their own masters.

I have had two masters. My first master's name was Anthony. I do not remember his first name. He was generally called Captain Anthony—a title which, I presume, he acquired by sailing a craft on the Chesapeake Bay. He was not considered a rich slaveholder. He owned two or three farms, and about thirty slaves. His farms and slaves were under the care of an overseer.[3] The overseer's name was Plummer. Mr. Plummer was a miserable drunkard, a profane swearer, and a savage monster. He always went armed with a cowskin and a heavy cudgel. I have known him to cut and slash the women's heads so horribly, that even master would be enraged at his cruelty, and would threaten to whip him if he did not mind himself. Master, however, was not a humane slaveholder. It required extraordinary barbarity on the part of an overseer to affect him. He was a cruel man, hardened by a long life of slaveholding. He would at times seem to take great pleasure in whipping a slave. I have often been awakened at the dawn of day by the most heart-rending shrieks of an own aunt of mine, whom he used to tie up to a joist, and whip upon her naked back till she was literally covered with blood. No words, no tears, no prayers, from his gory victim, seemed to move his iron heart from its bloody purpose. The louder she screamed, the harder he whipped; and where the blood ran fastest, there he whipped longest. He would whip her to make her scream, and whip her to make her hush; and not until overcome by fatigue, would he cease to swing the blood-clotted cowskin. I remember the first time I ever witnessed this horrible exhibition. I was quite a child, but I well remember it. I never shall forget it whilst I remember any thing. It was the first of a long series of such outrages, of which I was doomed to be a witness and a participant. It struck me with awful force. It was the blood-stained gate, the entrance to the hell of slavery, through which I was about to pass. It was a most terrible spectacle. I wish I could commit to paper the feelings with which I beheld it.

This occurrence took place very soon after I went to live with my old master, and under the following circumstances. Aunt Hester went out one night—where or for what I do not know—and happened to be absent when my master desired her presence. He had ordered her not to go out evenings, and warned her that she must never let him catch her in company with a young man, who was paying attention to her belonging to Colonel Lloyd. The young man's name was Ned Roberts, generally called Lloyd's Ned. Why master was so careful of her, may be safely left to conjecture. She was a woman of noble form, and of graceful proportions, having very few equals, and fewer superiors, in personal appearance, among the colored or white women of our neighborhood.

Aunt Hester had not only disobeyed his orders in going out, but had been found in company with Lloyd's Ned; which circumstance, I found, from what he said while whipping her, was the chief offence. Had he been a man of pure morals himself, he might have been thought interested in protecting the innocence of my aunt; but those who knew him will not suspect him of any such virtue. Before he commenced whipping Aunt Hester, he took her into the kitchen, and stripped her from neck to waist, leaving her neck, shoulders, and back, entirely naked. He then told her to cross her hands, calling her at the same time a d——d b——h. After crossing her hands, he tied them with a strong rope, and led her to a stool under a large hook in the joist, put in for the purpose. He made her get upon the stool, and tied her hands to the hook. She now stood fair for his infernal purpose. Her arms were stretched up at their full length, so that she stood upon the ends of her toes. He then said to her, "Now, you d——d b——h, I'll learn you how to disobey my orders!" and after rolling up his sleeves, he commenced to lay on the heavy cowskin, and soon the warm, red blood (amid heart-rending shrieks from her, and horrid oaths from him) came dripping to the floor. I was so terrified and horror-stricken at the sight, that I hid myself in a closet, and dared not venture out till long after the bloody transaction was over. I expected it would be my turn next. It was all new to me. I had never seen any thing like it before. I had always lived with my grandmother on the outskirts of the plantation, where she was put to raise the children of the younger women. I had therefore been, until now, out of the way of the bloody scenes that often occurred on the plantation.

CHAPTER II

MY MASTER'S FAMILY CONSISTED OF TWO SONS, ANDREW AND RICHARD; one daughter, Lucretia, and her husband, Captain Thomas Auld. They lived in one house, upon the home plantation of Colonel Edward Lloyd. My master was Colonel Lloyd's clerk and superintendent. He was what might be called the overseer of the overseers. I spent two years of childhood on this plantation in my old master's family. It was here that I witnessed the bloody transaction recorded in the first chapter; and as I received my first impressions of slavery on this plantation, I will give some description of it, and of slavery as it there existed. The plantation is about twelve miles north of Easton, in Talbot county, and is situated on the border of Miles River. The principal products raised upon it were tobacco, corn, and wheat. These were raised in great abundance; so that, with the products of this and the other farms belonging to him, he was able to keep in almost constant employment a large sloop, in carrying them to market at Baltimore. This sloop was named Sally Lloyd, in honor of one of the colonel's daughters. My master's son-in-law, Captain Auld, was master of the vessel; she was otherwise manned by the colonel's own slaves. Their names were Peter, Isaac, Rich, and Jake. These were esteemed very highly by the other slaves, and looked upon as the privileged ones of the plantation; for it was no small affair, in the eyes of the slaves, to be allowed to see Baltimore.

Colonel Lloyd kept from three to four hundred slaves on his home plantation, and owned a large number more on the neighboring farms belonging to him. The names of the farms nearest to the home plantation were Wye Town and New Design. "Wye Town" was under the overseership of a man named Noah Willis, New Design was under the overseership of a Mr. Townsend. The overseers of these, and all the rest of the farms, numbering over twenty, received advice and direction from the managers of the home plantation. This was the great business place. It was the seat of government for the whole twenty farms. All disputes among the overseers were settled here. If a slave was convicted of any high misdemeanor, became unmanageable, or evinced a determination to run away, he was brought immediately here, severely whipped, put on board the sloop, carried to Baltimore, and sold to Austin Woolfolk, or some other slave-trader, as a warning to the slaves remaining.

Here, too, the slaves of all the other farms received their monthly allowance of food, and their yearly clothing. The men and women slaves received, as their monthly allowance of food, eight pounds of pork, or its equivalent in fish, and one bushel of corn meal. Their yearly clothing consisted of two coarse linen shirts, one pair of linen trousers, like the shirts, one jacket, one pair of trousers for winter, made of coarse negro cloth, one pair of stockings, and one pair of shoes; the whole of which could not have cost more than seven dollars. The allowance of the slave children was given to their mothers, or the old women having the care of them. The children unable to work in the field had neither shoes, stockings, jackets, nor trousers, given to them; their clothing consisted of two coarse linen shirts per year. When these failed them, they went naked until the next allowance-day. Children from seven to ten years old, of both sexes, almost naked, might be seen at all seasons of the year.

There were no beds given the slaves, unless one coarse blanket be considered such, and none but the men and women had these. This, however, is not considered a very great privation. They find less diffi-culty from the want of beds, than from the want of time to sleep; for when their day's work in the field is done, the most of them having their washing, mending, and cooking to do, and having few or none of the ordinary facilities for doing either of these, very many of their sleeping hours are consumed in preparing for the field the coming day; and when this is done, old and young, male and female, married and single, drop down side by side, on one common bed—the cold, damp floor—each covering himself or herself with their miserable blankets; and here they sleep till they are summoned to the field by the driver's horn. At the sound of this, all must rise, and be off to the field. There must be no halting; every one must be at his or her post; and woe betides them who hear not this morning summons to the field; for if they are not awakened by the sense of hearing, they are by the sense of feeling: no age nor sex finds any favor. Mr. Severe, the overseer, used to stand by the door of the quarter, armed with a large hickory stick and heavy cowskin, ready to whip any one who was so unfortunate as not to hear, or, from any other cause, was prevented from being ready to start for the field at the sound of the horn.

Mr. Severe was rightly named: he was a cruel man. I have seen him whip a woman, causing the blood to run half an hour at the time; and this, too, in the midst of her crying children, pleading for their mother's release. He seemed to take pleasure in manifesting his fiendish barbarity. Added to his cruelty, he was a profane swearer. It was enough to chill the blood and stiffen the hair of an ordinary man to hear him talk. Scarce a sentence escaped him but that was commenced or concluded by some horrid oath. The field was the place to witness his cruelty and profanity. His presence made it both the field of blood and of blasphemy. From the rising till the going down of the sun, he was cursing, raving, cutting, and slashing among the slaves of the field, in the most frightful manner. His career was short. He died very soon after I went to Colonel Lloyd's; and he died as he lived, uttering, with his dying groans, bitter curses and horrid oaths. His death was regarded by the slaves as the result of a merciful providence.

Mr. Severe's place was filled by a Mr. Hopkins. He was a very different man. He was less cruel, less profane, and made less noise, than Mr. Severe. His course was characterized by no extraordinary demonstrations of cruelty. He whipped, but seemed to take no pleasure in it. He was called by the slaves a good overseer.

The home plantation of Colonel Lloyd wore the appearance of a country village. All the mechanical operations for all the farms were performed here. The shoemaking and mending, the blacksmithing, cartwrighting, coopering, weaving, and grain-grinding, were all performed by the slaves on the home plantation. The whole place wore a business-like aspect very unlike the neighboring farms. The number of houses, too, conspired to give it advantage over the neighboring farms. It was called by the slaves the *Great House Farm*. Few privileges were esteemed higher, by the slaves of the out-farms, than that of being selected to do errands at the Great House Farm. It was associated in their minds with greatness. A representative could not be prouder of his election to a seat in the American Congress, than a slave on one of the out-farms would be of his election to do errands at the Great House Farm. They regarded it as evidence of great confidence reposed in them by their overseers; and it was on this account, as well as a constant desire to be out of the field from under the driver's lash, that they esteemed it a high privilege, one worth careful living for. He was called the smartest and most trusty fellow, who had this honor conferred upon him the most frequently. The competitors for this office sought as diligently to please their overseers, as the office-seekers in the political parties seek to please and deceive the people. The same traits of character might be seen in Colonel Lloyd's slaves, as are seen in the slaves of the political parties.

The slaves selected to go to the Great House Farm, for the monthly allowance for themselves and their fellow-slaves, were peculiarly enthusiastic. While on their way, they would make the dense old woods, for miles around, reverberate with their wild songs, revealing at once the highest joy and the deepest sadness. They would compose and sing as they went along, consulting neither time nor tune. The thought that came up, came out—if not in the word, in the sound; and as frequently in the one as in the other. They would sometimes sing the most pathetic sentiment in the most rapturous tone, and the most rapturous sentiment in the most pathetic tone. Into all of their songs they would manage to weave something of the Great House Farm. Especially would they do this, when leaving home. They would then sing most exultingly the following words:

> I am going away to the Great House Farm!
> O, yea! O, yea! O!

This they would sing, as a chorus, to words which to many would seem unmeaning jargon, but which, nevertheless, were full of meaning to themselves. I have sometimes thought that the mere hearing of those songs would do more to impress some minds with the horrible character of slavery, than the reading of whole volumes of philosophy on the subject could do.

I did not, when a slave, understand the deep meaning of those rude and apparently incoherent songs. I was myself within the circle; so that I neither saw nor heard as those without might see and hear. They told a tale of woe which was then altogether beyond my feeble comprehension; they were tones loud, long, and deep; they breathed the prayer and complaint of souls boiling over with the bitterest anguish. Every tone was a testimony against slavery, and a prayer to God for deliverance from chains. The hearing of those wild notes always depressed my spirit, and filled me with ineffable sadness. I have frequently found myself in tears while hearing them. The mere recurrence to those songs, even now, afflicts me; and while I am writing these lines, an expression of feeling has already found its way down my cheek. To those songs I trace my first glimmering conception of the dehumanizing character of slavery. I can never get rid of that conception. Those songs still follow me, to deepen my hatred of slavery, and quicken my sympathies for my brethren in bonds. If any one wishes to be impressed with the soul-killing effects of slavery, let him go to Colonel Lloyd's plantation, and, on allowance-day, place himself in the deep pine woods, and there let him, in silence, analyze the sounds that shall pass through the chambers of his soul—and if he is not thus impressed, it will only be because "there is no flesh in his obdurate heart."

I have often been utterly astonished, since I came to the North, to find persons who could speak of the singing, among slaves, as evidence of their contentment and happiness. It is impossible to conceive of a greater mistake. Slaves sing most when they are most unhappy. The songs of the slave represent the sorrows of his heart; and he is relieved by them, only as an aching heart is relieved by its tears. At least, such is my experience. I have often sung to drown my sorrow, but seldom to express my happiness. Crying for joy, and singing for joy, were alike uncommon to me while in the jaws of slavery. The singing of a man cast away upon a desolate island might be as appropriately considered as evidence of contentment and happiness, as the singing of a slave; the songs of the one and of the other are prompted by the same emotion.

Chapter III

Colonel Lloyd kept a large and finely cultivated garden, which afforded almost constant employment for four men, besides the chief gardener, (Mr. M'Durmond). This garden was probably the greatest attraction of the place. During the summer months, people came from far and near—from Baltimore, Easton, and Annapolis—to see it. It abounded in fruits of almost every description, from the hardy apple of the North to the delicate orange of the South. This garden was not the least source of trouble on the plantation. Its excellent fruit was quite a temptation to the hungry swarms of boys, as well as the older slaves, belonging to the colonel, few of whom had the virtue or the vice to resist it. Scarcely a day passed, during the summer, but that some slave had to take the lash for stealing fruit. The colonel had to resort to all kinds of stratagems to keep his slaves out of the garden. The last and most successful one was that of tarring his fence all around; after which, if a slave was caught with any tar upon his person, it was deemed sufficient proof that he had either been into the garden, or had tried to get in. In either case, he was severely whipped by the chief gardener. This plan worked well; the slaves became as fearful of tar as of the lash. They seemed to realize the impossibility of touching *tar* without being defiled.

The colonel also kept a splendid riding equipage. His stable and carriage-house presented the appearance of some of our large city livery establishments. His horses were of the finest form and noblest blood.

His carriage-house contained three splendid coaches, three or four gigs, besides dearborns and barouches of the most fashionable style.

This establishment was under the care of two slaves—old Barney and young Barney—father and son. To attend to this establishment was their sole work. But it was by no means an easy employment; for in nothing was Colonel Lloyd more particular than in the management of his horses. The slightest inattention to these was unpardonable, and was visited upon those, under whose care they were placed, with the severest punishment; no excuse could shield them, if the colonel only suspected any want of attention to his horses—a supposition which he frequently indulged, and one which, of course, made the office of old and young Barney a very trying one. They never knew when they were safe from punishment. They were frequently whipped when least deserving, and escaped whipping when most deserving it. Every thing depended upon the looks of the horses, and the state of Colonel Lloyd's own mind when his horses were brought to him for use. If a horse did not move fast enough, or hold his head high enough, it was owing to some fault of his keepers. It was painful to stand near the stable-door, and hear the various complaints against the keepers when a horse was taken out for use. "This horse has not had proper attention. He has not been sufficiently rubbed and curried, or he has not been properly fed; his food was too wet or too dry; he got it too soon or too late; he was too hot or too cold; he had too much hay, and not enough of grain; or he had too much grain, and not enough of hay; instead of old Barney's attending to the horse, he had very improperly left it to his son." To all these complaints, no matter how unjust, the slave must answer never a word. Colonel Lloyd could not brook any contradiction from a slave. When he spoke, a slave must stand, listen, and tremble; and such was literally the case. I have seen Colonel Lloyd make old Barney, a man between fifty and sixty years of age, uncover his bald head, kneel down upon the cold, damp ground, and receive upon his naked and toil-worn shoulders more than thirty lashes at the time. Colonel Lloyd had three sons— Edward, Murray, and Daniel—and three sons-in-law, Mr. Winder, Mr. Nicholson, and Mr. Lowndes. All of these lived at the Great House Farm, and enjoyed the luxury of whipping the servants when they pleased, from old Barney down to William Wilkes, the coach-driver. I have seen Winder make one of the house-servants stand off from him a suitable distance to be touched with the end of his whip, and at every stroke raise great ridges upon his back.

To describe the wealth of Colonel Lloyd would be almost equal to describing the riches of Job. He kept from ten to fifteen house-servants. He was said to own a thousand slaves, and I think this estimate quite within the truth. Colonel Lloyd owned so many that he did not know them when he saw them; nor did all the slaves of the out-farms know him. It is reported of him, that, while riding along the road one day, he met a colored man, and addressed him in the usual manner of speaking to colored people on the public highways of the South: "Well, boy, whom do you belong to?" "To Colonel Lloyd," replied the slave. "Well, does the colonel treat you well?" "No, sir," was the ready reply. "What, does he work you too hard?" "Yes, sir." "Well, don't he give you enough to eat?" "Yes, sir, he gives me enough, such as it is."

The colonel, after ascertaining where the slave belonged, rode on; the man also went on about his business, not dreaming that he had been conversing with his master. He thought, said, and heard nothing more of the matter, until two or three weeks afterwards. The poor man was then informed by his overseer that, for having found fault with his master, he was now to be sold to a Georgia trader. He was immediately chained and handcuffed; and thus, without a moment's warning, he was snatched away, and forever sundered, from his family and friends, by a hand more unrelenting than death. This is the penalty of telling the truth, of telling the simple truth, in answer to a series of plain questions.

It is partly in consequence of such facts, that slaves, when inquired of as to their condition and the character of their masters, almost universally say they are contented, and that their masters are kind. The slaveholders have been known to send in spies among their slaves, to ascertain their views and feelings in regard to their condition. The frequency of this has had the effect to establish among the slaves the maxim, that a still tongue makes a wise head. They suppress the truth rather than take the consequences of telling it, and in so doing prove themselves a part of the human family. If they have any thing to say of their masters, it is generally in their masters' favor, especially when speaking to an untried man. I have been frequently asked, when a slave, if I had a kind master, and do not remember ever to have given a negative answer; nor did I, in pursuing this course, consider myself as uttering what was absolutely false; for I always measured the kindness of my master by the standard of kindness set up among slaveholders around us. Moreover, slaves are like other people, and imbibe prejudices quite common to others. They think their own better than that of others. Many, under the influence of this prejudice, think their own masters are better than the masters of other slaves; and this, too, in some cases, when the very reverse is true. Indeed, it is not uncommon for slaves even to fall out and quarrel among themselves about the relative goodness of their masters, each contending for the superior goodness of his own over that of the others. At the very same time, they mutually execrate their masters when viewed separately. It was so on our plantation. When Colonel Lloyd's slaves met the slaves of Jacob Jepson, they seldom parted without a quarrel about their masters; Colonel Lloyd's slaves contending that he was the richest, and Mr. Jepson's slaves that he was the smartest, and most of a man. Colonel Lloyd's slaves would boast his ability to buy and sell Jacob Jepson. Mr. Jepson's slaves would boast his ability to whip Colonel Lloyd. These quarrels would almost always end in a fight between the parties, and those that whipped were supposed to have gained the point at issue. They seemed to think that the greatness of their masters was transferable to themselves. It was considered as being bad enough to be a slave; but to be a poor man's slave was deemed a disgrace indeed!

CHAPTER IV

M R. HOPKINS REMAINED BUT A SHORT TIME IN THE OFFICE OF OVERSEER.
Why his career was so short, I do not know, but suppose he lacked the
necessary severity to suit Colonel Lloyd. Mr. Hopkins was succeeded
by Mr. Austin Gore, a man possessing, in an eminent degree, all those
traits of character indispensable to what is called a first-rate overseer.
Mr. Gore had served Colonel Lloyd, in the capacity of overseer, upon
one of the out-farms, and had shown himself worthy of the high station of overseer upon the home or Great House Farm.

Mr. Gore was proud, ambitious, and persevering. He was artful,
cruel, and obdurate. He was just the man for such a place, and it was
just the place for such a man. It afforded scope for the full exercise of
all his powers, and he seemed to be perfectly at home in it. He was one
of those who could torture the slightest look, word, or gesture, on the
part of the slave, into impudence, and would treat it accordingly.
There must be no answering back to him; no explanation was allowed
a slave, showing himself to have been wrongfully accused. Mr. Gore
acted fully up to the maxim laid down by slaveholders—"It is better
that a dozen slaves should suffer under the lash, than that the overseer
should be convicted, in the presence of the slaves, of having been at
fault." No matter how innocent a slave might be—it availed him nothing, when accused by Mr. Gore of any misdemeanor. To be accused
was to be convicted, and to be convicted was to be punished; the one
always following the other with immutable certainty. To escape punishment was to escape accusation; and few slaves had the fortune to do

either, under the overseership of Mr. Gore. He was just proud enough to demand the most debasing homage of the slave, and quite servile enough to crouch, himself, at the feet of the master. He was ambitious enough to be contented with nothing short of the highest rank of overseers, and persevering enough to reach the height of his ambition. He was cruel enough to inflict the severest punishment, artful enough to descend to the lowest trickery, and obdurate enough to be insensible to the voice of a reproving conscience. He was, of all the overseers, the most dreaded by the slaves. His presence was painful; his eye flashed confusion; and seldom was his sharp, shrill voice heard, without producing horror and trembling in their ranks.

Mr. Gore was a grave man, and, though a young man, he indulged in no jokes, said no funny words, seldom smiled. His words were in perfect keeping with his looks, and his looks were in perfect keeping with his words. Overseers will sometimes indulge in a witty word, even with the slaves; not so with Mr. Gore. He spoke but to command, and commanded but to be obeyed; he dealt sparingly with his words, and bountifully with his whip, never using the former where the latter would answer as well. When he whipped, he seemed to do so from a sense of duty, and feared no consequences. He did nothing reluctantly, no matter how disagreeable; always at his post, never inconsistent. He never promised but to fulfill. He was, in a word, a man of the most inflexible firmness and stone-like coolness.

His savage barbarity was equalled only by the consummate coolness with which he committed the grossest and most savage deeds upon the slaves under his charge. Mr. Gore once undertook to whip one of Colonel Lloyd's slaves, by the name of Demby. He had given Demby but few stripes, when, to get rid of the scourging, he ran and plunged himself into a creek, and stood there at the depth of his shoulders, refusing to come out. Mr. Gore told him that he would give him three calls, and that, if he did not come out at the third call, he would shoot him. The first call was given. Demby made no response, but stood his ground. The second and third calls were given with the same result. Mr. Gore then, without consultation or deliberation with any one, not even giving Demby an additional call, raised his musket to his face, taking deadly aim at his standing victim, and in an instant poor Demby was no more. His mangled body sank out of sight, and blood and brains marked the water where he had stood.

A thrill of horror flashed through every soul upon the plantation, excepting Mr. Gore. He alone seemed cool and collected. He was asked by Colonel Lloyd and my old master, why he resorted to this extraordinary expedient. His reply was, (as well as I can remember), that Demby had become unmanageable. He was setting a dangerous example to the other slaves—one which, if suffered to pass without some such demonstration on his part, would finally lead to the total subversion of all rule and order upon the plantation. He argued that if one slave refused to be corrected, and escaped with his life, the other slaves would soon copy the example; the result of which would be, the freedom of the slaves, and the enslavement of the whites. Mr. Gore's defence was satisfactory. He was continued in his station as overseer upon the home plantation. His fame as an overseer went abroad. His horrid crime was not even submitted to judicial investigation. It was committed in the presence of slaves, and they of course could neither institute a suit, nor testify against him; and thus the guilty perpetrator of one of the bloodiest and most foul murders goes unwhipped of justice, and uncensured by the community in which he lives. Mr. Gore lived in St. Michael's, Talbot county, Maryland, when I left there; and if he is still alive, he very probably lives there now; and if so, he is now, as he was then, as highly esteemed and as much respected as though his guilty soul had not been stained with his brother's blood.

I speak advisedly when I say this—that killing a slave, or any colored person, in Talbot county, Maryland, is not treated as a crime, either by the courts or the community. Mr. Thomas Lanman, of St. Michael's, killed two slaves, one of whom he killed with a hatchet, by knocking his brains out. He used to boast of the commission of the awful and bloody deed. I have heard him do so laughingly, saying, among other things, that he was the only benefactor of his country in the company, and that when others would do as much as he had done, we should be relieved of "the d——d niggers."

The wife of Mr. Giles Hicks, living but a short distance from where I used to live, murdered my wife's cousin, a young girl between fifteen and sixteen years of age, mangling her person in the most horrible manner, breaking her nose and breastbone with a stick, so that the poor girl expired in a few hours afterward. She was immediately buried, but had not been in her untimely grave but a few hours before she was taken up and examined by the coroner, who decided that she had come to her death by severe beating. The offence for which this girl was thus murdered was this: She had been set that night to mind Mrs. Hicks' baby, and during the night she fell asleep, and the baby cried. She, having lost her rest for several nights previous, did not hear the crying. They were both in the room with Mrs. Hicks. Mrs. Hicks, finding the girl slow to move, jumped from her bed, seized an oak stick of wood by the fireplace, and with it broke the girl's nose and breastbone, and thus ended her life. I will not say that this most horrid murder produced no sensation in the community. It did produce sensation, but not enough to bring the murderess to punishment. There was a warrant issued for her arrest, but it was never served. Thus she escaped not only punishment, but even the pain of being arraigned before a court for her horrid crime.

Whilst I am detailing bloody deeds which took place during my stay on Colonel Lloyd's plantation, I will briefly narrate another, which occurred about the same time as the murder of Demby by Mr. Gore.

Colonel Lloyd's slaves were in the habit of spending a part of their nights and Sundays in fishing for oysters, and in this way made up the deficiency of their scanty allowance. An old man belonging to Colonel Lloyd, while thus engaged, happened to get beyond the limits of Colonel Lloyd's, and on the premises of Mr. Beal Bondly. At this trespass, Mr. Bondly took offence, and with his musket came down to the shore, and blew its deadly contents into the poor old man.

Mr. Bondly came over to see Colonel Lloyd the next day, whether to pay him for his property, or to justify himself in what he had done, I know not. At any rate, this whole fiendish transaction was soon hushed up. There was very little said about it at all, and nothing done. It was a common saying, even among little white boys, that it was worth a half-cent to kill a "nigger," and a half-cent to bury one.

Chapter V

As to my own treatment while I lived on Colonel Lloyd's plantation, it was very similar to that of the other slave children. I was not old enough to work in the field, and there being little else than field work to do, I had a great deal of leisure time. The most I had to do was to drive up the cows at evening, keep the fowls out of the garden, keep the front yard clean, and run off errands for my old master's daughter, Mrs. Lucretia Auld. The most of my leisure time I spent in helping Master Daniel Lloyd in finding his birds, after he had shot them. My connection with Master Daniel was of some advantage to me. He became quite attached to me, and was a sort of protector of me. He would not allow the older boys to impose upon me, and would divide his cakes with me.

I was seldom whipped by my old master, and suffered little from any thing else than hunger and cold. I suffered much from hunger, but much more from cold. In hottest summer and coldest winter, I was kept almost naked—no shoes, no stockings, no jacket, no trousers, nothing on but a coarse tow linen shirt, reaching only to my knees. I had no bed. I must have perished with cold, but that, the coldest nights, I used to steal a bag which was used for carrying corn to the mill. I would crawl into this bag, and there sleep on the cold, damp, clay floor, with my head in and feet out. My feet have been so cracked with the frost, that the pen with which I am writing might be laid in the gashes.

We were not regularly allowanced. Our food was coarse corn meal boiled. This was called *mush*. It was put into a large wooden tray or trough, and set down upon the ground. The children were then called, like so many pigs, and like so many pigs they would come and devour the mush; some with oyster-shells, others with pieces of shingle, some with naked hands, and none with spoons. He that ate fastest got most; he that was strongest secured the best place; and few left the trough satisfied.

I was probably between seven and eight years old when I left Colonel Lloyd's plantation. I left it with joy. I shall never forget the ecstasy with which I received the intelligence that my old master (Anthony) had determined to let me go to Baltimore, to live with Mr. Hugh Auld, brother to my old master's son-in-law, Captain Thomas Auld. I received this information about three days before my departure. They were three of the happiest days I ever enjoyed. I spent the most part of all these three days in the creek, washing off the plantation scurf, and preparing myself for my departure.

The pride of appearance which this would indicate was not my own. I spent the time in washing, not so much because I wished to, but because Mrs. Lucretia had told me I must get all the dead skin off my feet and knees before I could go to Baltimore; for the people in Baltimore were very cleanly, and would laugh at me if I looked dirty. Besides, she was going to give me a pair of trousers, which I should not put on unless I got all the dirt off me. The thought of owning a pair of trousers was great indeed! It was almost a sufficient motive, not only to make me take off what would be called by pig-drovers the mange, but the skin itself. I went at it in good earnest, working for the first time with the hope of reward.

The ties that ordinarily bind children to their homes were all suspended in my case. I found no severe trial in my departure. My home was charmless; it was not home to me; on parting from it, I could not feel that I was leaving any thing which I could have enjoyed by staying. My mother was dead, my grandmother lived far off, so that I seldom saw her. I had two sisters and one brother, that lived in the same house with me; but the early separation of us from our mother had well nigh blotted the fact of our relationship from our memories. I looked for home elsewhere, and was confident of finding none which I should relish less than the one which I was leaving. If, however, I found in my new home hardship, hunger, whipping, and nakedness, I had the consolation that

I should not have escaped any one of them by staying. Having already had more than a taste of them in the house of my old master, and having endured them there, I very naturally inferred my ability to endure them elsewhere, and especially at Baltimore; for I had something of the feeling about Baltimore that is expressed in the proverb, that "being hanged in England is preferable to dying a natural death in Ireland." I had the strongest desire to see Baltimore. Cousin Tom, though not fluent in speech, had inspired me with that desire by his eloquent description of the place. I could never point out any thing at the Great House, no matter how beautiful or powerful, but that he had seen something at Baltimore far exceeding, both in beauty and strength, the object which I pointed out to him. Even the Great House itself, with all its pictures, was far inferior to many buildings in Baltimore. So strong was my desire, that I thought a gratification of it would fully compensate for whatever loss of comforts I should sustain by the exchange. I left without a regret, and with the highest hopes of future happiness.

We sailed out of Miles River for Baltimore on a Saturday morning. I remember only the day of the week, for at that time I had no knowledge of the days of the month, nor the months of the year. On setting sail, I walked aft, and gave to Colonel Lloyd's plantation what I hoped would be the last look. I then placed myself in the bows of the sloop, and there spent the remainder of the day in looking ahead, interesting myself in what was in the distance rather than in things near by or behind.

In the afternoon of that day, we reached Annapolis, the capital of the State. We stopped but a few moments, so that I had no time to go on shore. It was the first large town that I had ever seen, and though it would look small compared with some of our New England factory villages, I thought it a wonderful place for its size—more imposing even than the Great House Farm!

We arrived at Baltimore early on Sunday morning, landing at Smith's Wharf, not far from Bowley's Wharf. We had on board the sloop a large flock of sheep; and after aiding in driving them to the slaughterhouse of Mr. Curtis on Louden Slater's Hill, I was conducted by Rich, one of the hands belonging on board of the sloop, to my new home in Alliciana Street, near Mr. Gardner's ship-yard, on Fells Point.

Mr. and Mrs. Auld were both at home, and met me at the door with their little son Thomas, to take care of whom I had been given. And here I saw what I had never seen before; it was a white face beaming with the most kindly emotions; it was the face of my new mistress, Sophia Auld. I wish I could describe the rapture that flashed through my soul as I beheld it. It was a new and strange sight to me, brightening up my pathway with the light of happiness. Little Thomas was told, there was his Freddy—and I was told to take care of little Thomas; and thus I entered upon the duties of my new home with the most cheering prospect ahead.

I look upon my departure from Colonel Lloyd's plantation as one of the most interesting events of my life. It is possible, and even quite probable, that but for the mere circumstance of being removed from that plantation to Baltimore, I should have today, instead of being here seated by my own table, in the enjoyment of freedom and the happiness of home, writing this Narrative, been confined in the galling chains of slavery. Going to live at Baltimore laid the foundation, and opened the gateway, to all my subsequent prosperity. I have ever regarded it as the first plain manifestation of that kind providence which has ever since attended me, and marked my life with so many favors. I regarded the selection of myself as being somewhat remarkable. There were a number of slave children that might have been sent from the plantation to Baltimore. There were those younger, those older, and those of the same age. I was chosen from among them all, and was the first, last, and only choice.

I may be deemed superstitious, and even egotistical, in regarding this event as a special interposition of divine Providence in my favor. But I should be false to the earliest sentiments of my soul, if I suppressed the opinion. I prefer to be true to myself, even at the hazard of incurring the ridicule of others, rather than to be false, and incur my own abhorrence. From my earliest recollection, I date the entertainment of a deep conviction that slavery would not always be able to hold me within its foul embrace; and in the darkest hours of my career in slavery, this living word of faith and spirit of hope departed not from me, but remained like ministering angels to cheer me through the gloom. This good spirit was from God, and to him I offer thanksgiving and praise.

CHAPTER VI

MY NEW MISTRESS PROVED TO BE ALL SHE APPEARED WHEN I FIRST MET her at the door—a woman of the kindest heart and finest feelings. She had never had a slave under her control previously to myself, and prior to her marriage she had been dependent upon her own industry for a living. She was by trade a weaver; and by constant application to her business, she had been in a good degree preserved from the blighting and dehumanizing effects of slavery. I was utterly astonished at her goodness. I scarcely knew how to behave towards her. She was entirely unlike any other white woman I had ever seen. I could not approach her as I was accustomed to approach other white ladies. My early instruction was all out of place. The crouching servility, usually so acceptable a quality in a slave, did not answer when manifested toward her. Her favor was not gained by it; she seemed to be disturbed by it. She did not deem it impudent or unmannerly for a slave to look her in the face. The meanest slave was put fully at ease in her presence, and none left without feeling better for having seen her. Her face was made of heavenly smiles, and her voice of tranquil music.

But, alas! this kind heart had but a short time to remain such. The fatal poison of irresponsible power was already in her hands, and soon commenced its infernal work. That cheerful eye, under the influence of slavery, soon became red with rage; that voice, made all of sweet accord, changed to one of harsh and horrid discord; and that angelic face gave place to that of a demon.

Very soon after I went to live with Mr. and Mrs. Auld, she very kindly commenced to teach me the A, B, C. After I had learned this, she assisted me in learning to spell words of three or four letters. Just at this point of my progress, Mr. Auld found out what was going on, and at once forbade Mrs. Auld to instruct me further, telling her, among other things, that it was unlawful, as well as unsafe, to teach a slave to read. To use his own words, further, he said, "If you give a nigger an inch, he will take an ell. A nigger should know nothing but to obey his master—to do as he is told to do. Learning will *spoil* the best nigger in the world. Now." he said, "if you teach that nigger (speaking of myself) how to read, there would be no keeping him. It would forever unfit him to be a slave. He would at once become unmanageable, and of no value to his master. As to himself, it could do him no good, but a great deal of harm. It would make him discontented and unhappy." These words sank deep into my heart, stirred up sentiments within that lay slumbering, and called into existence an entirely new train of thought. It was a new and special revelation, explaining dark and mysterious things, with which my youthful understanding had struggled, but struggled in vain. I now understood what had been to me a most perplexing difficulty—to wit, the white man's power to enslave the black man. It was a grand achievement, and I prized it highly. From that moment, I understood the pathway from slavery to freedom. It was just what I wanted, and I got it at a time when I the least expected it. Whilst I was saddened by the thought of losing the aid of my kind mistress, I was gladdened by the invaluable instruction which, by the merest accident, I had gained from my master. Though conscious of the difficulty of learning without a teacher, I set out with high hope, and a fixed purpose, at whatever cost of trouble, to learn how to read. The very decided manner with which he spoke, and strove to impress his wife with the evil consequences of giving me instruction, served to convince me that he was deeply sensible of the truths he was uttering. It gave me the best assurance that I might rely with the utmost confidence on the results which, he said, would flow from teaching me to read. What he most dreaded, that I most desired. What he most loved, that I most hated. That which to him was a great evil, to be carefully shunned, was to me a great good, to be diligently sought; and the argument which he so warmly urged, against my learning to read, only served to inspire me with a desire and determination to learn. In learning to read, I owe almost as much to the bitter opposition of my master, as to the kindly aid of my mistress. I acknowledge the benefit of both.

I had resided but a short time in Baltimore before I observed a marked difference, in the treatment of slaves, from that which I had witnessed in the country. A city slave[1] is almost a freeman, compared with a slave on the plantation. He is much better fed and clothed, and enjoys privileges altogether unknown to the slave on the plantation. There is a vestige of decency, a sense of shame, that does much to curb and check those outbreaks of atrocious cruelty so commonly enacted upon the plantation. He is a desperate slaveholder, who will shock the humanity of his non-slaveholding neighbors with the cries of his lacerated slave. Few are willing to incur the odium attaching to the reputation of being a cruel master; and above all things, they would not be known as not giving a slave enough to eat. Every city slaveholder is anxious to have it known of him, that he feeds his slaves well; and it is due to them to say, that most of them do give their slaves enough to eat. There are, however, some painful exceptions to this rule. Directly opposite to us, on Philpot Street, lived Mr. Thomas Hamilton. He owned two slaves. Their names were Henrietta and Mary. Henrietta was about twenty-two years of age, Mary was about fourteen; and of all the mangled and emaciated creatures I ever looked upon, these two were the most so. His heart must be harder than stone, that could look upon these unmoved. The head, neck, and shoulders of Mary were literally cut to pieces. I have frequently felt her head, and found it nearly covered with festering sores, caused by the lash of her cruel mistress. I do not know that her master ever whipped her, but I have been an eye-witness to the cruelty of Mrs. Hamilton. I used to be in Mr. Hamilton's house nearly every day. Mrs. Hamilton used to sit in a large chair in the middle of the room, with a heavy cowskin always by her side, and scarce an hour passed during the day but was marked by the blood of one of these slaves. The girls seldom passed her without her saying, "Move faster, you *black gip!*" at the same time giving them a blow with the cowskin over the head or shoulders, often drawing the blood. She would then say, "Take that, you *black gip!*" continuing, "If you don't move faster, I'll move you!" Added to the cruel lashings to which these slaves were subjected, they were kept nearly half-starved. They seldom knew what it was to eat a full meal. I have seen Mary contending with the pigs for the offal thrown into the street. So much was Mary kicked and cut to pieces, that she was oftener called "*pecked*" than by her name.

CHAPTER VII

I LIVED IN MASTER HUGH'S FAMILY ABOUT SEVEN YEARS. DURING THIS
time, I succeeded in learning to read and write. In accomplishing
this, I was compelled to resort to various stratagems. I had no regular
teacher. My mistress, who had kindly commenced to instruct me, had,
in compliance with the advice and direction of her husband, not only
ceased to instruct, but had set her face against my being instructed by
any one else. It is due, however, to my mistress to say of her, that she
did not adopt this course of treatment immediately. She at first lacked
the depravity indispensable to shutting me up in mental darkness. It
was at least necessary for her to have some training in the exercise of
irresponsible power, to make her equal to the task of treating me as
though I were a brute.

My mistress was, as I have said, a kind and tender-hearted woman;
and in the simplicity of her soul she commenced, when I first went to
live with her, to treat me as she supposed one human being ought
to treat another. In entering upon the duties of a slaveholder, she did
not seem to perceive that I sustained to her the relation of a mere
chattel, and that for her to treat me as a human being was not only
wrong, but dangerously so. Slavery proved as injurious to her as it did
to me. When I went there, she was a pious, warm, and tender-hearted
woman. There was no sorrow or suffering for which she had not a tear.
She had bread for the hungry, clothes for the naked, and comfort for
every mourner that came within her reach. Slavery soon proved its
ability to divest her of these heavenly qualities. Under its influence,

the tender heart became stone, and the lamblike disposition gave way to one of tiger-like fierceness. The first step in her downward course was in her ceasing to instruct me. She now commenced to practice her husband's precepts. She finally became even more violent in her opposition than her husband himself. She was not satisfied with simply doing as well as he had commanded; she seemed anxious to do better. Nothing seemed to make her more angry than to see me with a newspaper. She seemed to think that here lay the danger. I have had her rush at me with a face made all up of fury, and snatch from me a newspaper, in a manner that fully revealed her apprehension. She was an apt woman; and a little experience soon demonstrated, to her satisfaction, that education and slavery were incompatible with each other.

From this time I was most narrowly watched. If I was in a separate room any considerable length of time, I was sure to be suspected of having a book, and was at once called to give an account of myself. All this, however, was too late. The first step had been taken. Mistress, in teaching me the alphabet, had given me the *inch*, and no precaution could prevent me from taking the *ell*.

The plan which I adopted, and the one by which I was most successful, was that of making friends of all the little white boys whom I met in the street. As many of these as I could, I converted into teachers. With their kindly aid, obtained at different times and in different places, I finally succeeded in learning to read. When I was sent on errands, I always took my book with me, and by doing one part of my errand quickly, I found time to get a lesson before my return. I used also to carry bread with me, enough of which was always in the house, and to which I was always welcome; for I was much better off in this regard than many of the poor white children in our neighborhood. This bread I used to bestow upon the hungry little urchins, who, in return, would give me that more valuable bread of knowledge. I am strongly tempted to give the names of two or three of those little boys, as a testimonial of the gratitude and affection I bear them; but prudence forbids; not that it would injure me, but it might embarrass them; for it is almost an unpardonable offence to teach slaves to read in this Christian country. It is enough to say of the dear little fellows, that they lived on Philpot Street, very near Durgin and Bailey's ship-yard.

I used to talk this matter of slavery over with them. I would sometimes say to them, I wished I could be as free as they would be when they got to be men. "You will be free as soon as you are twenty-one, *but I am a slave for life!* Have not I as good a right to be free as you have?" These words used to trouble them; they would express for me the liveliest sympathy, and console me with the hope that something would occur by which I might be free.

I was now about twelve years old, and the thought of being *a slave for life* began to bear heavily upon my heart. Just about this time, I got hold of a book entitled *The Columbian Orator.* Every opportunity I got, I used to read this book. Among much of other interesting matter, I found in it a dialogue between a master and his slave. The slave was represented as having run away from his master three times. The dialogue represented the conversation which took place between them, when the slave was retaken the third time. In this dialogue, the whole argument in behalf of slavery was brought forward by the master, all of which was disposed of by the slave. The slave was made to say some very smart as well as impressive things in reply to his master— things which had the desired though unexpected effect; for the conversation resulted in the voluntary emancipation of the slave on the part of the master.

In the same book, I met with one of Sheridan's mighty speeches on and in behalf of Catholic emancipation. These were choice documents to me. I read them over and over again with unabated interest. They gave tongue to interesting thoughts of my own soul, which had frequently flashed through my mind, and died away for want of utterance. The moral which I gained from the dialogue was the power of truth over the conscience of even a slaveholder. What I got from Sheridan was a bold denunciation of slavery, and a powerful vindication of human rights. The reading of these documents enabled me to utter my thoughts, and to meet the arguments brought forward to sustain slavery; but while they relieved me of one difficulty, they brought on another even more painful than the one of which I was relieved. The more I read, the more I was led to abhor and detest my enslavers. I could regard them in no other light than a band of successful robbers, who had left their homes, and gone to Africa, and stolen us from our homes, and in a strange land reduced us to slavery. I loathed them as being the meanest as well as the most wicked of men. As I read and contemplated the subject, behold! that very discontentment which Master Hugh had predicted would follow my learning to read had already come, to torment and sting my soul to unutterable anguish. As I writhed under it, I would at times feel that learning to read had been a curse rather than a blessing. It had given me a view of my wretched condition, without the remedy. It opened my eyes to the horrible pit, but to no ladder upon which to get out. In moments of agony, I envied my fellow-slaves for their stupidity. I have often wished myself a beast. I preferred the condition of the meanest reptile to my own. Any thing, no matter what, to get rid of thinking! It was this everlasting thinking of my condition that tormented me. There was no getting rid of it. It was pressed upon me by every object within sight or hearing, animate or inanimate. The silver trump of freedom had roused my soul to eternal wakefulness. Freedom now appeared, to disappear no more forever. It was heard in every sound, and seen in every thing. It was ever present to torment me with a sense of my wretched condition. I saw nothing without seeing it, I heard nothing without hearing it, and felt nothing without feeling it. It looked from every star, it smiled in every calm, breathed in every wind, and moved in every storm.

I often found myself regretting my own existence, and wishing myself dead; and but for the hope of being free, I have no doubt but that I should have killed myself, or done something for which I should have been killed. While in this state of mind, I was eager to hear any one speak of slavery. I was a ready listener. Every little while, I could hear something about the abolitionists. It was some time before I found what the word meant. It was always used in such connections as to make it an interesting word to me. If a slave ran away and succeeded in getting clear; or if a slave killed his master, set fire to a barn, or did any thing very wrong in the mind of a slaveholder, it was spoken of as the fruit of *abolition*. Hearing the word in this connection very often, I set about learning what it meant. The dictionary afforded me little or no help. I found it was "the act of abolishing"; but then I did not know what was to be abolished. Here I was perplexed. I did not dare to ask any one about its meaning, for I was satisfied that it was something they wanted me to know very little about. After a patient waiting, I got one of our city papers, containing an account of the number of petitions from the North, praying for the abolition of slavery in the District of Columbia, and of the slave trade between the States. From this time I understood the words *abolition* and *abolitionist*, and always drew near when that word was spoken, expecting to hear something of importance to myself and fellow-slaves. The light broke in upon me by degrees. I went one day down on the wharf of Mr. Waters; and seeing two Irishmen unloading a scow of stone, I went, unasked, and helped them. When we had finished, one of them came to me and asked me if I were a slave. I told him I was. He asked, "Are ye a slave for life?" I told him that I was. The good Irishman seemed to be deeply affected by the statement. He said to the other that it was a pity so fine a little fellow as myself should be a slave for life. He said it was a shame to hold me. They both advised me to run away to the North; that I should find friends there, and that I should be free. I pretended not to be interested in what they said, and treated them as if I did not understand them; for I feared they might be treacherous. White men have been known to encourage slaves to escape, and then, to get the reward, catch them and return them to their masters. I was afraid that these seemingly good men might use me so; but I nevertheless remembered their advice, and from that time I resolved to run away. I looked forward to a time at which it would be safe for me to escape. I was too young to think of doing so immediately; besides, I wished to learn how to write, as I might have occasion to write my own pass. I consoled myself with the hope that I should one day find a good chance. Meanwhile, I would learn to write.

The idea as to how I might learn to write was suggested to me by being in Durgin and Bailey's ship-yard, and frequently seeing the ship carpenters, after hewing, and getting a piece of timber ready for use, write on the timber the name of that part of the ship for which it was intended. When a piece of timber was intended for the larboard side, it would be marked thus—"L." When a piece was for the starboard side, it would be marked thus—"S." A piece for the larboard side forward, would be marked thus—"L. F." When a piece was for starboard side forward, it would be marked thus—"S. F." For larboard aft, it would be marked thus—"L. A." For starboard aft, it would be marked thus—"S. A." I soon learned the names of these letters, and for what they were intended when placed upon a piece of timber in the shipyard. I immediately commenced copying them, and in a short time was able to make the four letters named. After that, when I met with any boy who I knew could write, I would tell him I could write as well as he. The next word would be, "I don't believe you. Let me see you try it." I would then make the letters which I had been so fortunate as to learn, and ask him to beat that. In this way I got a good many lessons in writing, which it is quite possible I should never have gotten in any other way. During this time, my copy-book was the board fence, brick wall, and pavement; my pen and ink was a lump of chalk. With these, I learned mainly how to write. I then commenced and continued copying the Italics in *Webster's Spelling Book*, until I could make them all without looking on the book. By this time, my little Master Thomas had gone to school, and learned how to write, and had written over a number of copy-books. These had been brought home, and shown to some of our near neighbors, and then laid aside. My mistress used to go to class meeting at the Wilk Street meetinghouse every Monday afternoon, and leave me to take care of the house. When left thus, I used to spend the time in writing in the spaces left in Master Thomas' copy-book, copying what he had written. I continued to do this until I could write a hand very similar to that of Master Thomas. Thus, after a long, tedious effort for years, I finally succeeded in learning how to write.

CHAPTER VIII

IN A VERY SHORT TIME AFTER I WENT TO LIVE AT BALTIMORE, MY OLD master's youngest son Richard died; and in about three years and six months after his death, my old master, Captain Anthony, died, leav-only his son, Andrew, and daughter, Lucretia, to share his estate. He died while on a visit to see his daughter at Hillsborough. Cut off thus unexpectedly, he left no will as to the disposal of his property.[1] It was therefore necessary to have a valuation of the property, that it might be equally divided between Mrs. Lucretia and Master Andrew. I was immediately sent for, to be valued with the other property. Here again my feelings rose up in detestation of slavery. I had now a new conception of my degraded condition. Prior to this, I had become, if not insensible to my lot, at least partly so. I left Baltimore with a young heart overborne with sadness, and a soul full of apprehension. I took passage with Captain Rowe, in the schooner Wild Cat, and, after a sail of about twenty-four hours, I found myself near the place of my birth. I had now been absent from it almost, if not quite, five years. I, how-ever, remembered the place very well. I was only about five years old when I left it, to go and live with my old master on Colonel Lloyd's plantation; so that I was now between ten and eleven years old.

We were all ranked together at the valuation. Men and women, old and young, married and single, were ranked with horses, sheep, and swine. There were horses and men, cattle and women, pigs and chil-dren, all holding the same rank in the scale of being, and were all subjected to the same narrow examination. Silvery-headed age and sprightly youth, maids and matrons, had to undergo the same indelicate inspection. At this moment, I saw more clearly than ever the brutalizing effects of slavery upon both slave and slaveholder.

After the valuation, then came the division. I have no language to express the high excitement and deep anxiety which were felt among us poor slaves during this time. Our fate for life was now to be decided. We had no more voice in that decision than the brutes among whom we were ranked. A single word from the white men was enough—against all our wishes, prayers, and entreaties—to sunder forever the dearest friends, dearest kindred, and strongest ties known to human beings. In addition to the pain of separation, there was the horrid dread of falling into the hands of Master Andrew. He was known to us all as being a most cruel wretch—a common drunkard, who had, by his reckless mismanagement and profligate dissipation, already wasted a large portion of his father's property. We all felt that we might as well be sold at once to the Georgia traders, as to pass into his hands; for we knew that that would be our inevitable condition—a condition held by us all in the utmost horror and dread.

I suffered more anxiety than most of my fellow slaves. I had known what it was to be kindly treated; they had known nothing of the kind. They had seen little or nothing of the world. They were in very deed men and women of sorrow, and acquainted with grief. Their backs had been made familiar with the bloody lash, so that they had become callous; mine was yet tender; for while at Baltimore I got few whippings, and few slaves could boast of a kinder master and mistress than myself; and the thought of passing out of their hands into those of Master Andrew—a man who, but a few days before, to give me a sample of his bloody disposition, took my little brother by the throat, threw him on the ground, and with the heel of his boot stamped upon his head till the blood gushed from his nose and ears—was well calculated to make me anxious as to my fate. After he had committed this savage outrage upon my brother, he turned to me, and said that was the way he meant to serve me one of these days—meaning, I suppose, when I came into his possession.

Thanks to a kind Providence, I fell to the portion of Mrs. Lucretia, and was sent immediately back to Baltimore, to live again in the family of Master Hugh. Their joy at my return equalled their sorrow at my departure. It was a glad day to me. I had escaped a worse than lion's jaws. I was absent from Baltimore, for the purpose of valuation and division, just about one month, and it seemed to have been six.

Very soon after my return to Baltimore, my mistress, Lucretia, died, leaving her husband and one child, Amanda; and in a very short time after her death, Master Andrew died. Now all the property of my old master, slaves included, was in the hands of strangers—strangers who had had nothing to do with accumulating it. Not a slave was left free. All remained slaves, from the youngest to the oldest. If any one thing in my experience, more than another, served to deepen my conviction of the infernal character of slavery, and to fill me with unutterable loathing of slaveholders, it was their base ingratitude to my poor old grandmother. She had served my old master faithfully from youth to old age. She had been the source of all his wealth; she had peopled his plantation with slaves; she had become a great grandmother in his service. She had rocked him in infancy, attended him in childhood, served him through life, and at his death wiped from his icy brow the cold death-sweat, and closed his eyes forever. She was nevertheless left a slave—a slave for life[2]—a slave in the hands of strangers; and in their hands she saw her children, her grandchildren, and her great-grandchildren, divided, like so many sheep, without being gratified with the small privilege of a single word, as to their or her own destiny. And, to cap the climax of their base ingratitude and fiendish barbarity, my grandmother, who was now very old, having outlived my old master and all his children, having seen the beginning and end of all of them, and her present owners finding she was of but little value, her frame already racked with the pains of old age, and complete helplessness fast stealing over her once active limbs, they took her to the woods, built her a little hut, put up a little mud-chimney, and then made her welcome to the privilege of supporting herself there in perfect loneliness; thus virtually turning her out to die! If my poor old grandmother now lives, she lives to suffer in utter loneliness; she lives to remember and mourn over the loss of children, the loss of grandchildren, and the loss of great-grandchildren. They are, in the language of the slave's poet, Whittier—

> Gone, gone, sold and gone
> To the rice swamp dank and lone,
> Where the slave-whip ceaseless swings,
> Where the noisome insect stings,
> Where the fever-demon strews
> Poison with the falling dews,
> Where the sickly sunbeams glare
> Through the hot and misty air:
>> Gone, gone, sold and gone
>> To the rice swamp dank and lone,
>> From Virginia hills and waters—
>> Woe is me, my stolen daughters!

The hearth is desolate. The children, the unconscious children, who once sang and danced in her presence, are gone. She gropes her way, in the darkness of age, for a drink of water. Instead of the voices of her children, she hears by day the moans of the dove, and by night the screams of the hideous owl. All is gloom. The grave is at the door. And now, when weighed down by the pains and aches of old age, when the head inclines to the feet, when the beginning and ending of human existence meet, and helpless infancy and painful old age combine together—at this time, this most needful time, the time for the exercise of that tenderness and affection which children only can exercise towards a declining parent—my poor old grandmother, the devoted mother of twelve children, is left all alone, in yonder little hut, before a few dim embers. She stands—she sits—she staggers—she falls—she groans—she dies—and there are none of her children or grandchildren present, to wipe from her wrinkled brow the cold sweat of death, or to place beneath the sod her fallen remains. Will not a righteous God visit for these things?

In about two years after the death of Mrs. Lucretia, Master Thomas married his second wife. Her name was Rowena Hamilton. She was the eldest daughter of Mr. William Hamilton. Master now lived in St. Michael's. Not long after his marriage, a misunderstanding took place between himself and Master Hugh; and as a means of punishing his brother, he took me from him to live with himself at St. Michael's.

Here I underwent another most painful separation. It, however, was not so severe as the one I dreaded at the division of property; for, during this interval, a great change had taken place in Master Hugh and his once kind and affectionate wife. The influence of brandy upon him, and of slavery upon her, had effected a disastrous change in the characters of both; so that, as far as they were concerned, I thought I had little to lose by the change. But it was not to them that I was attached. It was to those little Baltimore boys that I felt the strongest attachment. I had received many good lessons from them, and was still receiving them, and the thought of leaving them was painful indeed. I was leaving, too, without the hope of ever being allowed to return. Master Thomas had said he would never let me return again. The barrier betwixt himself and brother he considered impassable.

I then had to regret that I did not at least make the attempt to carry out my resolution to run away; for the chances of success are tenfold greater from the city than from the country.

I sailed from Baltimore for St. Michael's in the sloop Amanda, Captain Edward Dodson. On my passage, I paid particular attention to the direction which the steamboats took to go to Philadelphia. I found, instead of going down, on reaching North Point they went up the bay, in a north-easterly direction. I deemed this knowledge of the utmost importance. My determination to run away was again revived. I resolved to wait only so long as the offering of a favorable opportunity. When that came, I was determined to be off.

CHAPTER IX

I HAVE NOW REACHED A PERIOD OF MY LIFE WHEN I CAN GIVE DATES. I left Baltimore, and went to live with Master Thomas Auld, at St. Michael's, in March, 1832. It was now more than seven years since I lived with him in the family of my old master, on Colonel Lloyd's plantation. We of course were now almost entire strangers to each other. He was to me a new master, and I to him a new slave. I was ignorant of his temper and disposition; he was equally so of mine. A very short time, however, brought us into full acquaintance with each other. I was made acquainted with his wife not less than with himself. They were well matched, being equally mean and cruel. I was now, for the first time during a space of more than seven years, made to feel the painful gnawings of hunger—a something which I had not experienced before since I left Colonel Lloyd's plantation. It went hard enough with me then, when I could look back to no period at which I had enjoyed a sufficiency. It was tenfold harder after living in Master Hugh's family, where I had always had enough to eat, and of that which was good. I have said Master Thomas was a mean man. He was so. Not to give a slave enough to eat, is regarded as the most aggravated development of meanness even among slaveholders. The rule is, no matter how coarse the food, only let there be enough of it. This is the theory; and in the part of Maryland from which I came, it is the general practice—though there are many exceptions. Master Thomas gave us enough of neither coarse nor fine food. There were four slaves of us in the kitchen—my sister Eliza, my aunt Priscilla, Henny, and myself; and we were allowed less than a half of a bushel of corn-meal per week, and very little else, either in the shape of meat or vegetables. It was not enough for us to subsist upon. We were therefore reduced to the wretched necessity of living at the expense of our neighbors. This we did by begging and stealing, whichever came handy in the time of need, the one being considered as legitimate as the other. A great many times have we poor creatures been nearly perishing with hunger, when food in abundance lay mouldering in the safe and smoke-house, and our pious mistress was aware of the fact; and yet that mistress and her husband would kneel every morning, and pray that God would bless them in basket and store!

Bad as all slaveholders are, we seldom meet one destitute of every element of character commanding respect. My master was one of this rare sort. I do not know of one single noble act ever performed by him. The leading trait in his character was meanness; and if there were any other element in his nature, it was made subject to this. He was mean; and, like most other mean men, he lacked the ability to conceal his meanness. Captain Auld was not born a slaveholder. He had been a poor man, master only of a Bay craft. He came into possession of all his slaves by marriage; and of all men, adopted slaveholders are the worst. He was cruel, but cowardly. He commanded without firmness. In the enforcement of his rules, he was at times rigid, and at times lax. At times, he spoke to his slaves with the firmness of Napoleon and the fury of a demon; at other times, he might well be mistaken for an inquirer who had lost his way. He did nothing of himself. He might have passed for a lion, but for his ears. In all things noble which he attempted, his own meanness shone most conspicuous. His airs, words, and actions, were the airs, words, and actions of born slavehold-ers, and, being assumed, were awkward enough. He was not even a good imitator. He possessed all the disposition to deceive, but wanted the power. Having no resources within himself, he was compelled to be the copyist of many, and being such, he was forever the victim of inconsistency; and of consequence he was an object of contempt, and was held as such even by his slaves. The luxury of having slaves of his own to wait upon him was something new and unprepared for. He was a slaveholder without the ability to hold slaves. He found himself incapable of managing his slaves either by force, fear, or fraud. We seldom called him "master"; we generally called him "Captain Auld," and were hardly disposed to title him at all. I doubt not that our conduct had much to do with making him appear awkward, and of consequence fretful. Our want of reverence for him must have perplexed him greatly. He wished to have us call him master, but lacked the firmness necessary to command us to do so. His wife used to insist upon our calling him so, but to no purpose. In August, 1832, my master attended a Methodist camp-meeting held in the Bayside, Talbot county, and there experienced religion. I indulged a faint hope that his conversion would lead him to emancipate his slaves, and that, if he did not do this, it would, at any rate, make him more kind and humane. I was disappointed in both these respects. It neither made him to be humane to his slaves, nor to emancipate them. If it had any effect on his character, it made him more cruel and hateful in all his ways; for I believe him to have been a much worse man after his conversion than before. Prior to his conversion, he relied upon his own depravity to shield and sustain him in his savage barbarity; but after his conversion, he found religious sanction and support for his slaveholding cruelty. He made the greatest pretensions to piety. His house was the house of prayer. He prayed morning, noon, and night. He very soon distinguished himself among his brethren, and was soon made a class-leader and exhorter. His activity in revivals was great, and he proved himself an instrument in the hands of the church in converting many souls. His house was the preacher's home. They used to take great pleasure in coming there to put up; for while he starved us, he stuffed them. We have had three or four preachers there at a time. The names of those who used to come most frequently while I lived there, were Mr. Storks, Mr. Ewery, Mr. Humphry, and Mr. Hickey. I have also seen Mr. George Cookman at our house. We slaves loved Mr. Cookman. We believed him to be a good man. We thought him instrumental in getting Mr. Samuel Harrison, a very rich slaveholder, to emancipate his slaves; and by some means got the impression that he was laboring to effect the emancipation of all the slaves. When he was at our house, we were sure to be called in to prayers. When the others were there, we were sometimes called in and sometimes not. Mr.

Cookman took more notice of us than either of the other ministers. He could not come among us without betraying his sympathy for us, and, stupid as we were, we had the sagacity to see it.

While I lived with my master in St. Michael's, there was a white young man, a Mr. Wilson, who proposed to keep a Sabbath school for the instruction of such slaves as might be disposed to learn to read the New Testament. We met but three times, when Mr. West and Mr. Fairbanks, both class-leaders, with many others, came upon us with sticks and other missiles, drove us off, and forbade us to meet again. Thus ended our little Sabbath school in the pious town of St. Michael's.

I have said my master found religious sanction for his cruelty. As an example, I will state one of many facts going to prove the charge. I have seen him tie up a lame young woman, and whip her with a heavy cowskin upon her naked shoulders, causing the warm red blood to drip; and, in justification of the bloody deed, he would quote this passage of Scripture—"He that knoweth his master's will, and doeth it not, shall be beaten with many stripes."

Master would keep this lacerated young woman tied up in this horrid situation four or five hours at a time. I have known him to tie her up early in the morning, and whip her before breakfast; leave her, go to his store, return at dinner, and whip her again, cutting her in the places already made raw with his cruel lash. The secret of master's cruelty toward "Henny" is found in the fact of her being almost helpless. When quite a child, she fell into the fire, and burned herself horribly. Her hands were so burnt that she never got the use of them. She could do very little but bear heavy burdens. She was to master a bill of expense; and as he was a mean man, she was a constant offence to him. He seemed desirous of getting the poor girl out of existence. He gave her away once to his sister; but, being a poor gift, she was not disposed to keep her. Finally, my benevolent master, to use his own words, "set her adrift to take care of herself." Here was a recently converted man, holding on upon the mother, and at the same time turning out her helpless child, to starve and die! Master Thomas was one of the many pious slaveholders who hold slaves for the very charitable purpose of taking care of them.

My master and myself had quite a number of differences. He found me unsuitable to his purpose. My city life, he said, had had a very pernicious effect upon me. It had almost ruined me for every good purpose, and fitted me for every thing which was bad. One of my greatest faults was that of letting his horse run away, and go down to his father-in-law's farm, which was about five miles from St. Michael's. I would then have to go after it. My reason for this kind of carelessness, or carefulness, was, that I could always get something to eat when I went there. Master William Hamilton, my master's father-in-law, always gave his slaves enough to eat. I never left there hungry, no matter how great the need of my speedy return. Master Thomas at length said he would stand it no longer. I had lived with him nine months, during which time he had given me a number of severe whippings, all to no good purpose. He resolved to put me out, as he said, to be broken; and, for this purpose, he let me for one year to a man named Edward Covey. Mr. Covey was a poor man, a farm-renter. He rented the place upon which he lived, as also the hands with which he tilled it. Mr. Covey had acquired a very high reputation for breaking young slaves,[1] and this reputation was of immense value to him. It enabled him to get his farm tilled with much less expense to himself than he could have had it done without such a reputation. Some slaveholders thought it not much loss to allow Mr. Covey to have their slaves one year, for the sake of the training to which they were subjected, without any other compensation. He could hire young help with great ease, in consequence of this reputation. Added to the natural good qualities of Mr. Covey, he was a professor of religion—a pious soul—a member and a class-leader in the Methodist church. All of this added weight to his reputation as a "nigger-breaker." I was aware of all the facts, having been made acquainted with them by a young man who had lived there. I nevertheless made the change gladly; for I was sure of getting enough to eat, which is not the smallest consideration to a hungry man.

CHAPTER X

I had left Master Thomas' house, and went to live with Mr. Covey, on the 1ˢᵗ of January, 1833. I was now, for the first time in my life, a field hand. In my new employment, I found myself even more awkward than a country boy appeared to be in a large city. I had been at my new home but one week before Mr. Covey gave me a very severe whipping, cutting my back, causing the blood to run, and raising ridges on my flesh as large as my little finger. The details of this affair are as follows: Mr. Covey sent me, very early in the morning of one of our coldest days in the month of January, to the woods, to get a load of wood. He gave me a team of unbroken oxen. He told me which was the in-hand ox, and which the off-hand one. He then tied the end of a large rope around the horns of the in-hand ox, and gave me the other end of it, and told me, if the oxen started to run, that I must hold on upon the rope. I had never driven oxen before, and of course I was very awkward. I, however, succeeded in getting to the edge of the woods with little difficulty; but I had got a very few rods into the woods, when the oxen took fright, and started full tilt, carrying the cart against trees, and over stumps, in the most frightful manner. I expected every moment that my brains would be dashed out against the trees. After running thus for a considerable distance, they finally upset the cart, dashing it with great force against a tree, and threw themselves into a dense thicket. How I escaped death, I do not know. There I was, entirely alone, in a thick wood, in a place new to me. My cart was upset and shattered, my oxen were entangled among the young trees, and there was none to help me. After a long spell of effort, I succeeded in getting my cart righted, my oxen disentangled, and again yoked to the cart. I now proceeded with my team to the place where I had, the day before, been chopping wood, and loaded my cart pretty heavily, thinking in this way to tame my oxen. I then proceeded on my way home. I had now consumed one half of the day. I got out of the woods safely, and now felt out of danger. I stopped my oxen to open the woods gate; and just as I did so, before I could get hold of my ox-rope, the oxen again started, rushed through the gate, catching it between the wheel and the body of the cart, tearing it to pieces, and coming within a few inches of crushing me against the gate-post. Thus twice, in one short day, I escaped death by the merest chance. On my return, I told Mr. Covey what had happened, and how it happened. He ordered me to return to the woods again immediately. I did so, and he followed on after me. Just as I got into the woods, he came up and told me to stop my cart, and that he would teach me how to trifle away my time, and break gates. He then went to a large gum-tree, and with his axe cut three large switches, and, after trimming them up neatly with his pocketknife, he ordered me to take off my clothes. I made him no answer, but stood with my clothes on. He repeated his order. I still made him no answer, nor did I move to strip myself. Upon this he rushed at me with the fierceness of a tiger, tore off my clothes, and lashed me till he had worn out his switches, cutting me so savagely as to leave the marks visible for a long time. This whipping was the first of a number just like it, and for similar offences.

I lived with Mr. Covey one year. During the first six months of that year, scarce a week passed without his whipping me. I was seldom free from a sore back. My awkwardness was almost always his excuse for whipping me. We were worked fully up to the point of endurance. Long before day we were up, our horses fed, and by the first approach of day we were off to the field with our hoes and ploughing teams. Mr. Covey gave us enough to eat, but scarce time to eat it. We were often less than five minutes taking our meals. We were often in the field from the first approach of day till its last lingering ray had left us; and at saving-fodder time, midnight often caught us in the field binding blades.

Covey would be out with us. The way he used to stand it, was this. He would spend the most of his afternoons in bed. He would then come out fresh in the evening, ready to urge us on with his words, example, and frequently with the whip. Mr. Covey was one of the few slaveholders who could and did work with his hands. He was a hardworking man. He knew by himself just what a man or a boy could do. There was no deceiving him. His work went on in his absence almost as well as in his presence; and he had the faculty of making us feel that he was ever present with us. This he did by surprising us. He seldom approached the spot where we were at work openly, if he could do it secretly. He always aimed at taking us by surprise. Such was his cunning, that we used to call him, among ourselves, "the snake." When we were at work in the cornfield, he would sometimes crawl on his hands and knees to avoid detection, and all at once he would rise nearly in our midst, and scream out, "Ha, ha! Come, come! Dash on, dash on!" This being his mode of attack, it was never safe to stop a single minute. His comings were like a thief in the night. He appeared to us as being ever at hand. He was under every tree, behind every stump, in every bush, and at every window, on the plantation. He would sometimes mount his horse, as if bound to St. Michael's, a distance of seven miles, and in half an hour afterwards you would see him coiled up in the corner of the wood-fence, watching every motion of the slaves. He would, for this purpose, leave his horse tied up in the woods. Again, he would sometimes walk up to us, and give us orders as though he was upon the point of starting on a long journey, turn his back upon us, and make as though he was going to the house to get ready; and, before he would get half way thither, he would turn short and crawl into a fence-corner, or behind some tree, and there watch us till the going down of the sun.

Mr. Covey's *forte* consisted in his power to deceive. His life was devoted to planning and perpetrating the grossest deceptions. Every thing he possessed in the shape of learning or religion, he made conform to his disposition to deceive. He seemed to think himself equal to deceiving the Almighty. He would make a short prayer in the morning, and a long prayer at night; and, strange as it may seem, few men would at times appear more devotional than he. The exercises of his family devotions were always commenced with singing; and, as he was a very poor singer himself, the duty of raising the hymn generally came upon me. He would read his hymn, and nod at me to commence. I would at times do so; at others, I would not. My noncompliance would almost always produce much confusion. To show himself independent of me, he would start and stagger through with his hymn in the most discordant manner. In this state of mind, he prayed with more than ordinary spirit. Poor man! Such was his disposition, and success at deceiving, I do verily believe that he sometimes deceived himself into the solemn belief, that he was a sincere worshipper of the most high God; and this, too, at a time when he may be said to have been guilty of compelling his woman slave to commit the sin of adultery. The facts in the case are these: Mr. Covey was a poor man; he was just commencing in life; he was only able to buy one slave; and, shocking as is the fact, he bought her, as he said, for *a breeder*. This woman was named Caroline. Mr. Covey bought her from Mr. Thomas Lowe, about six miles from St. Michael's. She was a large, able-bodied woman, about twenty years old. She had already given birth to one child, which proved her to be just what he wanted. After buying her, he hired a married man of Mr. Samuel Harrison, to live with him one year; and him he used to fasten up with her every night! The result was, that, at the end of the year, the miserable woman gave birth to twins. At this result Mr. Covey seemed to be highly pleased, both with the man and the wretched woman. Such was his joy, and that of his wife, that nothing they could do for Caroline during her confinement was too good, or too hard, to be done. The children were regarded as being quite an addition to his wealth.

If at any one time of my life more than another, I was made to drink the bitterest dregs of slavery, that time was during the first six months of my stay with Mr. Covey. We were worked in all weathers. It was never too hot or too cold; it could never rain, blow, hail, or snow, too hard for us to work in the field. Work, work, work, was scarcely more the order of the day than of the night. The longest days were too short for him, and the shortest nights too long for him. I was somewhat unmanageable when I first went there, but a few months of this discipline tamed me. Mr. Covey succeeded in breaking me. I was broken in body, soul, and spirit. My natural elasticity was crushed, my intellect languished, the disposition to read departed, the cheerful spark that lingered about my eye died; the dark night of slavery closed in upon me; and behold a man transformed into a brute!

Sunday was my only leisure time. I spent this in a sort of beast-like stupor, between sleep and wake, under some large tree. At times I would rise up, a flash of energetic freedom would dart through my soul, accompanied with a faint beam of hope, that flickered for a moment, and then vanished. I sank down again, mourning over my wretched condition. I was sometimes prompted to take my life, and that of Covey, but was prevented by a combination of hope and fear. My sufferings on this plantation seem now like a dream rather than a stern reality.

Our house stood within a few rods of the Chesapeake Bay, whose broad bosom was ever white with sails from every quarter of the habitable globe. Those beautiful vessels, robed in purest white, so delightful to the eye of freemen, were to me so many shrouded ghosts, to terrify and torment me with thoughts of my wretched condition. I have often, in the deep stillness of a summer's Sabbath, stood all alone upon the lofty banks of that noble bay, and traced, with saddened heart and tearful eye, the countless number of sails moving off to the mighty ocean. The sight of these always affected me powerfully. My thoughts would compel utterance; and there, with no audience but the Almighty, I would pour out my soul's complaint, in my rude way, with an apostrophe to the moving multitude of ships:

"You are loosed from your moorings, and are free; I am fast in my chains, and am a slave! You move merrily before the gentle gale, and I sadly before the bloody whip! You are freedom's swift-winged angels, that fly round the world; I am confined in bands of iron! O, that I were free! O, that I were on one of your gallant decks, and under your protecting wing! Alas! Betwixt me and you, the turbid waters roll. Go on, go on. O that I could also go! Could I but swim! If I could fly! O, why was I born a man, of whom to make a brute! The glad ship is gone; she hides in the dim distance. I am left in the hottest hell of unending slavery. O God, save me! God, deliver me! Let me be free! Is there any God? Why am I a slave? I will run away. I will not stand it. Get caught, or get clear, I'll try it. I had as well die with ague as the fever. I have only one life to lose. I had as well be killed running as die standing. Only think of it; one hundred miles straight north, and I am free! Try it? Yes! God helping me, I will. It cannot be that I shall live and die a slave. I will take the water. This very bay shall yet bear me into freedom. The steamboats steered in a northeast course from North Point. I will do the same; and when I get to the head of the bay, I will turn my canoe adrift, and walk straight through Delaware into Pennsylvania. When I get there, I shall not be required to have a pass; I can travel without being disturbed. Let but the first opportunity offer, and, come what will, I am off. Meanwhile, I will try to bear up under the yoke. I am not the only slave in the world. Why should I fret? I can bear as much as any of them. Besides, I am but a boy, and all boys are bound to some one. It may be that my misery in slavery will only increase my happiness when I get free. There is a better day coming."

Thus I used to think, and thus I used to speak to myself; goaded almost to madness at one moment, and at the next reconciling myself to my wretched lot.

I have already intimated that my condition was much worse, during the first six months of my stay at Mr. Covey's, than in the last six. The circumstances leading to the change in Mr. Covey's course toward me form an epoch in my humble history. You have seen how a man was made a slave; you shall see how a slave was made a man. On one of the hottest days of the month of August, 1833, Bill Smith, William Hughes, a slave named Eli, and myself, were engaged in fanning wheat. Hughes was clearing the fanned wheat from before the fan. Eli was turning, Smith was feeding, and I was carrying wheat to the fan. The work was simple, requiring strength rather than intellect; yet, to one entirely unused to such work, it came very hard. About three o'clock of that day, I broke down; my strength failed me; I was seized with a violent aching of the head, attended with extreme dizziness; I trembled in every limb. Finding what was coming, I nerved myself up, feeling it would never do to stop work. I stood as long as I could stagger to the hopper with grain. When I could stand no longer, I fell, and felt as if held down by an immense weight. The fan of course stopped; every one had his own work to do; and no one could do the work of the other, and have his own go on at the same time.

Mr. Covey was at the house, about one hundred yards from the treading-yard where we were fanning. On hearing the fan stop, he left immediately, and came to the spot where we were. He hastily inquired what the matter was. Bill answered that I was sick, and there was no one to bring wheat to the fan. I had by this time crawled away under the side of the post and rail-fence by which the yard was enclosed, hoping to find relief by getting out of the sun. He then asked where I was. He was told by one of the hands. He came to the spot, and, after looking at me awhile, asked me what was the matter. I told him as well as I could, for I scarce had strength to speak. He then gave me a savage kick in the side, and told me to get up. I tried to do so, but fell back in the attempt. He gave me another kick, and again told me to rise. I again tried, and succeeded in gaining my feet; but, stooping to get the tub with which I was feeding the fan, I again staggered and fell. While down in this situation, Mr. Covey took up the hickory slat with which Hughes had been striking off the half-bushel measure, and with it gave me a heavy blow upon the head, making a large wound, and the blood ran freely; and with this again told me to get up. I made no effort to comply, having now made up my mind to let him do his worst. In a short time after receiving this blow, my head grew better. Mr. Covey had now left me to my fate. At this moment I resolved, for the first time, to go to my master, enter a complaint, and ask his protection. In order to do this, I must that afternoon walk seven miles; and this, under the circumstances, was truly a severe undertaking. I was exceedingly feeble; made so as much by the kicks and blows which I received, as by the severe fit of sickness to which I had been subjected. I, however, watched my chance, while Covey was looking in an opposite direction, and started for St. Michael's: I succeeded in getting a considerable distance on my way to the woods, when Covey discovered me, and called after me to come back, threatening what he would do if I did not come. I disregarded both his calls and his threats, and made my way to the woods as fast as my feeble state would allow; and thinking I might be overhauled by him if I kept the road, I walked through the woods, keeping far enough from the road to avoid detection, and near enough to prevent losing my way. I had not gone far before my little strength again failed me. I could go no farther. I fell down, and lay for a considerable time. The blood was yet oozing from the wound on my head. For a time I thought I should bleed to death; and think now that I should have done so, but that the blood so matted my hair as to stop the wound. After lying there about three quarters of an hour, I nerved myself up again, and started on my way, through bogs and briers, barefooted and bareheaded, tearing my feet sometimes at nearly every step; and after a journey of about seven miles, occupying some five hours to perform it, I arrived at master's store. I then presented an appearance enough to affect any but a heart of iron. From the crown of my head to my feet, I was covered with blood. My hair was all clotted with dust and blood; my shirt was stiff with blood. My legs and feet were torn in sundry places with briers and thorns, and were also covered with blood. I suppose I looked like a man who had escaped a den of wild beasts, and barely escaped them. In this state I appeared before my master, humbly entreating him to interpose his authority for my protection. I told him all the circumstances as well as I could, and it seemed, as I spoke, at times to affect him. He would then walk the floor and seek to justify Covey by saying he expected I deserved it. He asked me what I wanted. I told him, to let me get a new home; that as sure as I lived with Mr. Covey again, I should live with but to die with him; that Covey would surely kill me; he was in a fair way for me. Master Thomas ridiculed the idea that there was any danger of Mr. Covey's killing me, and said that he knew Mr. Covey, that he was a good man, and that he could not think of taking me from him; that, should he do so, he would lose the whole year's wages; that I belonged to Mr. Covey for one year, and that I must go back to him, come what might; and that I must not trouble him with any more stories, or that he would himself *get hold of me*. After threatening me thus, he gave me a very large dose of salts, telling me that I might remain in St. Michael's that night, (it being quite late), but that I must be off back to Mr. Covey's early in the morning; and that if I did not, he would *get hold of me*, which meant that he would whip me. I remained all night, and, according to his orders, I started off to Covey's in the morning, (Saturday morning), wearied in body and broken in spirit. I got no supper that night, or breakfast that morning. I reached Covey's about nine o'clock; and just as I was getting over the fence that divided Mrs. Kemp's fields from ours, out ran Covey with his cowskin, to give me another whipping. Before he could reach me, I succeeded in getting to the cornfield; and as the corn was very high, it afforded me the means of hiding. He seemed very angry, and searched for me a long time. My behavior was altogether unaccountable. He finally gave up the chase, thinking, I suppose, that I must come home for something to eat; he would give himself no further trouble in looking for me. I spent that day mostly in the woods, having the alternative before me—to go home and be whipped to death, or stay in the woods and be starved to death. That night, I fell in with Sandy Jenkins, a slave with whom I was somewhat acquainted. Sandy had a free wife who lived about four miles from Mr. Covey's; and it being Saturday, he was on his way to see her. I told him my circumstances, and he very kindly invited me to go home with him. I went home with him, and talked this whole matter over, and got his advice as to what course it was best for me to pursue. I found Sandy an old adviser. He told me, with great solemnity, I must go back to Covey; but that before I went, I must go with him into another part of the woods, where there was a certain *root*, which, if I would take some of it with me, carrying it *always on my right side,* would render it impossible for Mr. Covey, or any other white man, to whip me. He said he had carried it for years; and since he had done so, he had never received a blow, and never expected to while he carried it. I at first rejected the idea, that the simple carrying of a root in my pocket would have any such effect as he had said, and was not disposed to take it; but Sandy impressed the necessity with much earnestness, telling me it could do no harm, if it did no good. To please him, I at length took the root, and, according to his direction, carried it upon my right side. This was Sunday morning. I immediately started for home; and upon entering the yard gate, out came Mr. Covey on his way to meeting. He spoke to me very kindly, bade me drive the pigs from a lot near by, and passed on towards the church. Now, this singular conduct of Mr. Covey really made me begin to think that there was something in the *root* which Sandy had given me; and had it been on any other day than Sunday, I could have attributed the conduct to no other cause than the influence of that root; and as it was, I was half inclined to think the *root* to be something more than I at first had taken it to be. All went well till Monday morning. On this morning, the virtue of the *root* was fully tested. Long before daylight, I was called to go and rub, curry, and feed, the horses. I obeyed, and was glad to obey. But whilst thus engaged, whilst in the act of throwing down some blades from the loft, Mr. Covey entered the stable with a long rope; and just as I was half out of the loft, he caught hold of my legs, and was about tying me. As soon as I found what he was up to, I gave a sudden spring, and as I did so, he holding to my legs, I was brought sprawling on the stable floor. Mr. Covey seemed now to think he had me, and could do what he pleased; but at this moment—from whence came the spirit I don't know—I resolved to fight; and, suiting my action to the resolution, I seized Covey hard by the throat; and as I did so, I rose. He held on to me, and I to him. My resistance was so entirely unexpected that Covey seemed taken all aback. He trembled like a leaf. This gave me assurance, and I held him uneasy, causing the blood to run where I touched him with the ends of my fingers. Mr. Covey soon called out to Hughes for help. Hughes came, and, while Covey held me, attempted to tie my right hand. While he was in the act of doing so, I watched my chance, and gave him a heavy kick close under the ribs. This kick fairly sickened Hughes, so that he left me in the hands of Mr. Covey. This kick had the effect of not only weakening Hughes, but Covey also. When he saw Hughes bending over with pain, his courage quailed. He asked me if I meant to persist in my resistance. I told him I did, come what might; that he had used me like a brute for six months, and that I was determined to be used so no longer. With that, he strove to drag me to a stick that was lying just out of the stable door. He meant to knock me down. But just as he was leaning over to get the stick, I seized him with both hands by his collar, and brought him by a sudden snatch to the ground. By this time, Bill came. Covey called upon him for assistance. Bill wanted to know what he could do. Covey said, "Take hold of him, take hold of him!" Bill said his master hired him out to work, and not to help to whip me; so he left Covey and myself to fight our own battle out. We were at it for nearly two hours. Covey at length let me go, puffing and blowing at a great rate, saying that if I had not resisted, he would not have whipped me half so much. The truth was, that he had not whipped me at all. I considered him as getting entirely the worst end of the bargain; for he had drawn no blood from me, but I had from him. The whole six months afterwards, that I spent with Mr. Covey, he never laid the weight of his finger upon me in anger. He would occasionally say, he didn't want to get hold of me again. "No," thought I, "you need not; for you will come off worse than you did before."

This battle with Mr. Covey was the turning-point in my career as a slave. It rekindled the few expiring embers of freedom, and revived within me a sense of my own manhood. It recalled the departed self-confidence, and inspired me again with a determination to be free. The gratification afforded by the triumph was a full compensation for whatever else might follow, even death itself. He only can understand the deep satisfaction which I experienced, who has himself repelled by force the bloody arm of slavery. I felt as I never felt before. It was a glorious resurrection, from the tomb of slavery, to the heaven of freedom. My long-crushed spirit rose, cowardice departed, bold defiance took its place; and I now resolved that, however long I might remain a slave in form, the day had passed forever when I could be a slave in fact. I did not hesitate to let it be known of me, that the white man who expected to succeed in whipping, must also succeed in killing me.

From this time I was never again what might be called fairly whipped, though I remained a slave four years afterwards. I had several fights, but was never whipped.

It was for a long time a matter of surprise to me why Mr. Covey did not immediately have me taken by the constable to the whipping-post, and there regularly whipped for the crime of raising my hand against a white man in defence of myself. And the only explanation I can now think of does not entirely satisfy me; but such as it is, I will give it. Mr. Covey enjoyed the most unbounded reputation for being a first-rate overseer and negro-breaker. It was of considerable importance to him. That reputation was at stake; and had he sent me—a boy about sixteen years old—to the public whipping-post, his reputation would have been lost; so, to save his reputation, he suffered me to go unpunished.

My term of actual service to Mr. Edward Covey ended on Christmas day, 1833. The days between Christmas and New Year's day are allowed as holidays;[1] and, accordingly, we were not required to perform any labor, more than to feed and take care of the stock. This time we regarded as our own, by the grace of our masters; and we therefore used or abused it nearly as we pleased. Those of us who had families at a distance, were generally allowed to spend the whole six days in their society. This time, however, was spent in various ways. The staid, sober, thinking and industrious ones of our number would employ themselves in making corn-brooms, mats, horse-collars, and baskets; and another class of us would spend the time in hunting opossums, hares, and coons. But by far the larger part engaged in such sports and merriments as playing ball, wrestling, running foot-races, fiddling, dancing, and drinking whisky; and this latter mode of spending the time was by far the most agreeable to the feelings of our masters. A slave who would work during the holidays was considered by our masters as scarcely deserving them. He was regarded as one who rejected the favor of his master. It was deemed a disgrace not to get drunk at Christmas; and he was regarded as lazy indeed, who had not provided himself with the necessary means, during the year, to get whisky enough to last him through Christmas.

From what I know of the effect of these holidays upon the slave, I believe them to be among the most effective means in the hands of the slaveholder in keeping down the spirit of insurrection. Were the slaveholders at once to abandon this practice, I have not the slightest doubt it would lead to an immediate insurrection among the slaves. These holidays serve as conductors, or safety-valves, to carry off the rebellious spirit of enslaved humanity. But for these, the slave would be forced up to the wildest desperation; and woe betide the slaveholder, the day he ventures to remove or hinder the operation of those conductors! I warn him that, in such an event, a spirit will go forth in their midst, more to be dreaded than the most appalling earthquake.

The holidays are part and parcel of the gross fraud, wrong, and inhumanity of slavery. They are professedly a custom established by the benevolence of the slaveholders; but I undertake to say, it is the result of selfishness, and one of the grossest frauds committed upon the down-trodden slave. They do not give the slaves this time because they would not like to have their work during its continuance, but because they know it would be unsafe to deprive them of it. This will be seen by the fact, that the slaveholders like to have their slaves spend those days just in such a manner as to make them as glad of their ending as of their beginning. Their object seems to be, to disgust their slaves with freedom, by plunging them into the lowest depths of dissipation. For instance, the slaveholders not only like to see the slave drink of his own accord, but will adopt various plans to make him drunk. One plan is, to make bets on their slaves, as to who can drink the most whisky without getting drunk; and in this way they succeed in getting whole multitudes to drink to excess. Thus, when the slave asks for virtuous freedom, the cunning slaveholder, knowing his ignorance, cheats him with a dose of vicious dissipation, artfully labelled with the name of liberty. The most of us used to drink it down, and the result was just what might be supposed: many of us were led to think that there was little to choose between liberty and slavery. We felt, and very properly too, that we had almost as well be slaves to man as to rum. So, when the holidays ended, we staggered up from the filth of our wallowing, took a long breath, and marched to the field—feeling, upon the whole, rather glad to go, from what our master had deceived us into a belief was freedom, back to the arms of slavery.

I have said that this mode of treatment is a part of the whole system of fraud and inhumanity of slavery. It is so. The mode here adopted to disgust the slave with freedom, by allowing him to see only the abuse of it, is carried out in other things. For instance, a slave loves molasses; he steals some. His master, in many cases, goes off to town, and buys a large quantity; he returns, takes his whip, and commands the slave to eat the molasses, until the poor fellow is made sick at the very mention of it. The same mode is sometimes adopted to make the slaves refrain from asking for more food than their regular allowance. A slave runs through his allowance, and applies for more. His master is enraged at him; but, not willing to send him off without food, gives him more than is necessary, and compels him to eat it within a given time. Then, if he complains that he cannot eat it, he is said to be satisfied neither full nor fasting, and is whipped for being hard to please!

I have an abundance of such illustrations of the same principle, drawn from my own observation, but think the cases I have cited sufficient. The practice is a very common one.

On the first of January, 1834, I left Mr. Covey, and went to live with Mr. William Freeland, who lived about three miles from St. Michael's. I soon found Mr. Freeland a very different man from Mr. Covey. Though not rich, he was what would be called an educated southern gentleman. Mr. Covey, as I have shown, was a well-trained negro-breaker and slave-driver. The former (slaveholder though he was) seemed to possess some regard for honor, some reverence for justice, and some respect for humanity. The latter seemed totally insensible to all such sentiments. Mr. Freeland had many of the faults peculiar to slaveholders, such as being very passionate and fretful; but I must do him the justice to say, that he was exceedingly free from those degrading vices to which Mr. Covey was constantly addicted. The one was open and frank, and we always knew where to find him. The other was a most artful deceiver, and could be understood only by such as were skillful enough to detect his cunningly devised frauds. Another advantage I gained in my new master was, he made no pretensions to, or profession of, religion; and this, in my opinion, was truly a great advantage. I assert most unhesitatingly, that the religion of the South is a mere covering for the most horrid crimes—a justifier of the most appalling barbarity—a sanctifier of the most hateful frauds—and a dark shelter under which the darkest, foulest, grossest, and most infernal deeds of slaveholders find the strongest protection. Were I to be again reduced to the chains of slavery, next to that enslavement, I should regard being the slave of a religious master the greatest calamity that could befall me. For of all slaveholders with whom I have ever met, religious slaveholders are the worst. I have ever found them the meanest and basest, the most cruel and cowardly, of all others. It was my unhappy lot not only to belong to a religious slaveholder, but to live in a community of such religionists. Very near Mr. Freeland lived the Rev. Daniel Weeden, and in the same neighborhood lived the Rev. Rigby Hopkins. These were members and ministers in the Reformed Methodist Church. Mr. Weeden owned, among others, a woman slave, whose name I have forgotten. This woman's back, for weeks, was kept literally raw, made so by the lash of this merciless, *religious* wretch. He used to hire hands. His maxim was, Behave well or behave ill, it is the duty of a master occasionally to whip a slave, to remind him of his master's authority. Such was his theory, and such his practice.

Mr. Hopkins was even worse than Mr. Weeden. His chief boast was his ability to manage slaves. The peculiar feature of his government was that of whipping slaves in advance of deserving it. He always managed to have one or more of his slaves to whip every Monday morning. He did this to alarm their fears, and strike terror into those who escaped. His plan was to whip for the smallest offences, to prevent the commission of large ones. Mr. Hopkins could always find some excuse for whipping a slave. It would astonish one, unaccustomed to a slave-holding life, to see with what wonderful ease a slaveholder can find things, of which to make occasion to whip a slave. A mere look, word, or motion—a mistake, accident, or want of power—are all matters for which a slave may be whipped at any time. Does a slave look dissatisfied? It is said, he has the devil in him, and it must be whipped out. Does he speak loudly when spoken to by his master? Then he is getting high-minded, and should be taken down a button-hole lower. Does he forget to pull off his hat at the approach of a white person? Then he is wanting in reverence, and should be whipped for it. Does he ever venture to vindicate his conduct, when censured for it? Then he is guilty of impudence—one of the greatest crimes of which a slave can be guilty. Does he ever venture to suggest a different mode of doing things from that pointed out by his master? He is indeed presumptuous, and getting above himself; and nothing less than a flogging will do for him. Does he, while ploughing, break a plough—or, while hoeing, break a hoe? It is owing to his carelessness, and for it a slave must always be whipped. Mr. Hopkins could always find something of this sort to justify the use of the lash, and he seldom failed to embrace such opportunities. There was not a man in the whole county, with whom the slaves who had the getting their own home, would not prefer to live, rather than with this Rev. Mr. Hopkins. And yet there was not a man any where round, who made higher professions of religion, or was more active in revivals—more attentive to the class, love-feast, prayer and preaching meetings, or more devotional in his family—

that prayed earlier, later, louder, and longer—than this same reverend slave-driver, Rigby Hopkins.

But to return to Mr. Freeland, and to my experience while in his employment. He, like Mr. Covey, gave us enough to eat; but, unlike Mr. Covey, he also gave us sufficient time to take our meals. He worked us hard, but always between sunrise and sunset. He required a good deal of work to be done, but gave us good tools with which to work. His farm was large, but he employed hands enough to work it, and with ease, compared with many of his neighbors. My treatment, while in his employment, was heavenly, compared with what I experienced at the hands of Mr. Edward Covey.

Mr. Freeland was himself the owner of but two slaves. Their names were Henry Harris and John Harris. The rest of his hands he hired. These consisted of myself, Sandy Jenkins,* and Handy Caldwell. Henry and John were quite intelligent, and in a very little while after I went there, I succeeded in creating in them a strong desire to learn how to read. This desire soon sprang up in the others also. They very soon mustered up some old spelling-books, and nothing would do but that I must keep a Sabbath school. I agreed to do so, and accordingly devoted my Sundays to teaching these my loved fellow-slaves how to read. Neither of them knew his letters when I went there. Some of the slaves of the neighboring farms found what was going on, and also availed themselves of this little opportunity to learn to read. It was understood, among all who came, that there must be as little display about it as possible. It was necessary to keep our religious masters at St. Michael's unacquainted with the fact, that, instead of spending the Sabbath in wrestling, boxing, and drinking whisky, we were trying to learn how to read the will of God; for they had much rather see us engaged in those degrading sports, than to see us behaving like intellectual, moral, and accountable beings. My blood boils as I think of the

---

* This is the same man who gave me the roots to prevent my being whipped by Mr. Covey. He was "a clever soul." We used frequently to talk about the fight with Covey, and as often as we did so, he would claim my success as the result of the roots which he gave me. This superstition is very common among the more ignorant slaves. A slave seldom dies but that his death is attributed to trickery.

bloody manner in which Messrs. Wright Fairbanks and Garrison West, both class-leaders, in connection with many others, rushed in upon us with sticks and stones, and broke up our virtuous little Sabbath school, at St. Michael's—all calling themselves Christians! Humble followers of the Lord Jesus Christ! But I am again digressing.

I held my Sabbath school at the house of a free colored man, whose name I deem it imprudent to mention; for should it be known, it might embarrass him greatly, though the crime of holding the school was committed ten years ago. I had at one time over forty scholars, and those of the right sort, ardently desiring to learn. They were of all ages, though mostly men and women. I look back to those Sundays with an amount of pleasure not to be expressed. They were great days to my soul. The work of instructing my dear fellow-slaves was the sweetest engagement with which I was ever blessed. We loved each other, and to leave them at the close of the Sabbath was a severe cross indeed. When I think that these precious souls are today shut up in the prison-house of slavery, my feelings overcome me, and I am almost ready to ask, "Does a righteous God govern the universe? And for what does he hold the thunders in his right hand, if not to smite the oppressor, and deliver the spoiled out of the hand of the spoiler?" These dear souls came not to Sabbath school because it was popular to do so, nor did I teach them because it was reputable to be thus engaged. Every moment they spent in that school, they were liable to be taken up, and given thirty-nine lashes. They came because they wished to learn. Their minds had been starved by their cruel masters. They had been shut up in mental darkness. I taught them, because it was the delight of my soul to be doing something that looked like bettering the condition of my race. I kept up my school nearly the whole year I lived with Mr. Freeland; and, beside my Sabbath school, I devoted three evenings in the week, during the winter, to teaching the slaves at home. And I have the happiness to know, that several of those who came to Sabbath school learned how to read; and that one, at least, is now free through my agency.

The year passed off smoothly. It seemed only about half as long as the year which preceded it. I went through it without receiving a single blow. I will give Mr. Freeland the credit of being the best master I ever had, *till I became my own master.* For the ease with which I passed the year, I was, however, somewhat indebted to the society of my fellow-slaves. They were noble souls; they not only possessed loving hearts, but brave ones. We were linked and interlinked with each other. I loved them with a love stronger than any thing I have experienced since. It is sometimes said that we slaves do not love and confide in each other. In answer to this assertion, I can say, I never loved any or confided in any people more than my fellow-slaves, and especially those with whom I lived at Mr. Freeland's. I believe we would have died for each other. We never undertook to do any thing, of any importance, without a mutual consultation. We never moved separately. We were one; and as much so by our tempers and dispositions, as by the mutual hardships to which we were necessarily subjected by our condition as slaves.

At the close of the year 1834, Mr. Freeland again hired me of my master, for the year 1835. But, by this time, I began to want to live *upon free land* as well as *with Freeland;* and I was no longer content, therefore, to live with him or any other slaveholder. I began, with the commencement of the year, to prepare myself for a final struggle, which should decide my fate one way or the other. My tendency was upward. I was fast approaching manhood, and year after year had passed, and I was still a slave. These thoughts roused me—I must do something. I therefore resolved that 1835 should not pass without witnessing an attempt, on my part, to secure my liberty. But I was not willing to cherish this determination alone. My fellow-slaves were dear to me. I was anxious to have them participate with me in this, my life-giving determination. I therefore, though with great prudence, commenced early to ascertain their views and feelings in regard to their condition, and to imbue their minds with thoughts of freedom. I bent myself to devising ways and means for our escape, and meanwhile strove, on all fitting occasions, to impress them with the gross fraud and inhumanity of slavery. I went first to Henry, next to John, then to the others. I found, in them all, warm hearts and noble spirits. They were ready to hear, and ready to act when a feasible plan should be proposed. This was what I wanted. I talked to them of our want of manhood, if we submitted to our enslavement without at least one noble effort to be free. We met often, and consulted frequently, and told our hopes and fears, recounted the difficulties, real and imagined, which we should be called on to meet. At times we were almost disposed to give up, and try to content ourselves with our wretched lot; at others, we were firm and unbending in our determination to go. Whenever we suggested any plan, there was shrinking—the odds were fearful. Our path was beset with the greatest obstacles; and if we succeeded in gaining the end of it, our right to be free was yet questionable—we were yet liable to be returned to bondage. We could see no spot, this side of the ocean, where we could be free. We knew nothing about Canada. Our knowledge of the North did not extend farther than New York; and to go there, and be forever harassed with the frightful liability of being returned to slavery—with the certainty of being treated tenfold worse than before—the thought was truly a horrible one, and one which it was not easy to overcome. The case sometimes stood thus: At every gate through which we were to pass, we saw a watchman—at every ferry a guard—on every bridge a sentinel—and in every wood a patrol. We were hemmed in upon every side. Here were the difficulties, real or imagined—the good to be sought, and the evil to be shunned. On the one hand, there stood slavery, a stern reality, glaring frightfully upon us—its robes already crimsoned with the blood of millions, and even now feasting itself greedily upon our own flesh. On the other hand, away back in the dim distance, under the flickering light of the North Star, behind some craggy hill or snow-covered mountain, stood a doubtful freedom—half frozen—beckoning us to come and share its hospitality. This in itself was sometimes enough to stagger us; but when we permitted ourselves to survey the road, we were frequently appalled. Upon either side we saw grim death, assuming the most horrid shapes. Now it was starvation, causing us to eat our own flesh; now we were contending with the waves, and were drowned; now we were overtaken, and torn to pieces by the fangs of the terrible bloodhound. We were stung by scorpions, chased by wild beasts, bitten by snakes, and finally, after having nearly reached the desired spot—after swimming rivers, encountering wild beasts, sleeping in the woods, suffering hunger and nakedness—we were overtaken by our pursuers, and, in our resistance, we were shot dead upon the spot! I say, this picture sometimes appalled us, and made us

"rather bear those ills we had,
Than fly to others, that we knew not of."

In coming to a fixed determination to run away, we did more than Patrick Henry, when he resolved upon liberty or death. With us it was a doubtful liberty at most, and almost certain death if we failed. For my part, I should prefer death to hopeless bondage.

Sandy, one of our number, gave up the notion, but still encouraged us. Our company then consisted of Henry Harris, John Harris, Henry Bailey, Charles Roberts, and myself. Henry Bailey was my uncle, and belonged to my master. Charles married my aunt: he belonged to my master's father-in-law, Mr. William Hamilton.

The plan we finally concluded upon was, to get a large canoe belonging to Mr. Hamilton, and upon the Saturday night previous to Easter holidays, paddle directly up the Chesapeake Bay. On our arrival at the head of the bay, a distance of seventy or eighty miles from where we lived, it was our purpose to turn our canoe adrift, and follow the guidance of the North Star till we got beyond the limits of Maryland. Our reason for taking the water route was, that we were less liable to be suspected as runaways; we hoped to be regarded as fishermen; whereas, if we should take the land route, we should be subjected to interruptions of almost every kind. Any one having a white face, and being so disposed, could stop us, and subject us to examination.

The week before our intended start, I wrote several protections, one for each of us. As well as I can remember, they were in the following words, to wit:

This is to certify that I, the undersigned, have given the bearer, my servant, full liberty to go to Baltimore, and spend the Easter holidays. Written with mine own hand, &c., 1835.

William Hamilton,
Near St. Michael's, in Talbot county, Maryland

We were not going to Baltimore; but, in going up the bay, we went toward Baltimore, and these protections were only intended to protect us while on the bay.

As the time drew near for our departure, our anxiety became more and more intense. It was truly a matter of life and death with us. The strength of our determination was about to be fully tested. At this time, I was very active in explaining every difficulty, removing every doubt, dispelling every fear, and inspiring all with the firmness indispensable to success in our undertaking; assuring them that half was gained the instant we made the move; we had talked long enough; we were now ready to move; if not now, we never should be; and if we did not intend to move now, we had as well fold our arms, sit down, and acknowledge ourselves fit only to be slaves. This, none of us were prepared to acknowledge. Every man stood firm; and at our last meeting, we pledged ourselves afresh, in the most solemn manner, that, at the time appointed, we would certainly start in pursuit of freedom. This was in the middle of the week, at the end of which we were to be off. We went, as usual, to our several fields of labor, but with bosoms highly agitated with thoughts of our truly hazardous undertaking. We tried to conceal our feelings as much as possible; and I think we succeeded very well.

After a painful waiting, the Saturday morning, whose night was to witness our departure, came. I hailed it with joy, bring what sadness it might. Friday night was a sleepless one for me. I probably felt more anxious than the rest, because I was, by common consent, at the head of the whole affair. The responsibility of success or failure lay heavily upon me. The glory of the one, and the confusion of the other, were alike mine. The first two hours of that morning were such as I never experienced before, and hope never to again. Early in the morning, we went, as usual, to the field. We were spreading manure; and all at once, while thus engaged, I was overwhelmed with an indescribable feeling, in the fulness of which I turned to Sandy, who was near by, and said, "We are betrayed!" "Well," said he, "that thought has this moment struck me." We said no more. I was never more certain of any thing.

The horn was blown as usual, and we went up from the field to the house for breakfast. I went for the form, more than for want of any thing to eat that morning. Just as I got to the house, in looking out at the lane gate, I saw four white men, with two colored men. The white men were on horseback, and the colored ones were walking behind, as if tied. I watched them a few moments till they got up to our lane gate. Here they halted, and tied the colored men to the gatepost. I was not yet certain as to what the matter was. In a few moments, in rode Mr. Hamilton, with a speed betokening great excitement. He came to the door, and inquired if Master William was in. He was told he was at the barn. Mr. Hamilton, without dismounting, rode up to the barn with extraordinary speed. In a few moments, he and Mr. Freeland returned to the house. By this time, the three constables rode up, and in great haste dismounted, tied their horses, and met Master William and Mr. Hamilton returning from the barn; and after talking awhile, they all walked up to the kitchen door. There was no one in the kitchen but myself and John. Henry and Sandy were up at the barn. Mr. Freeland put his head in at the door, and called me by name, saying, there were some gentlemen at the door who wished to see me. I stepped to the door, and inquired what they wanted. They at once seized me, and, without giving me any satisfaction, tied me—lashing my hands closely together. I insisted upon knowing what the matter was. They at length said, that they had learned I had been in a "scrape," and that I was to be examined before my master; and if their information proved false, I should not be hurt.

In a few moments, they succeeded in tying John. They then turned to Henry, who had by this time returned, and commanded him to cross his hands. "I won't!" said Henry, in a firm tone, indicating his readiness to meet the consequences of his refusal. "Won't you?" said Tom Graham, the constable. "No, I won't!" said Henry, in a still stronger tone. With this, two of the constables pulled out their shining pistols, and swore, by their Creator, that they would make him cross his hands or kill him. Each cocked his pistol, and, with fingers on the trigger, walked up to Henry, saying, at the same time, if he did not cross his hands, they would blow his damned heart out. "Shoot me, shoot me!" said Henry; "you can't kill me but once. Shoot, shoot—and be damned! *I won't be tied!*" This he said in a tone of loud defiance; and at the same time, with a motion as quick as lightning, he with one single stroke dashed the pistols from the hand of each constable. As he did this, all hands fell upon him, and, after beating him some time, they finally overpowered him, and got him tied.

During the scuffle, I managed, I know not how, to get my pass out, and, without being discovered, put it into the fire. We were all now tied; and just as we were to leave for Easton jail, Betsy Freeland, mother of William Freeland, came to the door with her hands full of biscuits, and divided them between Henry and John. She then delivered herself of a speech, to the following effect: addressing herself to me, she said, "*You devil! You yellow devil!* It was you that put it into the heads of Henry and John to run away. But for you, you long-legged mulatto devil! Henry nor John would never have thought of such a thing." I made no reply, and was immediately hurried off towards St. Michael's. Just a moment previous to the scuffle with Henry, Mr. Hamilton suggested the propriety of making a search for the protections which he had understood Frederick had written for himself and the rest. But, just at the moment he was about carrying his proposal into effect, his aid was needed in helping to tie Henry; and the excitement attending the scuffle caused them either to forget, or to deem it unsafe, under the circumstances, to search. So we were not yet convicted of the intention to run away.

When we got about half way to St. Michael's, while the constables having us in charge were looking ahead, Henry inquired of me what he should do with his pass. I told him to eat it with his biscuit, and own nothing; and we passed the word around. "*Own nothing;*" and "*Own nothing!*" said we all. Our confidence in each other was unshaken. We were resolved to succeed or fail together, after the calamity had befallen us as much as before. We were now prepared for any thing. We were to be dragged that morning fifteen miles behind horses, and then to be placed in the Easton jail. When we reached St. Michael's, we underwent a sort of examination. We all denied that we ever intended to run away. We did this more to bring out the evidence against us, than from any hope of getting clear of being sold; for, as I have said, we were ready for that. The fact was, we cared but little where we went, so we went together. Our greatest concern was about separation. We dreaded that more than any thing this side of death. We found the evidence against us to be the testimony of one person; our master would not tell who it was; but we came to a unanimous decision among ourselves as to who their informant was. We were sent off to the jail at Easton. When we got there, we were delivered up to the sheriff, Mr. Joseph Graham, and by him placed in jail. Henry, John, and myself, were placed in one room together—Charles, and Henry Bailey, in another. Their object in separating us was to hinder concert.

We had been in jail scarcely twenty minutes, when a swarm of slave traders, and agents for slave traders, flocked into jail to look at us, and to ascertain if we were for sale. Such a set of beings I never saw before! I felt myself surrounded by so many fiends from perdition. A band of pirates never looked more like their father, the devil. They laughed and grinned over us, saying, "Ah, my boys! We have got you, haven't we?" And after taunting us in various ways, they one by one went into an examination of us, with intent to ascertain our value. They would impudently ask us if we would not like to have them for our masters. We would make them no answer, and leave them to find out as best they could. Then they would curse and swear at us telling us that they could take the devil out of us in a very little while, if we were only in their hands.

While in jail, we found ourselves in much more comfortable quarters than we expected when we went there. We did not get much to eat, nor that which was very good; but we had a good clean room, from the windows of which we could see what was going on in the street, which was very much better than though we had been placed in one of the dark, damp cells. Upon the whole, we got along very well, so far as the jail and its keeper were concerned. Immediately after the holidays were over, contrary to all our expectations, Mr. Hamilton and Mr. Freeland came up to Easton, and took Charles, the two Henrys, and John, out of jail, and carried them home, leaving me alone. I regarded this separation as a final one. It caused me more pain than any thing else in the whole transaction. I was ready for any thing rather than separation. I supposed that they had consulted together, and had decided that, as I was the whole cause of the intention of the others to run away, it was hard to make the innocent suffer with the guilty; and that they had, therefore, concluded to take the others home, and sell me, as a warning to the others that remained. It is due to the noble Henry to say, he seemed almost as reluctant at leaving the prison as at leaving home to come to the prison. But we knew we should, in all probability, be separated, if we were sold; and since he was in their hands, he concluded to go peaceably home.

I was now left to my fate. I was all alone, and within the walls of a stone prison. But a few days before, and I was full of hope. I expected to have been safe in a land of freedom; but now I was covered with gloom, sunk down to the utmost despair. I thought the possibility of freedom was gone. I was kept in this way about one week, at the end of which, Captain Auld, my master, to my surprise and utter astonishment, came up, and took me out, with the intention of sending me, with a gentleman of his acquaintance, into Alabama. But, from some cause or other, he did not send me to Alabama, but concluded to send me back to Baltimore, to live again with his brother Hugh, and to learn a trade.

Thus, after an absence of three years and one month, I was once more permitted to return to my old home at Baltimore. My master sent me away, because there existed against me a very great prejudice in the community, and he feared I might be killed.

In a few weeks after I went to Baltimore, Master Hugh hired me to Mr. William Gardner, an extensive ship-builder, on Fell's Point. I was put there to learn how to calk. It, however, proved a very unfavorable place for the accomplishment of this object. Mr. Gardner was engaged that spring in building two large man-of-war brigs, professedly for the Mexican government. The vessels were to be launched in the July of that year, and in failure thereof, Mr. Gardner was to lose a considerable sum; so that when I entered, all was hurry. There was no time to learn any thing. Every man had to do that which he knew how to do. In entering the shipyard, my orders from Mr. Gardner were, to do whatever the carpenters commanded me to do. This was placing me at the beck and call of about seventy-five men. I was to regard all these as masters. Their word was to be my law. My situation was a most trying one. At times I needed a dozen pair of hands. I was called a dozen ways in the space of a single minute. Three or four voices would strike my ear at the same moment. It was—"Fred., come help me to cant this timber here." "Fred., come carry this timber yonder." "Fred., bring that roller here." "Fred., go get a fresh can of water." "Fred., come help saw off the end of this timber." "Fred., go quick, and get the crowbar." "Fred., hold on the end of this fall." "Fred., go to the blacksmith's shop, and get a new punch." "Hurra, Fred.! Run and bring me a cold chisel." "I say, Fred., bear a hand, and get up a fire as quick as lightning under that steam-box." "Halloo, nigger! Come, turn this grindstone." "Come, come! Move, move! And *bowse* this timber forward." "I say, darky, blast your eyes, why don't you heat up some pitch?" "Halloo! Halloo! Halloo!" (Three voices at the same time.) "Come here! Go there! Hold on where you are! Damn you, if you move, I'll knock your brains out!"

This was my school for eight months; and I might have remained there longer, but for a most horrid fight I had with four of the white apprentices, in which my left eye was nearly knocked out, and I was horribly mangled in other respects. The facts in the case were these: Until a very little while after I went there, white and black ship-carpenters worked side by side, and no one seemed to see any impropriety in it. All hands seemed to be very well satisfied. Many of the black carpenters were freemen.[2] Things seemed to be going on very well. All at once, the white carpenters knocked off, and said they would not work with free colored workmen. Their reason for this, as alleged, was, that if free colored carpenters were encouraged, they would soon take the trade into their own hands, and poor white men would be thrown out of employment. They therefore felt called upon at once to put a stop to it. And, taking advantage of Mr. Gardner's necessities, they broke off, swearing they would work no longer, unless he would discharge his black carpenters. Now, though this did not extend to me in form, it did reach me in fact. My fellow-apprentices very soon began to feel it degrading to them to work with me. They began to put on airs, and talk about the "niggers" taking the country, saying we all ought to be killed; and, being encouraged by the journey-men, they commenced making my condition as hard as they could, by hectoring me around, and sometimes striking me. I, of course, kept the vow I made after the fight with Mr. Covey, and struck back again, regardless of consequences; and while I kept them from combining, I succeeded very well; for I could whip the whole of them, taking them separately. They, however, at length combined, and came upon me, armed with sticks, stones, and heavy handspikes. One came in front with a half brick. There was one at each side of me, and one behind me. While I was attending to those in front, and on either side, the one behind ran up with the handspike, and struck me a heavy blow upon the head. It stunned me. I fell, and with this they all ran upon me, and fell to beating me with their fists. I let them lay on for a while, gathering strength. In an instant, I gave a sudden surge, and rose to my hands and knees. Just as I did that, one of their number gave me, with his heavy boot, a powerful kick in the left eye. My eyeball seemed to have burst. When they saw my eye closed, and badly swollen, they left me. With this I seized the handspike, and for a time pursued them. But here the carpenters interfered, and I thought I might as well give it up. It was impossible to stand my hand against so many. All this took place in sight of not less than fifty white ship-carpenters, and not one interposed a friendly word; but some cried, "Kill the damned nigger! Kill him! Kill him! He struck a white person." I found my only chance for life was in flight. I succeeded in getting away without an additional blow, and barely so; for to strike a white man is death by Lynch law— and that was the law in Mr. Gardner's ship-yard; nor is there much of any other out of Mr. Gardner's ship-yard.

I went directly home, and told the story of my wrongs to Master Hugh; and I am happy to say of him, irreligious as he was, his conduct was heavenly, compared with that of his brother Thomas under similar circumstances. He listened attentively to my narration of the circum-stances leading to the savage outrage, and gave many proofs of his strong indignation at it. The heart of my once overkind mistress was again melted into pity. My puffed-out eye and blood-covered face moved her to tears. She took a chair by me, washed the blood from my face, and, with a mother's tenderness, bound up my head, covering the wounded eye with a lean piece of fresh beef. It was almost compensation for my suffering to witness, once more, a manifestation of kindness from this, my once affectionate old mistress. Master Hugh was very much enraged. He gave expression to his feelings by pouring out curses upon the heads of those who did the deed. As soon as I got a little the better of my bruises, he took me with him to Esquire Watson's, on Bond Street, to see what could be done about the matter. Mr. Watson inquired who saw the assault committed. Master Hugh told him it was done in

Mr. Gardner's ship-yard at midday, where there were a large company of men at work. "As to that," he said, "the deed was done, and there was no question as to who did it." His answer was, he could do nothing in the case, unless some white man would come forward and testify. He could issue no warrant on my word. If I had been killed in the presence of a thousand colored people, their testimony combined would have been insufficient to have arrested one of the murderers. Master Hugh, for once, was compelled to say this state of things was too bad. Of course, it was impossible to get any white man to volunteer his testimony in my behalf, and against the white young men. Even those who may have sympathized with me were not prepared to do this. It required a degree of courage unknown to them to do so; for just at that time, the slightest manifestation of humanity toward a colored person was denounced as abolitionism, and that name subjected its bearer to frightful liabilities. The watchwords of the bloody minded in that region, and in those days, were, "Damn the abolitionists!" and "Damn the niggers!" There was nothing done, and probably nothing would have been done if I had been killed. Such was, and such remains, the state of things in the Christian city of Baltimore.

Master Hugh, finding he could get no redress, refused to let me go back again to Mr. Gardner. He kept me himself, and his wife dressed my wound till I was again restored to health. He then took me into the ship-yard of which he was foreman, in the employment of Mr. Walter Price. There I was immediately set to calking, and very soon learned the art of using my mallet and irons. In the course of one year from the time I left Mr. Gardner's, I was able to command the highest wages given to the most experienced calkers. I was now of some importance to my master. I was bringing him from six to seven dollars per week. I sometimes brought him nine dollars per week: my wages were a dollar and a half a day. After learning how to calk, I sought my own employment, made my own contracts, and collected the money which I earned. My pathway became much more smooth than before; my condition was now much more comfortable. When I could get no calking to do, I did nothing. During these leisure times, those old notions about freedom would steal over me again. When in Mr. Gardner's employment, I was kept in such a perpetual whirl of excitement, I could think of nothing, scarcely, but my life; and in thinking of my life, I almost forgot my liberty. I have observed this in my experience of slavery—that whenever my condition was improved, instead of its increasing my contentment, it only increased my desire to be free, and set me to thinking of plans to gain my freedom. I have found that, to make a contented slave, it is necessary to make a thoughtless one. It is necessary to darken his moral and mental vision, and, as far as possible, to annihilate the power of reason. He must be able to detect no inconsistencies in slavery; he must be made to feel that slavery is right; and he can be brought to that only when he ceases to be a man.

I was now getting, as I have said, one dollar and fifty cents per day. I contracted for it; I earned it; it was paid to me; it was rightfully my own; yet, upon each returning Saturday night, I was compelled to deliver every cent of that money to Master Hugh. And why? Not because he earned it—not because he had any hand in earning it— not because I owed it to him—nor because he possessed the slightest shadow of a right to it; but solely because he had the power to compel me to give it up. The right of the grim-visaged pirate upon the high seas is exactly the same.

CHAPTER XI

I NOW COME TO THAT PART OF MY LIFE DURING WHICH I PLANNED, AND finally succeeded in making, my escape from slavery. But before narrating any of the peculiar circumstances, I deem it proper to make known my intention not to state all the facts connected with the transaction. My reasons for pursuing this course may be understood from the following: First, were I to give a minute statement of all the facts, it is not only possible, but quite probable, that others would thereby be involved in the most embarrassing difficulties. Secondly, such a statement would most undoubtedly induce greater vigilance on the part of slaveholders than has existed heretofore among them; which would, of course, be the means of guarding a door whereby some dear brother bondman might escape his galling chains. I deeply regret the necessity that impels me to suppress any thing of importance connected with my experience in slavery. It would afford me great pleasure indeed, as well as materially add to the interest of my narrative, were I at liberty to gratify a curiosity, which I know exists in the minds of many, by an accurate statement of all the facts pertaining to my most fortunate escape. But I must deprive myself of this pleasure, and the curious of the gratification which such a statement would afford. I would allow myself to suffer under the greatest imputations which evil-minded men might suggest, rather than exculpate myself, and thereby run the hazard of closing the slightest avenue by which a brother slave might clear himself of the chains and fetters of slavery.

I have never approved of the very public manner in which some of our western friends have conducted what they call the *underground railroad,* but which I think, by their open declarations, has been made most emphatically the *upperground railroad.* I honor those good men and women for their noble daring, and applaud them for willingly subjecting themselves to bloody persecution, by openly avowing their participation in the escape of slaves. I, however, can see very little good resulting from such a course, either to themselves or the slaves escaping; while, upon the other hand, I see and feel assured that those open declarations are a positive evil to the slaves remaining, who are seeking to escape. They do nothing towards enlightening the slave, whilst they do much towards enlightening the master. They stimulate him to greater watchfulness, and enhance his power to capture his slave. We owe something to the slave south of the line as well as to those north of it; and in aiding the latter on their way to freedom, we should be careful to do nothing which would be likely to hinder the former from escaping from slavery. I would keep the merciless slave-holder profoundly ignorant of the means of flight adopted by the slave. I would leave him to imagine himself surrounded by myriads of invisible tormentors, ever ready to snatch from his infernal grasp his trembling prey. Let him be left to feel his way in the dark; let darkness commensurate with his crime hover over him; and let him feel that at every step he takes, in pursuit of the flying bondman, he is running the frightful risk of having his hot brains dashed out by an invisible agency. Let us render the tyrant no aid; let us not hold the light by which he can trace the footprints of our flying brother. But enough of this. I will now proceed to the statement of those facts, connected with my escape, for which I am alone responsible, and for which no one can be made to suffer but myself.

In the early part of the year 1838, I became quite restless. I could see no reason why I should, at the end of each week, pour the reward of my toil into the purse of my master. When I carried to him my weekly wages, he would, after counting the money, look me in the face with a robber-like fierceness, and ask, "Is this all?" He was satisfied with nothing less than the last cent. He would, however, when I made him six dollars, sometimes give me six cents, to encourage me. It had the opposite effect. I regarded it as a sort of admission of my right to the whole. The fact that he gave me any part of my wages was proof, to my mind, that he believed me entitled to the whole of them. I always felt worse for having received any thing; for I feared that the giving me a few cents would ease his conscience, and make him feel himself to be a pretty honorable sort of robber. My discontent grew upon me. I was ever on the look-out for means of escape; and, finding no direct means, I determined to try to hire my time, with a view of getting money with which to make my escape. In the spring of 1838, when Master Thomas came to Baltimore to purchase his spring goods, I got an opportunity, and applied to him to allow me to hire my time. He unhesitatingly refused my request, and told me this was another stratagem by which to escape. He told me I could go nowhere but that he could get me; and that, in the event of my running away, he should spare no pains in his efforts to catch me. He exhorted me to content myself, and be obedient. He told me, if I would be happy, I must lay out no plans for the future. He said, if I behaved myself properly, he would take care of me. Indeed, he advised me to complete thoughtlessness of the future, and taught me to depend solely upon him for happiness. He seemed to see fully the pressing necessity of setting aside my intellectual nature, in order to contentment in slavery. But in spite of him, and even in spite of myself, I continued to think, and to think about the injustice of my enslavement, and the means of escape.

About two months after this, I applied to Master Hugh for the privilege of hiring my time.[1] He was not acquainted with the fact that I had applied to Master Thomas, and had been refused. He too, at first, seemed disposed to refuse; but, after some reflection, he granted me the privilege, and proposed the following terms: I was to be allowed all my time, make all contracts with those for whom I worked, and find my own employment; and, in return for this liberty, I was to pay him three dollars at the end of each week; find myself in calking tools, and in board and clothing. My board was two dollars and a half per week. This, with the wear and tear of clothing and calking tools, made my regular expenses about six dollars per week. This amount I was compelled to make up, or relinquish the privilege of hiring my time. Rain or shine, work or no work, at the end of each week the money must be forthcoming, or I must give up my privilege. This arrangement, it will be perceived, was decidedly in my master's favor. It relieved him of all need of looking after me. His money was sure. He received all the benefits of slaveholding without its evils; while I endured all the evils of a slave, and suffered all the care and anxiety of a freeman. I found it a hard bargain. But, hard as it was, I thought it better than the old mode of getting along. It was a step towards freedom to be allowed to bear the responsibilities of a freeman, and I was determined to hold on upon it. I bent myself to the work of making money. I was ready to work at night as well as day, and by the most untiring perseverance and industry, I made enough to meet my expenses, and lay up a little money every week. I went on thus from May till August. Master Hugh then refused to allow me to hire my time longer. The ground for his refusal was a failure on my part, one Saturday night, to pay him for my week's time. This failure was occasioned by my attending a camp meeting about ten miles from Baltimore. During the week, I had entered into an engagement with a number of young friends to start from Baltimore to the camp ground early Saturday evening; and being detained by my employer, I was unable to get down to Master Hugh's without disappointing the company. I knew that Master Hugh was in no special need of the money that night. I therefore decided to go to camp meeting, and upon my return pay him the three dollars. I stayed at the camp meeting one day longer than I intended when I left. But as soon as I returned, I called upon him to pay him what he considered his due. I found him very angry; he could scarce restrain his wrath. He said he had a great mind to give me a severe whipping. He wished to know how I dared go out of the city without asking his permission. I told him I hired my time, and while I paid him the price which he asked for it, I did not know that I was bound to ask him when and where I should go. This reply troubled him; and, after reflecting a few moments, he turned to me, and said I should hire my time no longer; that the next thing he should know of, I would be running away. Upon the same plea, he told me to bring my tools and clothing home forthwith. I did so; but instead of seeking work, as I had been accustomed to do previously to hiring my time, I spent the whole week without the performance of a single stroke of work. I did this in retaliation. Saturday night, he called upon me as usual for my week's wages. I told him I had no wages; I had done no work that week. Here we were upon the point of coming to blows. He raved, and swore his determination to get hold of me. I did not allow myself a single word; but was resolved, if he laid the weight of his hand upon me, it should be blow for blow. He did not strike me, but told me that he would find me in constant employment in future. I thought the matter over during the next day, Sunday, and finally resolved upon the third day of September, as the day upon which I would make a second attempt to secure my freedom. I now had three weeks during which to prepare for my journey. Early on Monday morning, before Master Hugh had time to make any engagement for me, I went out and got employment of Mr. Butler, at his ship-yard near the drawbridge, upon what is called the City Block, thus making it unnecessary for him to seek employment for me. At the end of the week, I brought him between eight and nine dollars. He seemed very well pleased, and asked why I did not do the same the week before. He little knew what my plans were. My object in working steadily was to remove any suspicion he might entertain of my intent to run away; and in this I succeeded admirably. I suppose he thought I was never better satisfied with my condition than at the very time during which I was planning my escape. The second week passed, and again I carried him my full wages; and so well pleased was he, that he gave me twenty-five cents, (quite a large sum for a slaveholder to give a slave), and bade me to make a good use of it. I told him I would.

Things went on without very smoothly indeed, but within there was trouble. It is impossible for me to describe my feelings as the time of my contemplated start drew near. I had a number of warm-hearted friends in Baltimore—friends that I loved almost as I did my life—and the thought of being separated from them forever was painful beyond expression. It is my opinion that thousands would escape from slavery, who now remain, but for the strong cords of affection that bind them to their friends. The thought of leaving my friends was decidedly the most painful thought with which I had to contend. The love of them was my tender point, and shook my decision more than all things else. Besides the pain of separation, the dread and apprehension of a failure exceeded what I had experienced at my first attempt. The appalling defeat I then sustained returned to torment me. I felt assured that, if I failed in this attempt, my case would be a hopeless one—it would seal my fate as a slave forever. I could not hope to get off with any thing less than the severest punishment, and being placed beyond the means of escape. It required no very vivid imagination to depict the most frightful scenes through which I should have to pass, in case I failed. The wretchedness of slavery, and the blessedness of freedom, were perpetually before me. It was life and death with me. But I remained firm, and, according to my resolution, on the third day of September, 1838, I left my chains, and succeeded in reaching New York without the slightest interruption of any kind. How I did so—what means I adopted—what direction I travelled, and by what mode of conveyance—I must leave unexplained, for the reasons before mentioned.

I have been frequently asked how I felt when I found myself in a free State. I have never been able to answer the question with any satisfaction to myself. It was a moment of the highest excitement I ever experienced. I suppose I felt as one may imagine the unarmed mariner to feel when he is rescued by a friendly man-of-war from the pursuit of a pirate. In writing to a dear friend, immediately after my arrival at New York, I said I felt like one who had escaped a den of hungry lions. This state of mind, however, very soon subsided; and I was again seized with a feeling of great insecurity and loneliness. I was yet liable to be taken back, and subjected to all the tortures of slavery. This in itself was enough to damp the ardor of my enthusiasm. But the loneliness overcame me. There I was in the midst of thousands, and yet a perfect stranger; without home and without friends, in the midst of thousands of my own brethren—children of a common Father, and yet I dared not to unfold to any one of them my sad condition. I was afraid to speak to any one for fear of speaking to the wrong one, and thereby falling into the hands of money-loving kidnappers, whose business it was to lie in wait for the panting fugitive, as the ferocious beasts of the forest lie in wait for their prey. The motto which I adopted when I started from slavery was this—"Trust no man!" I saw in every white man an enemy, and in almost every colored man cause for distrust. It was a most painful situation; and, to understand it, one must needs experience it, or imagine himself in similar circumstances. Let him be a fugitive slave in a strange land—a land given up to be the hunting-ground for slaveholders—whose inhabitants are legalized kidnappers—where he is every moment subjected to the terrible liability of being seized upon by his fellow-men, as the hideous crocodile seizes upon his prey!—I say, let him place himself in my situation—without home or friends—without money or credit—wanting shelter, and no one to give it—wanting bread, and no money to buy it—and at the same time let him feel that he is pursued by merciless men-hunters, and in total darkness as to what to do, where to go, or where to stay—perfectly helpless both as to the means of defence and means of escape—in the midst of plenty, yet suffering the terrible gnawings of hunger—in the midst of houses, yet having no home—among fellow-men, yet feeling as if in the midst of wild beasts, whose greediness to swallow up the trembling and half-famished fugitive is only equalled by that with which the monsters of the deep swallow up the helpless fish upon which they subsist—I say, let him be placed in this most trying situation—the situation in which I was placed—then, and not till then, will he fully appreciate the hardships of, and know how to sympathize with, the toil-worn and whip-scarred fugitive slave.

Thank Heaven, I remained but a short time in this distressed situation. I was relieved from it by the humane hand of Mr. DAVID RUGGLES, whose vigilance, kindness, and perseverance, I shall never forget. I am glad of an opportunity to express, as far as words can, the love and gratitude I bear him. Mr. Ruggles is now afflicted with blindness, and is himself in need of the same kind offices which he was once so forward in the performance of toward others. I had been in New York but a few days, when Mr. Ruggles sought me out, and very kindly took me to his boarding-house at the corner of Church and Lespenard Streets. Mr. Ruggles was then very deeply engaged in the memorable *Darg* case, as well as attending to a number of other fugitive slaves, devising ways and means for their successful escape; and, though watched and hemmed in on almost every side, he seemed to be more than a match for his enemies.

Very soon after I went to Mr. Ruggles, he wished to know of me where I wanted to go; as he deemed it unsafe for me to remain in New York. I told him I was a calker, and should like to go where I could get work. I thought of going to Canada; but he decided against it, and in favor of my going to New Bedford, thinking I should be able to get work there at my trade. At this time, Anna,* my intended wife, came on; for I wrote to her immediately after my arrival at New York, (notwithstanding my homeless, houseless, and helpless condition), informing her of my successful flight, and wishing her to come on forthwith. In a few days after her arrival, Mr. Ruggles called in the Rev. J. W. C. Pennington, who, in the presence of Mr. Ruggles, Mrs. Michaels, and two or three others, performed the marriage ceremony, and gave us a certificate, of which the following is an exact copy:

This may certify, that I joined together in holy matrimony Frederick Johnson† and Anna Murray, as man and wife, in the presence of Mr. David Ruggles and Mrs. Michaels.

James W. C. Pennington
New York, September 15, 1838

Upon receiving this certificate, and a five-dollar bill from Mr. Ruggles, I shouldered one part of our baggage, and Anna took up the other, and we set out forthwith to take passage on board of the steam-boat John W. Richmond for Newport, on our way to New Bedford. Mr. Ruggles gave me a letter to a Mr. Shaw in Newport, and told me, in case my money did not serve me to New Bedford, to stop in Newport and obtain further assistance; but upon our arrival at Newport, we were so anxious to get to a place of safety, that, notwithstanding we lacked the necessary money to pay our fare, we decided to take seats in the stage, and promise to pay when we got to New Bedford. We were encouraged to do this by two excellent gentlemen, residents of New Bedford, whose names I afterward ascertained to be Joseph Ricketson and William C. Taber. They seemed at once to understand

---

* She was free.
† I had changed my name from Frederick BAILEY to that of JOHNSON.

our circumstances, and gave us such assurance of their friendliness as put us fully at ease in their presence. It was good indeed to meet with such friends, at such a time. Upon reaching New Bedford, we were directed to the house of Mr. Nathan Johnson, by whom we were kindly received, and hospitably provided for. Both Mr. and Mrs. Johnson took a deep and lively interest in our welfare. They proved themselves quite worthy of the name of abolitionists. When the stage-driver found us unable to pay our fare, he held on upon our baggage as security for the debt. I had but to mention the fact to Mr. Johnson, and he forthwith advanced the money.

We now began to feel a degree of safety, and to prepare ourselves for the duties and responsibilities of a life of freedom. On the morning after our arrival at New Bedford, while at the breakfast table, the question arose as to what name I should be called by. The name given me by my mother was, "Frederick Augustus Washington Bailey." I, however, had dispensed with the two middle names long before I left Maryland so that I was generally known by the name of "Frederick Bailey." I started from Baltimore bearing the name of "Stanley." When I got to New York, I again changed my name to "Frederick Johnson," and thought that would be the last change. But when I got to New Bedford, I found it necessary again to change my name. The reason of this necessity was, that there were so many Johnsons in New Bedford, it was already quite difficult to distinguish between them. I gave Mr. Johnson the privilege of choosing me a name, but told him he must not take from me the name of "Frederick." I must hold on to that, to preserve a sense of my identity. Mr. Johnson had just been reading the *Lady of the Lake*, and at once suggested that my name be "Douglass." From that time until now I have been called "Frederick Douglass"; and as I am more widely known by that name than by either of the others, I shall continue to use it as my own.

I was quite disappointed at the general appearance of things in New Bedford. The impression which I had received respecting the character and condition of the people of the North, I found to be singularly erroneous. I had very strangely supposed, while in slavery, that few of the comforts, and scarcely any of the luxuries, of life were enjoyed at the North, compared with what were enjoyed by the slaveholders of the

South. I probably came to this conclusion from the fact that northern people owned no slaves. I supposed that they were about upon a level with the non-slaveholding population of the South. I knew *they* were exceedingly poor, and I had been accustomed to regard their poverty as the necessary consequence of their being non-slaveholders. I had somehow imbibed the opinion that, in the absence of slaves, there could be no wealth, and very little refinement. And upon coming to the North, I expected to meet with a rough, hard-handed, and uncultivated population, living in the most Spartan-like simplicity, knowing nothing of the ease, luxury, pomp, and grandeur of southern slaveholders. Such being my conjectures, any one acquainted with the appearance of New Bedford may very readily infer how palpably I must have seen my mistake.

In the afternoon of the day when I reached New Bedford, I visited the wharves, to take a view of the shipping. Here I found myself surrounded with the strongest proofs of wealth. Lying at the wharves, and riding in the stream, I saw many ships of the finest model, in the best order, and of the largest size. Upon the right and left, I was walled in by granite warehouses of the widest dimensions, stowed to their utmost capacity with the necessaries and comforts of life. Added to this, almost every body seemed to be at work, but noiselessly so, compared with what I had been accustomed to in Baltimore. There were no loud songs heard from those engaged in loading and unloading ships. I heard no deep oaths or horrid curses on the laborer. I saw no whipping of men; but all seemed to go smoothly on. Every man appeared to understand his work, and went at it with a sober, yet cheerful earnestness, which betokened the deep interest which he felt in what he was doing, as well as a sense of his own dignity as a man. To me this looked exceedingly strange. From the wharves I strolled around and over the town, gazing with wonder and admiration at the splendid churches, beautiful dwellings, and finely cultivated gardens; evincing an amount of wealth, comfort, taste, and refinement, such as I had never seen in any part of slaveholding Maryland.

Every thing looked clean, new, and beautiful. I saw few or no dilapidated houses, with poverty-stricken inmates; no half-naked children and barefooted women, such as I had been accustomed to see in

Hillsborough, Easton, St. Michael's, and Baltimore. The people looked more able, stronger, healthier, and happier, than those of Maryland. I was for once made glad by a view of extreme wealth, without being saddened by seeing extreme poverty. But the most astonishing as well as the most interesting thing to me was the condition of the colored people, a great many of whom, like myself, had escaped thither as a refuge from the hunters of men. I found many who had not been seven years out of their chains, living in finer houses, and evidently enjoying more of the comforts of life, than the average of slaveholders in Maryland. I will venture to assert, that my friend Mr. Nathan Johnson (of whom I can say with a grateful heart, "I was hungry, and he gave me meat; I was thirsty, and he gave me drink; I was a stranger, and he took me in") lived in a neater house; dined at a better table; took, paid for, and read, more newspapers; better understood the moral, religious, and political character of the nation—than nine tenths of the slaveholders in Talbot county Maryland. Yet Mr. Johnson was a working man. His hands were hardened by toil, and not his alone, but those also of Mrs. Johnson. I found the colored people much more spirited than I had supposed they would be. I found among them a determination to protect each other from the blood-thirsty kidnapper, at all hazards. Soon after my arrival, I was told of a circumstance which illustrated their spirit. A colored man and a fugitive slave were on unfriendly terms. The former was heard to threaten the latter with informing his master of his whereabouts. Straightway a meeting was called among the colored people, under the stereotyped notice, "Business of importance!" The betrayer was invited to attend. The people came at the appointed hour, and organized the meeting by appointing a very religious old gentleman as president, who, I believe, made a prayer, after which he addressed the meeting as follows: *"Friends, we have got him here, and I would recommend that you young men just take him outside the door, and kill him!"* With this, a number of them bolted at him; but they were intercepted by some more timid than themselves, and the betrayer escaped their vengeance, and has not been seen in New Bedford since. I believe there have been no more such threats, and should there be hereafter, I doubt not that death would be the consequence.

I found employment, the third day after my arrival, in stowing a sloop with a load of oil. It was new, dirty, and hard work for me; but I went at it with a glad heart and a willing hand. I was now my own master. It was a happy moment, the rapture of which can be understood only by those who have been slaves. It was the first work, the reward of which was to be entirely my own. There was no Master Hugh standing ready, the moment I earned the money, to rob me of it. I worked that day with a pleasure I had never before experienced. I was at work for myself and newly married wife. It was to me the starting-point of a new existence. When I got through with that job, I went in pursuit of a job of calking; but such was the strength of prejudice against color, among the white calkers, that they refused to work with me, and of course I could get no employment.* Finding my trade of no immediate benefit, I threw off my calking habiliments, and prepared myself to do any kind of work I could get to do. Mr. Johnson kindly let me have his wood-horse and saw, and I very soon found myself a plenty of work. There was no work too hard—none too dirty. I was ready to saw wood, shovel coal, carry wood, sweep the chimney, or roll oil casks—all of which I did for nearly three years in New Bedford, before I became known to the anti-slavery world.

In about four months after I went to New Bedford, there came a young man to me, and inquired if I did not wish to take the *Liberator*. I told him I did; but, just having made my escape from slavery, I remarked that I was unable to pay for it then. I, however, finally became a subscriber to it. The paper came, and I read it from week to week with such feelings as it would be quite idle for me to attempt to describe. The paper became my meat and my drink. My soul was set all on fire. Its sympathy for my brethren in bonds—its scathing denunciations of slaveholders—its faithful exposures of slavery—and its powerful attacks upon the upholders of the institution—sent a thrill of joy through my soul, such as I had never felt before!

I had not long been a reader of the *Liberator*, before I got a pretty correct idea of the principles, measures and spirit of the anti-slavery

---

* I am told that colored persons can now get employment at calking in New Bedford—a result of anti-slavery effort.

reform. I took right hold of the cause. I could do but little; but what I could, I did with a joyful heart, and never felt happier than when in an anti-slavery meeting. I seldom had much to say at the meetings, because what I wanted to say was said so much better by others. But, while attending an anti-slavery convention at Nantucket, on the 11th of August, 1841, I felt strongly moved to speak, and was at the same time much urged to do so by Mr. William C. Coffin, a gentleman who had heard me speak in the colored people's meeting at New Bedford. It was a severe cross, and I took it up reluctantly. The truth was, I felt myself a slave, and the idea of speaking to white people weighed me down. I spoke but a few moments, when I felt a degree of freedom, and said what I desired with considerable ease. From that time until now, I have been engaged in pleading the cause of my brethren—with what success, and with what devotion, I leave those acquainted with my labors to decide.

APPENDIX

I FIND, SINCE READING OVER THE FOREGOING NARRATIVE, THAT I
have, in several instances, spoken in such a tone and manner,
respecting religion, as may possibly lead those unacquainted with my
religious views to suppose me an opponent of all religion. To remove
the liability of such misapprehension, I deem it proper to append the
following brief explanation. What I have said respecting and against
religion, I mean strictly to apply to the *slaveholding religion* of this
land, and with no possible reference to Christianity proper; for,
between the Christianity of this land, and the Christianity of Christ,
I recognize the widest possible difference—so wide, that to receive
the one as good, pure, and holy, is of necessity to reject the other as
bad, corrupt, and wicked. To be the friend of the one, is of necessity
to be the enemy of the other. I love the pure, peaceable, and impartial Christianity of Christ: I therefore hate the corrupt, slaveholding,
women-whipping, cradle-plundering, partial and hypocritical Christianity of this land. Indeed, I can see no reason, but the most
deceitful one, for calling the religion of this land Christianity. I look
upon it as the climax of all misnomers, the boldest of all frauds, and
the grossest of all libels. Never was there a clearer case of "stealing the
livery of the court of heaven to serve the devil in." I am filled with
unutterable loathing when I contemplate the religious pomp and
show, together with the horrible inconsistencies, which every where
surround me. We have men-stealers for ministers, women-whippers

for missionaries, and cradle-plunderers for church members. The man who wields the blood-clotted cowskin during the week fills the pulpit on Sunday, and claims to be a minister of the meek and lowly Jesus. The man who robs me of my earnings at the end of each week meets me as a class-leader on Sunday morning, to show me the way of life, and the path of salvation. He who sells my sister, for purposes of prostitution, stands forth as the pious advocate of purity. He who proclaims it a religious duty to read the Bible denies me the right of learning to read the name of the God who made me. He who is the religious advocate of marriage robs whole millions of its sacred influence, and leaves them to the ravages of wholesale pollution. The warm defender of the sacredness of the family relation is the same that scatters whole families—sundering husbands and wives, parents and children, sisters and brothers—leaving the hut vacant, and the hearth desolate. We see the thief preaching against theft, and the adulterer against adultery. We have men sold to build churches, women sold to support the gospel, and babes sold to purchase Bibles for the *poor heathen! all for the glory of God and the good of souls!* The slave auctioneer's bell and the church-going bell chime in with each other, and the bitter cries of the heart-broken slave are drowned in the religious shouts of his pious master. Revivals of religion and revivals in the slave-trade go hand in hand together. The slave prison and the church stand near each other. The clanking of fetters and the rattling of chains in the prison, and the pious psalm and solemn prayer in the church, may be heard at the same time. The dealers in the bodies and souls of men erect their stand in the presence of the pulpit, and they mutually help each other. The dealer gives his blood-stained gold to support the pulpit, and the pulpit, in return, covers his infernal business with the garb of Christianity. Here we have religion and robbery the allies of each other—devils dressed in angels' robes, and hell presenting the semblance of paradise.

> Just God! and these are they,
> Who minister at thine altar. God of right!
> Men who their hands, with prayer and blessing, lay
> On Israel's ark of light.

What! preach, and kidnap men?
Give thanks, and rob thy own afflicted poor?
Talk of thy glorious liberty, and then
Bolt hard the captive's door?

What! servants of thy own
Merciful Son, who came to seek and save
The homeless and the outcast, fettering down
The tasked and plundered slave!

Pilate and Herod friends!
Chief priests and rulers, as of old, combine!
Just God and holy! Is that church which lends
Strength to the spoiler thine?

The Christianity of America is a Christianity, of whose votaries it may be as truly said, as it was of the ancient scribes and Pharisees. "They bind heavy burdens, and grievous to be borne, and lay them on men's shoulders, but they themselves will not move them with one of their fingers. All their works they do for to be seen of men. They love the uppermost rooms at feasts, and the chief seats in the synagogues, . . . and to be called of men, Rabbi, Rabbi. But woe unto you, scribes and Pharisees, hypocrites! For ye shut up the kingdom of heaven against men; for ye neither go in yourselves, neither suffer ye them that are entering to go in. Ye devour widows' houses, and for a pretence make long prayers; therefore ye shall receive the greater damnation. Ye compass sea and land to make one proselyte, and when he is made, ye make him twofold more the child of hell than yourselves. Woe unto you, scribes and Pharisees, hypocrites! For ye pay tithe of mint, and anise, and cumin, and have omitted the weightier matters of the law, judgment, mercy, and faith; these ought ye to have done, and not to leave the other undone. Ye blind guides! Which strain at a gnat, and swallow a camel. Woe unto you, scribes and Pharisees, hypocrites! For ye make clean the outside of the cup and of the platter; but within, they are full of extortion and excess. Woe unto you, scribes and Pharisees, hypocrites! For ye are like unto whited sepulchres, which indeed appear beautiful outward, but are within full of dead men's bones, and of all uncleanness. Even so ye also outwardly appear righteous unto men, but within ye are full of hypocrisy and iniquity."

Dark and terrible as is this picture, I hold it to be strictly true of the overwhelming mass of professed Christians in America. They strain at a gnat, and swallow a camel. Could any thing be more true of our churches? They would be shocked at the proposition of fellowshipping a *sheep*-stealer; and at the same time they hug to their communion a *man*-stealer, and brand me with being an infidel, if I find fault with them for it. They attend with Pharisaical strictness to the outward forms of religion, and at the same time neglect the weightier matters of the law, judgment, mercy, and faith. They are always ready to sacrifice, but seldom to show mercy. They are they who are represented as professing to love God whom they have not seen, whilst they hate their brother whom they have seen. They love the heathen on the other side of the globe. They can pray for him, pay money to have the Bible put into his hand, and missionaries to instruct him; while they despise and totally neglect the heathen at their own doors.

Such is, very briefly, my view of the religion of this land; and to avoid any misunderstanding, growing out of the use of general terms, I mean by the religion of this land, that which is revealed in the words, deeds, and actions, of those bodies, north and south, calling themselves Christian churches, and yet in union with slaveholders. It is against religion, as presented by these bodies, that I have felt it my duty to testify.

I conclude these remarks by copying the following portrait of the religion of the South, (which is, by communion and fellowship, the religion of the North), which I soberly affirm is "true to the life," and without caricature or the slightest exaggeration. It is said to have been drawn, several years before the present anti-slavery agitation began, by a northern Methodist preacher, who, while residing at the South, had an opportunity to see slaveholding morals, manners, and piety, with his own eyes. "Shall I not visit for these things? saith the Lord. Shall not my soul be avenged on such a nation as this?"

A PARODY

Come, saints and sinners, hear me tell
How pious priests whip Jack and Nell,

And women buy and children sell,
And preach all sinners down to hell,
    And sing of heavenly union.

They'll bleat and baa, dona like goats,
Gorge down black sheep, and strain at motes,
Array their backs in fine black coats,
Then seize their negroes by their throats,
    And choke, for heavenly union.

They'll church you if you sip a dram,
And damn you if you steal a lamb;
Yet rob old Tony, Doll, and Sam,
Of human rights, and bread and ham;
    Kidnapper's heavenly union.

They'll loudly talk of Christ's reward,
And bind his image with a cord,
And scold, and swing the lash abhorred,
And sell their brother in the Lord
    To handcuffed heavenly union.

They'll read and sing a sacred song,
And make a prayer both loud and long,
And teach the right and do the wrong,
Hailing the brother, sister throng,
    With words of heavenly union.

We wonder how such saints can sing,
Or praise the Lord upon the wing,
Who roar, and scold, and whip, and sting,
And to their slaves and mammon cling,
    In guilty conscience union.

They'll raise tobacco, corn, and rye,
And drive, and thieve, and cheat, and lie,

And lay up treasures in the sky,
By making switch and cowskin fly,
    In hope of heavenly union.

They'll crack old Tony on the skull,
And preach and roar like Bashan bull,
Or braying ass, of mischief full,
Then seize old Jacob by the wool,
    And pull for heavenly union.

A roaring, ranting, sleek man-thief,
Who lived on mutton, veal, and beef,
Yet never would afford relief
To needy, sable sons of grief,
    Was big with heavenly union.

"Love not the world," the preacher said,
And winked his eye, and shook his head;
He seized on Tom, and Dick, and Ned,
Cut short their meat, and clothes, and bread,
    Yet still loved heavenly union.

Another preacher whining spoke
Of One whose heart for sinners broke:
He tied old Nanny to an oak,
And drew the blood at every stroke,
    And prayed for heavenly union.

Two others oped their iron jaws.
And waved their children-stealing paws;
There sat their children in gewgaws;
By stinting negroes' backs and maws,
    They kept up heavenly union.

All good from Jack another takes,
And entertains their flirts and rakes,

> Who dress as sleek as glossy snakes,
> And cram their mouths with sweetened cakes;
> And this goes down for union.

Sincerely and earnestly hoping that this little book may do something toward throwing light on the American slave system, and hastening the glad day of deliverance to the millions of my brethren in bonds—faithfully relying upon the power of truth, love, and justice, for success in my humble efforts—and solemnly pledging my self anew to the sacred cause—I subscribe myself,

FREDERICK DOUGLASS
LYNN, MASS., APRIL 28, 1845

THE END

SELECTED ESSAYS
AND SPEECHES

My Escape from Slavery

In the first narrative of my experience in slavery, written nearly forty years ago, and in various writings since, I have given the public what I considered very good reasons for withholding the manner of my escape. In substance these reasons were, first, that such publication at any time during the existence of slavery might be used by the master against the slave, and prevent the future escape of any who might adopt the same means that I did. The second reason was, if possible, still more binding to silence: the publication of details would certainly have put in peril the persons and property of those who assisted. Murder itself was not more sternly and certainly punished in the State of Maryland than that of aiding and abetting the escape of a slave. Many colored men, for no other crime than that of giving aid to a fugitive slave, have, like Charles T. Torrey, perished in prison. The abolition of slavery in my native State and throughout the country, and the lapse of time, render the caution hitherto observed no longer necessary. But even since the abolition of slavery, I have sometimes thought it well enough to baffle curiosity by saying that while slavery existed there were good reasons for not telling the manner of my escape, and since slavery had ceased to exist, there was no reason for telling it. I shall now, however, cease to avail myself of this formula, and, as far as I can, endeavor to satisfy this very natural curiosity. I should, perhaps, have yielded to that feeling sooner, had there been anything very heroic or thrilling in the incidents connected with my escape, for I am sorry to say I have nothing of that sort to tell; and yet the courage that could risk betrayal and the bravery which was ready to encounter death, if need be, in pursuit of freedom, were essential features in the undertaking. My success was due to address rather than courage, to good luck rather than bravery. My means of escape were provided for me by the very men who were making laws to hold and bind me more securely in slavery.

It was the custom in the State of Maryland to require the free colored people to have what were called free papers. These instruments they were required to renew very often, and by charging a fee for this writing, considerable sums from time to time were collected by the State. In these papers the name, age, color, height, and form of the freeman were described, together with any scars or other marks upon his person which could assist in his identification. This device in some measure defeated itself—since more than one man could be found to answer the same general description. Hence many slaves could escape by personating the owner of one set of papers; and this was often done as follows: A slave, nearly or sufficiently answering the description set forth in the papers, would borrow or hire them till by means of them he could escape to a free State, and then, by mail or otherwise, would return them to the owner. The operation was a hazardous one for the lender as well as for the borrower. A failure on the part of the fugitive to send back the papers would imperil his benefactor, and the discovery of the papers in possession of the wrong man would imperil both the fugitive and his friend. It was, therefore, an act of supreme trust on the part of a freeman of color thus to put in jeopardy his own liberty that another might be free. It was, however, not unfrequently bravely done, and was seldom discovered. I was not so fortunate as to resemble any of my free acquaintances sufficiently to answer the description of their papers. But I had a friend—a sailor—who owned a sailor's protection, which answered somewhat the purpose of free papers—describing his person, and certifying to the fact that he was a free American sailor. The instrument had at its head the American eagle, which gave it the appearance at once of an authorized document. This protection, when in my hands, did not describe its bearer very accurately. Indeed, it called for a man much darker than myself, and close examination of it would have caused my arrest at the start.

In order to avoid this fatal scrutiny on the part of railroad officials, I arranged with Isaac Rolls, a Baltimore hackman, to bring my baggage to the Philadelphia train just on the moment of starting, and jumped upon the car myself when the train was in motion. Had I gone into the station and offered to purchase a ticket, I should have been instantly and carefully examined, and undoubtedly arrested. In choosing this plan I considered the jostle of the train, and the natural haste of the conductor, in a train crowded with passengers, and relied upon my skill and address in playing the sailor, as described in my protection, to do the rest. One element in my favor was the kind feeling which prevailed in Baltimore and other seaports at the time, toward "those who go down to the sea in ships." "Free trade and sailors' rights" just then expressed the sentiment of the country. In my clothing I was rigged out in sailor style. I had on a red shirt and a tarpaulin hat, and a black cravat tied in sailor fashion carelessly and loosely about my neck. My knowledge of ships and sailor's talk came much to my assistance, for I knew a ship from stem to stern, and from keelson to cross-trees, and could talk sailor like an "old salt." I was well on the way to Havre de Grace before the conductor came into the negro car to collect tickets and examine the papers of his black passengers. This was a critical moment in the drama. My whole future depended upon the decision of this conductor. Agitated though I was while this ceremony was proceeding, still, externally, at least, I was apparently calm and self-possessed. He went on with his duty—examining several colored passengers before reaching me. He was somewhat harsh in tome and peremptory in manner until he reached me, when, strange enough, and to my surprise and relief, his whole manner changed. Seeing that I did not readily produce my free papers, as the other colored persons in the car had done, he said to me, in friendly contrast with his bearing toward the others:

"I suppose you have your free papers?"

To which I answered:

"No sir; I never carry my free papers to sea with me."

"But you have something to show that you are a freeman, haven't you?"

"Yes, sir," I answered; "I have a paper with the American Eagle on it, and that will carry me around the world."

With this I drew from my deep sailor's pocket my seaman's protection, as before described. The merest glance at the paper satisfied him, and he took my fare and went on about his business. This moment of time was one of the most anxious I ever experienced. Had the conductor looked closely at the paper, he could not have failed to discover that it called for a very different-looking person from myself, and in that case it would have been his duty to arrest me on the instant, and send me back to Baltimore from the first station. When he left me with the assurance that I was all right, though much relieved, I realized that I was still in great danger: I was still in Maryland, and subject to arrest at any moment. I saw on the train several persons who would have known me in any other clothes, and I feared they might recognize me, even in my sailor "rig," and report me to the conductor, who would then subject me to a closer examination, which I knew well would be fatal to me.

Though I was not a murderer fleeing from justice, I felt perhaps quite as miserable as such a criminal. The train was moving at a very high rate of speed for that epoch of railroad travel, but to my anxious mind it was moving far too slowly. Minutes were hours, and hours were days during this part of my flight. After Maryland, I was to pass through Delaware—another slave State, where slave-catchers generally awaited their prey, for it was not in the interior of the State, but on its borders, that these human hounds were most vigilant and active. The border lines between slavery and freedom were the dangerous ones for the fugitives. The heart of no fox or deer, with hungry hounds on his trail in full chase, could have beaten more anxiously or noisily than did mine from the time I left Baltimore till I reached Philadelphia. The passage of the Susquehanna River at Havre de Grace was at that time made by ferry-boat, on board of which I met a young colored man by the name of Nichols, who came very near betraying me. He was a "hand" on the boat, but, instead of minding his business, he insisted upon knowing me, and asking me dangerous questions as to where I was going, when I was coming back, etc. I got away from my old and inconvenient acquaintance as soon as I could decently do so, and went to another part of the boat. Once across the river, I encountered a new danger. Only a few days before, I had been at work on a revenue cutter, in Mr. Price's shipyard in Baltimore, under the care of Captain McGowan. On the meeting at this point of the two trains, the one going south stopped on the track just opposite to the one going north, and it so happened that this Captain McGowan sat at a window where he could see me very distinctly, and would certainly have recognized me had he looked at me but for a second. Fortunately, in the hurry of the moment, he did not see me; and the trains soon passed each other on their respective ways. But this was not my only hair-breadth escape. A German blacksmith whom I knew well was on the train with me, and looked at me very intently, as if he thought he had seen me somewhere before in his travels. I really believe he knew me, but had no heart to betray me. At any rate, he saw me escaping and held his peace.

The last point of imminent danger, and the one I dreaded most, was Wilmington. Here we left the train and took the steam-boat for Philadelphia. In making the change here I again apprehended arrest, but no one disturbed me, and I was soon on the broad and beautiful Delaware, speeding away to the Quaker City. On reaching Philadelphia in the afternoon, I inquired of a colored man how I could get on to New York. He directed me to the William Street depot, and thither I went, taking the train that night. I reached New York Tuesday morning, having completed the journey in less than twenty-four hours.

My free life began on the third of September, 1838. On the morning of the fourth of that month, after an anxious and most perilous but safe journey, I found myself in the big city of New York, a FREE MAN—one more added to the mighty throng which, like the confused waves of the troubled sea, surged to and fro between the lofty walls of Broadway. Though dazzled with the wonders which met me on every hand, my thoughts could not be much withdrawn from my strange situation. For the moment, the dreams of my youth and the hopes of my manhood were completely fulfilled. The bonds that had held me to "old master" were broken. No man now had a right to call me his slave or assert mastery over me. I was in the rough and tumble of an outdoor world, to take my chance with the rest of its busy number. I have often been asked how I felt when first I found myself on free soil. There is scarcely anything in my experience about which I could not give a more satisfactory answer. A new world had opened upon me. If life is more than breath and the "quick round of blood," I lived more in that one day than in a year of my slave life. It was a time of joyous excitement which words can but tamely describe. In a letter written to a friend soon after reaching New York, I said: "I felt as one might feel upon escape from a den of hungry lions." Anguish and grief, like darkness and rain, may be depicted; but gladness and joy, like the rainbow, defy the skill of pen or pencil. During ten or fifteen years I had been, as it were, dragging a heavy chain which no strength of mine could break; I was not only a slave, but a slave for life. I might become a husband, a father, an aged man, but through all, from birth to death, from the cradle to the grave, I had felt myself doomed. All efforts I had previously made to secure my freedom had not only failed, but had seemed only to rivet my fetters the more firmly, and to render my escape more difficult. Baffled, entangled, and discouraged, I had at times asked myself the question, May not my condition after all be God's work, and ordered for a wise purpose, and if so, Is not submission my duty? A contest had in fact been going on in my mind for a long time, between the clear consciousness of right and the plausible make-shifts of theology and superstition. The one held me an abject slave—a prisoner for life, punished for some transgression in which I had no lot nor part; and the other counseled me to manly endeavor to secure my freedom. This contest was now ended; my chains were broken, and the victory brought me unspeakable joy.

But my gladness was short-lived, for I was not yet out of the reach and power of the slave-holders. I soon found that New York was not quite so free or so safe a refuge as I had supposed, and a sense of loneliness and insecurity again oppressed me most sadly. I chanced to meet on the street, a few hours after my landing, a fugitive slave whom I had once known well in slavery. The information received from him alarmed me. The fugitive in question was known in Baltimore as "Allender's Jake," but in New York he wore the more respectable name of "William Dixon." Jake, in law, was the property of Doctor Allender, and Tolly Allender, the son of the doctor, had once made an effort to recapture MR. DIXON, but had failed for want of evidence to support his claim. Jake told me the circumstances of this attempt, and how narrowly he escaped being sent back to slavery and torture. He told me that New York was then full of Southerners returning from the Northern watering-places; that the colored people of New York were not to be trusted; that there were hired men of my own color who would betray me for a few dollars; that there were hired men ever on the lookout for fugitives; that I must trust no man with my secret; that I must not think of going either upon the wharves or into any colored boardinghouse, for all such places were closely watched; that he was himself unable to help me; and, in fact, he seemed while speaking to me to fear lest I myself might be a spy and a betrayer. Under this apprehension, as I suppose, he showed signs of wishing to be rid of me, and with whitewash brush in hand, in search of work, he soon disappeared.

This picture, given by poor "Jake," of New York, was a damper to my enthusiasm. My little store of money would soon be exhausted, and since it would be unsafe for me to go on the wharves for work, and I had no introductions elsewhere, the prospect for me was far from cheerful. I saw the wisdom of keeping away from the ship-yards, for, if pursued, as I felt certain I should be, Mr. Auld, my "master," would naturally seek me there among the calkers. Every door seemed closed against me. I was in the midst of an ocean of my fellow-men, and yet a perfect stranger to every one. I was without home, without acquain-tance, without money, without credit, without work, and without any definite knowledge as to what course to take, or where to look for suc-cor. In such an extremity, a man had something besides his new-born freedom to think of. While wandering about the streets of New York, and lodging at least one night among the barrels on one of the wharves, I was indeed free—from slavery, but free from food and shel-ter as well. I kept my secret to myself as long as I could, but I was compelled at last to seek some one who would befriend me without taking advantage of my destitution to betray me. Such a person I found in a sailor named Stuart, a warm-hearted and generous fellow, who, from his humble home on Centre Street, saw me standing on the oppo-site sidewalk, near the Tombs prison. As he approached me, I ventured a remark to him which at once enlisted his interest in me. He took me to his home to spend the night, and in the morning went with me to Mr. David Ruggles, the secretary of the New York Vigilance Committee, a co-worker with Isaac T. Hopper, Lewis and Arthur Tappan, Theodore S. Wright, Samuel Cornish, Thomas Downing, Philip A. Bell, and other true men of their time. All these (save Mr. Bell, who still lives, and is editor and publisher of a paper called the "Elevator," in San Francisco) have finished their work on earth. Once in the hands of these brave and wise men, I felt comparatively safe. With Mr. Ruggles, on the corner of Lispenard and Church Streets, I was hidden several days, during which time my intended wife came on from Baltimore at my call, to share the burdens of life with me. She was a free woman, and came at once on getting the good news of my safety. We were married by Rev. J. W. C. Pennington, then a well-known and respected Presbyterian minister. I had no money with which to pay the marriage fee, but he seemed well pleased with our thanks.

Mr. Ruggles was the first officer on the "Underground Railroad" whom I met after coming North, and was, indeed, the only one with whom I had anything to do till I became such an officer myself. Learning that my trade was that of a calker, he promptly decided that the best place for me was in New Bedford, Mass. He told me that many ships for whaling voyages were fitted out there, and that I might there find work at my trade and make a good living. So, on the day of the marriage ceremony, we took our little luggage to the steamer John W. Richmond, which, at that time, was one of the line running between New York and Newport, R. I. Forty-three years ago colored travelers were not permitted in the cabin, nor allowed abaft the paddle-wheels of a steam vessel. They were compelled, whatever the weather might be, whether cold or hot, wet or dry, to spend the night on deck. Unjust as this regulation was, it did not trouble us much; we had fared much harder before. We arrived at Newport the next morning, and soon after an old fashioned stage-coach, with "New Bedford" in large yellow letters on its sides, came down to the wharf. I had not money enough to pay our fare, and stood hesitating what to do. Fortunately for us, there were two Quaker gentlemen who were about to take passage on the stage, Friends William C. Taber and Joseph Ricketson, who at once discerned our true situation, and, in a peculiarly quiet way, addressing me, Mr. Taber said: "Thee get in." I never obeyed an order with more alacrity, and we were soon on our way to our new home. When we reached "Stone Bridge" the passengers alighted for breakfast, and paid their fares to the driver. We took no breakfast, and, when asked for our fares, I told the driver I would make it right with him when we reached New Bedford. I expected some objection to this on his part, but he made none. When, however, we reached New Bedford, he took our baggage, including three music-books, two of them collections by Dyer, and one by Shaw, and held them until I was able to redeem them by paying to him the amount due for our rides. This was soon done, for Mr. Nathan Johnson not only received me kindly and hospitably, but, on being informed about our baggage, at once loaned me the two dollars with which to square accounts with the stage-driver. Mr. and Mrs. Nathan Johnson reached a good old age, and now rest from their labors. I am under many grateful obligations to them. They not only "took me in when a stranger" and "fed me when hungry," but taught me how to make an honest living. Thus, in a fortnight after my flight from Maryland, I was safe in New Bedford, a citizen of the grand old commonwealth of Massachusetts.

Once initiated into my new life of freedom and assured by Mr. Johnson that I need not fear recapture in that city, a comparatively unimportant question arose as to the name by which I should be known thereafter in my new relation as a free man. The name given me by my dear mother was no less pretentious and long than Frederick Augustus Washington Bailey. I had, however, while living in Maryland, dispensed with the Augustus Washington, and retained only Frederick Bailey. Between Baltimore and New Bedford, the better to conceal myself from the slave-hunters, I had parted with Bailey and called myself Johnson; but in New Bedford I found that the Johnson family was already so numerous as to cause some confusion in distinguishing them, hence a change in this name seemed desirable. Nathan Johnson, mine host, placed great emphasis upon this necessity, and wished me to allow him to select a name for me. I consented, and he called me by my present name—the one by which I have been known for three and forty years—Frederick Douglass. Mr. Johnson had just been reading the "Lady of the Lake," and so pleased was he with its great character that he wished me to bear his name. Since reading that charming poem myself, I have often thought that, considering the noble hospitality and manly character of Nathan Johnson—black man though he was—he, far more than I, illustrated the virtues of the Douglas of Scotland. Sure am I that, if any slave-catcher had entered his domicile with a view to my recapture, Johnson would have shown himself like him of the "stalwart hand."

The reader may be surprised at the impressions I had in some way conceived of the social and material condition of the people at the North. I had no proper idea of the wealth, refinement, enterprise, and high civilization of this section of the country. My "Columbian Orator," almost my only book, had done nothing to enlighten me concerning Northern society. I had been taught that slavery was the bottom fact of all wealth. With this foundation idea, I came naturally to the conclusion that poverty must be the general condition of the people of the free States. In the country from which I came, a white man holding no slaves was usually an ignorant and poverty-stricken man, and men of this class were contemptuously called "poor white trash." Hence I supposed that, since the non-slave-holders at the South were ignorant, poor, and degraded as a class, the non-slave-holders at the North must be in a similar condition. I could have landed in no part of the United States where I should have found a more striking and gratifying contrast, not only to life generally in the South, but in the condition of the colored people there, than in New Bedford. I was amazed when Mr. Johnson told me that there was nothing in the laws or constitution of Massachusetts that would prevent a colored man from being governor of the State, if the people should see fit to elect him. There, too, the black man's children attended the public schools with the white man's children, and apparently without objection from any quarter. To impress me with my security from recapture and return to slavery, Mr. Johnson assured me that no slave-holder could take a slave out of New Bedford; that there were men there who would lay down their lives to save me from such a fate.

The fifth day after my arrival, I put on the clothes of a common laborer, and went upon the wharves in search of work. On my way down Union Street I saw a large pile of coal in front of the house of Rev. Ephraim Peabody, the Unitarian minister. I went to the kitchen door and asked the privilege of bringing in and putting away this coal.

"What will you charge?" said the lady. "I will leave that to you, madam." "You may put it away," she said. I was not long in accomplishing the job, when the dear lady put into my hand TWO SILVER HALF-DOLLARS. To understand the emotion which swelled my heart as I clasped this money, realizing that I had no master who could take it from me, THAT IT WAS MINE—THAT MY HANDS WERE MY OWN, and could earn more of the precious coin, one must have been in some sense himself a slave. My next job was stowing a sloop at Uncle Gid. Howland's wharf with a cargo of oil for New York. I was not only a freeman, but a free working-man, and no "master" stood ready at the end of the week to seize my hard earnings.

The season was growing late and work was plenty. Ships were being fitted out for whaling, and much wood was used in storing them. The sawing this wood was considered a good job. With the help of old Friend Johnson (blessings on his memory) I got a saw and "buck," and went at it. When I went into a store to buy a cord with which to brace up my saw in the frame, I asked for a "fip's" worth of cord. The man behind the counter looked rather sharply at me, and said with equal sharpness, "You don't belong about here." I was alarmed, and thought I had betrayed myself. A fip in Maryland was six and a quarter cents, called fourpence in Massachusetts. But no harm came from the "fi'penny-bit" blunder, and I confidently and cheerfully went to work with my saw and buck. It was new business to me, but I never did better work, or more of it, in the same space of time on the plantation for Covey, the negro-breaker, than I did for myself in these earliest years of my freedom.

Notwithstanding the just and humane sentiment of New Bedford three and forty years ago, the place was not entirely free from race and color prejudice. The good influence of the Roaches, Rodmans, Arnolds, Grinnells, and Robesons did not pervade all classes of its people. The test of the real civilization of the community came when I applied for work at my trade, and then my repulse was emphatic and decisive. It so happened that Mr. Rodney French, a wealthy and enter-prising citizen, distinguished as an anti-slavery man, was fitting out a vessel for a whaling voyage, upon which there was a heavy job of calk-ing and coppering to be done. I had some skill in both branches, and applied to Mr. French for work. He, generous man that he was, told me he would employ me, and I might go at once to the vessel. I obeyed him, but upon reaching the float-stage, where others [sic] calkers were at work, I was told that every white man would leave the ship, in her unfinished condition, if I struck a blow at my trade upon her. This uncivil, inhuman, and selfish treatment was not so shocking and scandalous in my eyes at the time as it now appears to me. Slavery had inured me to hardships that made ordinary trouble sit lightly upon me. Could I have worked at my trade I could have earned two dollars a day, but as a common laborer I received but one dollar. The difference was of great importance to me, but if I could not get two dollars, I was glad to get one; and so I went to work for Mr. French as a common laborer. The consciousness that I was free—no longer a slave—kept me cheerful under this, and many similar proscriptions, which I was destined to meet in New Bedford and elsewhere on the free soil of Massachusetts. For instance, though colored children attended the schools, and were treated kindly by their teachers, the New Bedford Lyceum refused, till several years after my residence in that city, to allow any colored person to attend the lectures delivered in its hall. Not until such men as Charles Sumner, Theodore Parker, Ralph Waldo Emerson, and Horace Mann refused to lecture in their course while there was such a restriction, was it abandoned.

Becoming satisfied that I could not rely on my trade in New Bedford to give me a living, I prepared myself to do any kind of work that came to hand. I sawed wood, shoveled coal, dug cellars, moved rubbish from backyards, worked on the wharves, loaded and unloaded vessels, and scoured their cabins.

I afterward got steady work at the brass-foundry owned by Mr. Richmond. My duty here was to blow the bellows, swing the crane, and empty the flasks in which castings were made; and at times this was hot and heavy work. The articles produced here were mostly for ship work, and in the busy season the foundry was in operation night and day. I have often worked two nights and every working day of the week. My foreman, Mr. Cobb, was a good man, and more than once protected me from abuse that one or more of the hands was disposed to throw upon me. While in this situation I had little time for mental improvement. Hard work, night and day, over a furnace hot enough to keep the metal running like water, was more favorable to action than thought; yet here I often nailed a newspaper to the post near my bellows, and read while I was performing the up and down motion of the heavy beam by which the bellows was inflated and discharged. It was the pursuit of knowledge under difficulties, and I look back to it now, after so many years, with some complacency and a little wonder that I could have been so earnest and persevering in any pursuit other than for my daily bread. I certainly saw nothing in the conduct of those around to inspire me with such interest: they were all devoted exclusively to what their hands found to do. I am glad to be able to say that, during my engagement in this foundry, no complaint was ever made against me that I did not do my work, and do it well. The bellows which I worked by main strength was, after I left, moved by a steam-engine.

RECEPTION SPEECH

At Finsbury Chapel, Moorfields, England
May 12, 1846

I FEEL EXCEEDINGLY GLAD OF THE OPPORTUNITY NOW AFFORDED ME OF presenting the claims of my brethren in bonds in the United States, to so many in London and from various parts of Britain, who have assembled here on the present occasion. I have nothing to commend me to your consideration in the way of learning, nothing in the way of education, to entitle me to your attention; and you are aware that slavery is a very bad school for rearing teachers of morality and religion. Twenty-one years of my life have been spent in slavery—personal slavery—surrounded by degrading influences, such as can exist nowhere beyond the pale of slavery; and it will not be strange, if under such circumstances, I should betray, in what I have to say to you, a deficiency of that refinement which is seldom or ever found, except among persons that have experienced superior advantages to those which I have enjoyed. But I will take it for granted that you know something about the degrading influences of slavery, and that you will not expect great things from me this evening, but simply such facts as I may be able to advance immediately in connection with my own experience of slavery.

Now, what is this system of slavery? This is the subject of my lecture this evening—what is the character of this institution? I am about to answer the inquiry, what is American slavery? I do this the more readily, since I have found persons in this country who have identified the term slavery with that which I think it is not, and in some instances, I have feared, in so doing, have rather (unwittingly, I know) detracted much from the horror with which the term slavery is contemplated. It is common in this country to distinguish every bad thing by the name of slavery. Intemperance is slavery; to be deprived of the right to vote is slavery, says one; to have to work hard is slavery, says another; and I do not know but that if we should let them go on, they would say that to eat when we are hungry, to walk when we desire to have exercise, or to minister to our necessities, or have necessities at all, is slavery.

I do not wish for a moment to detract from the horror with which the evil of intemperance is contemplated—not at all; nor do I wish to throw the slightest obstruction in the way of any political freedom that any class of persons in this country may desire to obtain. But I am here to say that I think the term slavery is sometimes abused by identifying it with that which it is not. Slavery in the United States is the granting of that power by which one man exercises and enforces a right of property in the body and soul of another. The condition of a slave is simply that of the brute beast. He is a piece of property—a marketable commodity, in the language of the law, to be bought or sold at the will and caprice of the master who claims him to be his property; he is spoken of, thought of, and treated as property. His own good, his conscience, his intellect, his affections, are all set aside by the master. The will and the wishes of the master are the law of the slave. He is as much a piece of property as a horse. If he is fed, he is fed because he is property. If he is clothed, it is with a view to the increase of his value as property. Whatever of comfort is necessary to him for his body or soul that is inconsistent with his being property, is carefully wrested from him, not only by public opinion, but by the law of the country. He is carefully deprived of everything that tends in the slightest degree to detract from his value as property. He is deprived of education. God has given him an intellect; the slaveholder declares it shall not be cultivated. If his moral perception leads him in a course contrary to his value as property, the slaveholder declares he shall not exercise it. The marriage institution cannot exist among slaves, and one-sixth of the population of democratic America is denied its privileges by the law of the land. What is to be thought of a nation boasting of its liberty, boasting of its humanity, boasting of its Christianity, boasting of its love of justice and purity, and yet having within its own borders three millions of persons denied by law the right of marriage?—what must be the condition of that people?

I need not lift up the veil by giving you any experience of my own. Every one that can put two ideas together, must see the most fearful results from such a state of things as I have just mentioned. If any of these three millions find for themselves companions, and prove themselves honest, upright, virtuous persons to each other, yet in these cases—few as I am bound to confess they are—the virtuous live in constant apprehension of being torn asunder by the merciless men-stealers that claim them as their property. This is American slavery; no marriage—no education—the light of the gospel shut out from the dark mind of the bondman—and he forbidden by law to learn to read. If a mother shall teach her children to read, the law in Louisiana proclaims that she may be hanged by the neck. If the father attempt to give his son a knowledge of letters, he may be punished by the whip in one instance, and in another be killed, at the discretion of the court. Three millions of people shut out from the light of knowledge! It is easy for you to conceive the evil that must result from such a state of things.

I now come to the physical evils of slavery. I do not wish to dwell at length upon these, but it seems right to speak of them, not so much to influence your minds on this question, as to let the slaveholders of America know that the curtain which conceals their crimes is being lifted abroad; that we are opening the dark cell, and leading the people into the horrible recesses of what they are pleased to call their domestic institution. We want them to know that a knowledge of their whippings, their scourgings, their brandings, their chainings, is not confined to their plantations, but that some Negro of theirs has broken loose from his chains—has burst through the dark incrustation of slavery, and is now exposing their deeds of deep damnation to the gaze of the Christian people of England.

The slaveholders resort to all kinds of cruelty. If I were disposed, I have matter enough to interest you on this question for five or six evenings, but I will not dwell at length upon these cruelties. Suffice it to say, that all of the peculiar modes of torture that were resorted to in the West India islands, are resorted to, I believe, even more frequently, in the United States of America. Starvation, the bloody whip, the chain, the gag, the thumb-screw, cat-hauling, the cat-o'-nine-tails, the dungeon, the blood-hound, are all in requisition to keep the slave in his condition as a slave in the United States. If any one has a doubt upon this point, I would ask him to read the chapter on slavery in Dickens' *Notes on America*. If any man has a doubt upon it, I have here the "testimony of a thousand witnesses," which I can give at any length, all going to prove the truth of my statement. The blood-hound is regularly trained in the United States, and advertisements are to be found in the southern papers of the Union, from persons advertising themselves as blood-hound trainers, and offering to hunt down slaves at fifteen dollars apiece, recommending their hounds as the fleetest in the neighborhood, never known to fail. Advertisements are from time to time inserted, stating that slaves have escaped with iron collars about their necks, with bands of iron about their feet, marked with the lash, branded with red-hot irons, the initials of their master's name burned into their flesh; and the masters advertise the fact of their being thus branded with their own signature, thereby proving to the world, that, however damning it may appear to non-slavers, such practices are not regarded discreditable among the slaveholders themselves. Why, I believe if a man should brand his horse in this country—burn the initials of his name into any of his cattle, and publish the ferocious deed here—that the united execrations of Christians in Britain would descend upon him. Yet in the United States, human beings are thus branded. As Whittier says—

> . . . Our countrymen in chains,
>   The whip on woman's shrinking flesh,
> Our soil yet reddening with the stains
>   Caught from her scourgings warm and fresh.

The slave-dealer boldly publishes his infamous acts to the world. Of all things that have been said of slavery to which exception has been taken by slaveholders, this, the charge of cruelty, stands foremost, and yet there is no charge capable of clearer demonstration, than that of the most barbarous inhumanity on the part of the slaveholders toward their slaves. And all this is necessary; it is necessary to resort to these cruelties, in order to *make the slave a slave,* and to *keep him a slave.* Why, my experience all goes to prove the truth of what you will call a marvelous proposition, that the better you treat a slave, the more you destroy his value *as a slave,* and enhance the probability of his eluding the grasp of the slaveholder; the more kindly you treat him, the more wretched you make him, while you keep him in the condition of a slave. My experience, I say, confirms the truth of this proposition. When I was treated exceedingly ill; when my back was being scourged daily; when I was whipped within an inch of my life—*life* was all I cared for. "Spare my life," was my continual prayer. When I was looking for the blow about to be inflicted upon my head, I was not thinking of my liberty; it was my life. But, as soon as the blow was not to be feared, then came the longing for liberty. If a slave has a bad master, his ambition is to get a better; when he gets a better, he aspires to have the best; and when he gets the best, he aspires to be his own master. But the slave must be brutalized to keep him as a slave. The slaveholder feels this necessity. I admit this necessity. If it be right to hold slaves at all, it is right to hold them in the only way in which they can be held; and this can be done only by shutting out the light of education from their minds, and brutalizing their persons.

The whip, the chain, the gag, the thumb-screw, the blood-hound, the stocks, and all the other bloody paraphernalia of the slave system, are indispensably necessary to the relation of master and slave. The slave must be subjected to these, or he ceases to be a slave. Let him know that the whip is burned; that the fetters have been turned to some useful and profitable employment; that the chain is no longer for his limbs; that the blood-hound is no longer to be put upon his track; that his master's authority over him is no longer to be enforced by taking his life—and immediately he walks out from the house of bondage and asserts his freedom as a man. The slaveholder finds it necessary to have these implements to keep the slave in bondage; finds it necessary to be able to say, "Unless you do so and so; unless you do as I bid you—I will take away your life!"

Some of the most awful scenes of cruelty are constantly taking place in the middle states of the Union. We have in those states what are called the slave-breeding states. Allow me to speak plainly. Although it is harrowing to your feelings, it is necessary that the facts of the case should be stated. We have in the United States slave-breeding states. The very state from which the minister from our court to yours comes, is one of these states—Maryland, where men, women, and children are reared for the market, just as horses, sheep, and swine are raised for the market. Slave-rearing is there looked upon as a legitimate trade; the law sanctions it, public opinion upholds it, the church does not condemn it. It goes on in all its bloody horrors, sustained by the auctioneer's block. If you would see the cruelties of this system, hear the following narrative. Not long since the following scene occurred. A slave-woman and a slave-man had united themselves as man and wife in the absence of any law to protect them as man and wife. They had lived together by the permission, not by right, of their master, and they had reared a family. The master found it expedient, and for his interest, to sell them. He did not ask them their wishes in regard to the matter at all; they were not consulted. The man and woman were brought to the auctioneer's block, under the sound of the hammer. The cry was raised, "Here goes; who bids cash?" Think of it—a man and wife to be sold! The woman was placed on the auctioneer's block; her limbs, as is customary, were brutally exposed to the purchasers, who examined her with all the freedom with which they would examine a horse. There stood the husband, powerless; no right to his wife; the master's right preëminent. She was sold. He was next brought to the auctioneer's block. His eyes followed his wife in the distance; and he looked beseechingly, imploringly, to the man that had bought his wife, to buy him also. But he was at length bid off to another person. He was about to be separated forever from her he loved. No word of his, no work of his, could save him from this separation. He asked permission of his new master to go and take the hand of his wife at parting. It was denied him. In the agony of his soul he rushed from the man who had just bought him, that he might take a farewell of his wife; but his way was obstructed, he was struck over the head with a loaded whip, and was held for a moment; but his agony was too great. When he was let go, he fell a corpse at the feet of his master. His heart was broken. Such scenes are the everyday fruits of American slavery.

Some two years since, the Hon. Seth M. Gates, an anti-slavery gentleman of the state of New York, a representative in the congress of the United States, told me he saw with his own eyes the following circumstance. In the national District of Columbia, over which the star-spangled emblem is constantly waving, where orators are ever holding forth on the subject of American liberty, American democracy, American republicanism, there are two slave prisons. When going across a bridge, leading to one of these prisons, he saw a young woman run out, bare-footed and bare-headed, and with very little clothing on. She was running with all speed to the bridge he was approaching. His eye was fixed upon her, and he stopped to see what was the matter. He had not paused long before he saw three men run out after her. He now knew what the nature of the case was; a slave escaping from her chains—a young woman, a sister—escaping from the bondage in which she had been held. She made her way to the bridge, but had not reached it, ere from the Virginia side there came two slaveholders. As soon as they saw them, her pursuers called out, "Stop her!" True to their Virginian instincts, they came to the rescue of their brother kidnappers, across the bridge. The poor girl now saw that there was no chance for her. It was a trying time. She knew if she went back, she must be a slave forever—she must be dragged down to the scenes of pollution which the slaveholders continually provide for most of the poor, sinking, wretched young women, whom they call their property. She formed her resolution; and just as those who were about to take her, were going to put hands upon her, to drag her back, she leaped over the balustrades of the bridge, and down she went to rise no more. She chose death, rather than to go back into the hands of those Christian slaveholders from whom she had escaped.

Can it be possible that such things as these exist in the United States? Are not these the exceptions? Are any such scenes as this general? Are not such deeds condemned by the law and denounced by public opinion? Let me read to you a few of the laws of the slaveholding states of America. I think no better exposure of slavery can be made than is made by the laws of the states in which slavery exists. I prefer reading the laws to making any statement in confirmation of what I have said myself; for the slaveholders cannot object to this testimony, since it is the calm, the cool, the deliberate enactment of their wisest heads, of their most clear-sighted, their own constituted representatives. "If more than seven slaves together are found in any road without a white person, twenty lashes apiece; for visiting a plantation without a written pass, ten lashes; for letting loose a boat from where it is made fast, thirty-nine lashes for the first offense; and for the second, shall have cut off from his head one ear; for keeping or carrying a club, thirty-nine lashes; for having any article for sale, without a ticket from his master, ten lashes; for traveling in any other than the most usual and accustomed road, when going alone to any place, forty lashes; for traveling in the night without a pass, forty lashes."

I am afraid you do not understand the awful character of these lashes. You must bring it before your mind. A human being in a perfect state of nudity, tied hand and foot to a stake, and a strong man standing behind with a heavy whip, knotted at the end, each blow cutting into the flesh, and leaving the warm blood dripping to the feet; and for these trifles. "For being found in another person's negro-quarters, forty lashes; for hunting with dogs in the woods, thirty lashes; for being on horseback without the written permission of his master, twenty-five lashes; for riding or going abroad in the night, or riding horses in the day time, without leave, a slave may be whipped, cropped, or branded in the cheek with the letter R, or otherwise punished, such punishment not extending to life, or so as to render him unfit for labor." The laws referred to, may be found by consulting Brevard's Digest; Haywood's Manual; Virginia Revised Code; Prince's Digest; Missouri Laws; Mississippi Revised Code. A man, for going to visit his brethren, without the permission of his master—and in many instances he may not have that permission; his master, from caprice or other reasons, may not be willing to allow it—may be caught on his way, dragged to a post, the branding-iron heated, and the name of his master or the letter R branded into his cheek or on his forehead.

They treat slaves thus, on the principle that they must punish for light offenses, in order to prevent the commission of larger ones. I wish you to mark that in the single state of Virginia there are seventy-one crimes for which a colored man may be executed; while there are only three of these crimes, which, when committed by a white man, will subject him to that punishment. There are many of these crimes which if the white man did not commit, he would be regarded as a scoundrel and a coward. In the state of Maryland, there is a law to this effect: that if a slave shall strike his master, he may be hanged, his head severed from his body, his body quartered, and his head and quarters set up in the most prominent places in the neighborhood. If a colored woman, in the defense of her own virtue, in defense of her own person, should shield herself from the brutal attacks of her tyrannical master, or make the slightest resistance, she may be killed on the spot. No law whatever will bring the guilty man to justice for the crime.

But you will ask me, can these things be possible in a land professing Christianity? Yes, they are so; and this is not the worst. No; a darker feature is yet to be presented than the mere existence of these facts. I have to inform you that the religion of the southern states, at this time, is the great supporter, the great sanctioner of the bloody atrocities to which I have referred. While America is printing tracts and Bibles; sending missionaries abroad to convert the heathen; expending her money in various ways for the promotion of the gospel in foreign lands—the slave not only lies forgotten, uncared for, but is trampled under foot by the very churches of the land. What have we in America? Why, we have slavery made part of the religion of the land. Yes, the pulpit there stands up as the great defender of this cursed *institution*, as it is called. Ministers of religion come forward and torture the hallowed pages of inspired wisdom to sanction the bloody deed. They stand forth as the foremost, the strongest defenders of this "institution."

As a proof of this, I need not do more than state the general fact, that slavery has existed under the droppings of the sanctuary of the South for the last two hundred years, and there has not been any war between the *religion* and the *slavery* of the South. Whips, chains, gags, and thumb-screws have all lain under the droppings of the sanctuary, and instead of rusting from off the limbs of the bondman, those droppings have served to preserve them in all their strength. Instead of preaching the gospel against this tyranny, rebuke, and wrong, ministers of religion have sought, by all and every means, to throw in the back-ground whatever in the Bible could be construed into opposition to slavery, and to bring forward that which they could torture into its support.

This I conceive to be the darkest feature of slavery, and the most difficult to attack, because it is identified with religion, and exposes those who denounce it to the charge of infidelity. Yes, those with whom I have been laboring, namely, the old organization anti-slavery society of America, have been again and again stigmatized as infidels, and for what reason? Why, solely in consequence of the faithfulness of their attacks upon the slaveholding religion of the southern states, and the northern religion that sympathizes with it. I have found it difficult to speak on this matter without persons coming forward and saying, "Douglass, are you not afraid of injuring the cause of Christ? You do not desire to do so, we know; but are you not undermining religion?" This has been said to me again and again, even since I came to this country, but I cannot be induced to leave off these exposures. I love the religion of our blessed Savior. I love that religion that comes from above, in the "wisdom of God," which is first pure, then peaceable, gentle, and easy to be entreated, full of mercy and good fruits, without partiality and without hypocrisy. I love that religion that sends its votaries to bind up the wounds of him that has fallen among thieves. I love that religion that makes it the duty of its disciples to visit the fatherless and the widow in their affliction. I love that religion that is based upon the glorious principle, of love to God and love to man; which makes its followers do unto others as they themselves would be done by. If you demand liberty to yourself, it says, grant it to your neighbors. If you claim a right to think for yourself, it says, allow your neighbors the same right. It is because I love this religion that I hate the slaveholding, the woman-whipping, the mind-darkening, the soul-destroying religion that exists in the southern states of America. It is because I regard the one as good, and pure, and holy, that I cannot but regard the other as bad, corrupt, and wicked. Loving the one I must hate the other; holding to the one I must reject the other.

I may be asked, why I am so anxious to bring this subject before the British public—why I do not confine my efforts to the United States? My answer is, first, that slavery is the common enemy of mankind, and all mankind should be made acquainted with its abominable character. My next answer is, that the slave is a man, and, as such, is entitled to your sympathy as a brother. All the feelings, all the susceptibilities, all the capacities, which you have, he has. He is a part of the human family. He has been the prey—the common prey—of christendom for the last three hundred years, and it is but right, it is but just, it is but proper, that his wrongs should be known throughout the world.

I have another reason for bringing this matter before the British public, and it is this: slavery is a system of wrong, so blinding to all around, so hardening to the heart, so corrupting to the morals, so deleterious to religion, so sapping to all the principles of justice in its immediate vicinity, that the community surrounding it lack the moral stamina necessary to its removal. It is a system of such gigantic evil, so strong, so overwhelming in its power, that no one nation is equal to its removal. It requires the humanity of Christianity, the morality of the world to remove it. Hence, I call upon the people of Britain to look at this matter, and to exert the influence I am about to show they possess, for the removal of slavery from America. I can appeal to them, as strongly by their regard for the slaveholder as for the slave, to labor in this cause. I am here, because you have an influence on America that no other nation can have. You have been drawn together by the power of steam to a marvelous extent; the distance between London and Boston is now reduced to some twelve or fourteen days, so that the denunciations against slavery, uttered in London this week, may be heard in a fortnight in the streets of Boston, and reverberating amidst the hills of Massachusetts. There is nothing said here against slavery that will not be recorded in the United States.

I am here, also, because the slaveholders do not want me to be here; they would rather that I were not here. I have adopted a maxim laid down by Napoleon, never to occupy ground which the enemy would like me to occupy. The slaveholders would much rather have me, if I will denounce slavery, denounce it in the northern states, where their friends and supporters are, who will stand by and mob me for denouncing it. They feel something as the man felt, when he uttered his prayer, in which he made out a most horrible case for himself, and one of his neighbors touched him and said, "My friend,

I always had the opinion of you that you have now expressed for yourself—that you are a very great sinner." Coming from himself, it was all very well, but coming from a stranger it was rather cutting.

The slaveholders felt that when slavery was denounced among themselves, it was not so bad; but let one of the slaves get loose, let him summon the people of Britain, and make known to them the conduct of the slaveholders toward their slaves, and it cuts them to the quick, and produces a sensation such as would be produced by nothing else. The power I exert now is something like the power that is exerted by the man at the end of the lever; my influence now is just in proportion to the distance that I am from the United States. My exposure of slavery abroad will tell more upon the hearts and con-sciences of slaveholders, than if I was attacking them in America; for almost every paper that I now receive from the United States, comes teeming with statements about this fugitive Negro, calling him a "glib-tongued scoundrel," and saying that he is running out against the institutions and people of America.

I deny the charge that I am saying a word against the institutions of America, or the people, as such. What I have to say is against slavery and slaveholders. I feel at liberty to speak on this subject. I have on my back the marks of the lash; I have four sisters and one brother now under the galling chain. I feel it my duty to cry aloud and spare not. I am not averse to having the good opinion of my fellow-creatures. I am not averse to being kindly regarded by all men; but I am bound, even at the hazard of making a large class of religionists in this country hate me, oppose me, and malign me as they have done—I am bound by the prayers, and tears, and entreaties of three millions of kneeling bonds-men, to have no compromise with men who are in any shape or form connected with the slaveholders of America.

I expose slavery in this country, because to expose it is to kill it. Slavery is one of those monsters of darkness to whom the light of truth is death. Expose slavery, and it dies. Light is to slavery what the heat of the sun is to the root of a tree; it must die under it. All the slaveholder asks of me is silence. He does not ask me to go abroad and preach *in favor* of slavery; he does not ask any one to do that. He would not say that slavery is a good thing, but the best under the circumstances. The slaveholders want total darkness on the subject. They want the hatchway shut down, that the monster may crawl in his den of darkness, crushing human hopes and happiness, destroying the bondman at will, and having no one to reprove or rebuke him. Slavery shrinks from the light; it hateth the light, neither cometh to the light, lest its deeds should be reproved. To tear off the mask from this abominable system, to expose it to the light of heaven, aye, to the heat of the sun, that it may burn and wither it out of existence, is my object in coming to this country. I want the slaveholder surrounded, as by a wall of anti-slavery fire, so that he may see the condemnation of himself and his system glaring down in letters of light. I want him to feel that he has no sympathy in England, Scotland, or Ireland; that he has none in Canada, none in Mexico, none among the poor wild Indians; that the voice of the civilized, aye, and savage world is against him. I would have condemnation blaze down upon him in every direction, till, stunned and overwhelmed with shame and confusion, he is compelled to let go the grasp he holds upon the persons of his victims, and restore them to their long-lost rights.

LETTER TO HIS OLD MASTER

To My Old Master, Thomas Auld,
September 3, 1848

SIR—THE LONG AND INTIMATE, THOUGH BY NO MEANS FRIENDLY, relation which unhappily subsisted between you and myself, leads me to hope that you will easily account for the great liberty which I now take in addressing you in this open and public manner. The same fact may remove any disagreeable surprise which you may experience on again finding your name coupled with mine, in any other way than in an advertisement, accurately describing my person, and offering a large sum for my arrest. In thus dragging you again before the public, I am aware that I shall subject myself to no inconsiderable amount of censure. I shall probably be charged with an unwarrantable, if not a wanton and reckless disregard of the rights and properties of private life. There are those north as well as south who entertain a much higher respect for rights which are merely conventional, than they do for rights which are personal and essential. Not a few there are in our country, who, while they have no scruples against robbing the laborer of the hard earned results of his patient industry, will be shocked by the extremely indelicate manner of bringing your name before the public. Believing this to be the case, and wishing to meet every reasonable or plausible objection to my conduct, I will frankly state the ground upon which I justify myself in this instance, as well as on former occasions when I have thought proper to mention your name in public. All will agree that a man guilty of theft, robbery, or murder, has forfeited the right to concealment and private life; that the community have a right to subject such persons to the most complete exposure. However much they may desire retirement, and aim to conceal themselves and their movements from the popular gaze, the public have a right to ferret them out, and bring their conduct before the proper tribunals of the country for investigation. Sir, you will undoubtedly make the proper application of these generally admitted principles, and will easily see the light in which you are regarded by me; I will not therefore manifest ill temper, by calling you hard names. I know you to be a man of some intelligence, and can readily determine the precise estimate which I entertain of your character. I may therefore indulge in language which may seem to others indirect and ambiguous, and yet be quite well understood by yourself.

I have selected this day on which to address you, because it is the anniversary of my emancipation; and knowing no better way, I am led to this as the best mode of celebrating that truly important event. Just ten years ago this beautiful September morning, yon bright sun beheld me a slave—a poor degraded chattel—trembling at the sound of your voice, lamenting that I was a man, and wishing myself a brute. The hopes which I had treasured up for weeks of a safe and successful escape from your grasp, were powerfully confronted at this last hour by dark clouds of doubt and fear, making my person shake and my bosom to heave with the heavy contest between hope and fear. I have no words to describe to you the deep agony of soul which I experienced on that never-to-be-forgotten morning—for I left by daylight. I was making a leap in the dark. The probabilities, so far as I could by reason determine them, were stoutly against the undertaking. The preliminaries and precautions I had adopted previously, all worked badly. I was like one going to war without weapons—ten chances of defeat to one of victory. One in whom I had confided, and one who had promised me assistance, appalled by fear at the trial hour, deserted me, thus leaving the responsibility of success or failure solely with myself. You, sir, can never know my feelings. As I look back to them, I can scarcely realize that I have passed through a scene so trying. Trying, however, as they were, and gloomy as was the prospect, thanks be to the Most High, who is ever the God of the oppressed, at the moment which was to determine my whole earthly career, His grace was sufficient; my mind was made up. I embraced the golden opportunity, took the morning tide at the flood, and a free man, young, active, and strong, is the result.

I have often thought I should like to explain to you the grounds upon which I have justified myself in running away from you. I am almost ashamed to do so now, for by this time you may have discovered them yourself. I will, however, glance at them. When yet but a child about six years old, I imbibed the determination to run away. The very first mental effort that I now remember on my part, was an attempt to solve the mystery—why am I a slave? and with this question my youthful mind was troubled for many days, pressing upon me more heavily at times than others. When I saw the slave-driver whip a slave-woman, cut the blood out of her neck, and heard her piteous cries, I went away into the corner of the fence, wept and pondered over the mystery. I had, through some medium, I know not what, got some idea of God, the Creator of all mankind, the black and the white, and that he had made the blacks to serve the whites as slaves. How he could do this and be *good*, I could not tell. I was not satisfied with this theory, which made God responsible for slavery, for it pained me greatly, and I have wept over it long and often. At one time, your first wife, Mrs. Lucretia, heard me sighing and saw me shedding tears, and asked of me the matter, but I was afraid to tell her. I was puzzled with this question, till one night while sitting in the kitchen, I heard some of the old slaves talking of their parents having been stolen from Africa by white men, and were sold here as slaves. The whole mystery was solved at once. Very soon after this, my Aunt Jinny and Uncle Noah ran away, and the great noise made about it by your father-in-law, made me for the first time acquainted with the fact, that there were free states as well as slave states. From that time, I resolved that I would some day run away. The morality of the act I dispose of as follows: I am myself; you are yourself; we are two distinct persons, equal persons. What you are, I am. You are a man, and so am I. God created both, and made us separate beings. I am not by nature bond to you, or you to me. Nature does not make your existence depend upon me, or mine to depend upon yours. I cannot walk upon your legs, or you upon mine. I cannot breathe for you, or you for me; I must breathe for myself, and you for yourself. We are distinct persons, and are each equally provided with faculties necessary to our individual existence. In leaving you, I took nothing but what belonged to me, and in no way lessened your means for obtaining an *honest* living. Your faculties remained yours, and mine became useful to their rightful owner. I therefore see no wrong in any part of the transaction. It is true, I went off secretly; but that was more your fault than mine. Had I let you into the secret, you would have defeated the enterprise entirely; but for this, I should have been really glad to have made you acquainted with my intentions to leave.

You may perhaps want to know how I like my present condition. I am free to say, I greatly prefer it to that which I occupied in Maryland. I am, however, by no means prejudiced against the state as such. Its geography, climate, fertility, and products, are such as to make it a very desirable abode for any man; and but for the existence of slavery there, it is not impossible that I might again take up my abode in that state. It is not that I love Maryland less, but freedom more. You will be surprised to learn that people at the North labor under the strange delusion that if the slaves were emancipated at the South, they would flock to the North. So far from this being the case, in that event, you would see many old and familiar faces back again to the South. The fact is, there are few here who would not return to the South in the event of emancipation. We want to live in the land of our birth, and to lay our bones by the side of our fathers; and nothing short of an intense love of personal freedom keeps us from the South. For the sake of this, most of us would live on a crust of bread and a cup of cold water.

Since I left you, I have had a rich experience. I have occupied stations which I never dreamed of when a slave. Three out of the ten years since I left you, I spent as a common laborer on the wharves of New Bedford, Massachusetts. It was there I earned my first free dollar. It was mine. I could spend it as I pleased. I could buy hams or herring with it, without asking any odds of anybody. That was a precious dollar to me. You remember when I used to make seven, or eight, or even nine dollars a week in Baltimore, you would take every cent of it from me every Saturday night, saying that I belonged to you, and my earnings also. I never liked this conduct on your part—to say the best, I thought it a little mean. I would not have served you so. But let that pass. I was a little awkward about counting money in New England fashion when I first landed in New Bedford. I came near betraying myself several times. I caught myself saying phip, for fourpence; and at one time a man actually charged me with being a runaway, whereupon I was silly enough to become one by running away from him, for I was greatly afraid he might adopt measures to get me again into slavery, a condition I then dreaded more than death.

I soon learned, however, to count money, as well as to make it, and got on swimmingly. I married soon after leaving you; in fact, I was engaged to be married before I left you; and instead of finding my companion a burden, she was truly a helpmate. She went to live at service, and I to work on the wharf, and though we toiled hard the first winter, we never lived more happily. After remaining in New Bedford for three years, I met with William Lloyd Garrison, a person of whom you have *possibly* heard, as he is pretty generally known among slaveholders. He put it into my head that I might make myself serviceable to the cause of the slave, by devoting a portion of my time to telling my own sorrows, and those of other slaves, which had come under my observation. This was the commencement of a higher state of existence than any to which I had ever aspired. I was thrown into society the most pure, enlightened, and benevolent, that the country affords. Among these I have never forgotten you, but have invariably made you the topic of conversation— thus giving you all the notoriety I could do. I need not tell you that the opinion formed of you in these circles is far from being favorable. They have little respect for your honesty, and less for your religion.

But I was going on to relate to you something of my interesting experience. I had not long enjoyed the excellent society to which I have referred, before the light of its excellence exerted a beneficial influence on my mind and heart. Much of my early dislike of white persons was removed, and their manners, habits, and customs, so entirely unlike what I had been used to in the kitchen-quarters on the plantations of the South, fairly charmed me, and gave me a strong disrelish for the coarse and degrading customs of my former condition. I therefore made an effort so to improve my mind and deportment, as to be somewhat fitted to the station to which I seemed almost providentially called. The transition from degradation to respectability was indeed great, and to get from one to the other without carrying some marks of one's former condition, is truly a difficult matter. I would not have you think that I am now entirely clear of all plantation peculiarities, but my friends here, while they entertain the strongest dislike to them, regard me with that charity to which my past life somewhat entitles me, so that my condition in this respect is exceedingly pleasant. So far as my domestic affairs are concerned, I can boast of as comfortable a dwelling as your own. I have an industrious and neat companion, and four dear children—the oldest a girl of nine years, and three fine boys, the oldest eight, the next six, and the youngest four years old. The three oldest are now going regularly to school—two can read and write, and the other can spell, with tolerable correctness, words of two syllables. Dear fellows! they are all in comfortable beds, and are sound asleep, perfectly secure under my own roof. There are no slaveholders here to rend my heart by snatching them from my arms, or blast a mother's dearest hopes by tearing them from her bosom. These dear children are ours—not to work up into rice, sugar, and tobacco, but to watch over, regard, and protect, and to rear them up in the nurture and admonition of the gospel—to train them up in the paths of wisdom and virtue, and, as far as we can, to make them useful to the world and to themselves. Oh! sir, a slaveholder never appears to me so completely an agent of hell, as when I think of and look upon my dear children. It is then that my feelings rise above my control. I meant to have said more with respect to my own prosperity and happiness, but thoughts and feelings which this recital has quickened, unfit me to proceed further in that direction. The grim horrors of slavery rise in all their ghastly terror before me; the wails of millions pierce my heart and chill my blood. I remember the chain, the gag, the bloody whip; the death-like gloom overshadowing the broken spirit of the fettered bondman; the appalling liability of his being torn away from wife and children, and sold like a beast in the market. Say not that this is a picture of fancy. You well know that I wear stripes on my back, inflicted by your direction; and that you, while we were brothers in the same church, caused this right hand, with which I am now penning this letter, to be closely tied to my left, and my person dragged, at the pistol's mouth, fifteen miles, from the Bay Side to Easton, to be sold like a beast in the market, for the alleged crime of intending to escape from your possession. All this, and more, you remember, and know to be perfectly true, not only of yourself, but of nearly all of the slaveholders around you.

At this moment, you are probably the guilty holder of at least three of my own dear sisters, and my only brother, in bondage. These you regard as your property. They are recorded on your ledger, or perhaps have been sold to human flesh-mongers, with a view to filling your own ever-hungry purse. Sir, I desire to know how and where these dear sisters are. Have you sold them? or are they still in your possession? What has become of them? are they living or dead? And my dear old grandmother, whom you turned out like an old horse to die in the woods—is she still alive? Write and let me know all about them. If my grandmother be still alive, she is of no service to you, for by this time she must be nearly eighty years old—too old to be cared for by one to whom she has ceased to be of service; send her to me at Rochester, or bring her to Philadelphia, and it shall be the crowning happiness of my life to take care of her in her old age. Oh! she was to me a mother and a father, so far as hard toil for my comfort could make her such. Send me my grandmother! that I may watch over and take care of her in her old age. And my sisters—let me know all about them. I would write to them, and learn all I want to know of them, without disturbing you in any way, but that, through your unrighteous conduct, they have been entirely deprived of the power to read and write. You have kept them in utter ignorance, and have therefore robbed them of the sweet enjoyments of writing or receiving letters from absent friends and relatives. Your wickedness and cruelty, committed in this respect on your fellow-creatures, are greater than all the stripes you have laid upon my back or theirs. It is an outrage upon the soul, a war upon the immortal spirit, and one for which you must give account at the bar of our common Father and Creator.

The responsibility which you have assumed in this regard is truly awful, and how you could stagger under it these many years is marvelous. Your mind must have become darkened, your heart hardened, your conscience seared and petrified, or you would have long since thrown off the accursed load, and sought relief at the hands of a sin-forgiving God. How, let me ask, would you look upon me, were I, some dark night, in company with a band of hardened villains, to enter the precincts of your elegant dwelling, and seize the person of your own lovely daughter, Amanda, and carry her off from your family, friends, and all the loved ones of her youth—make her my slave—compel her to work, and I take her wages—place her name on my ledger as property—disregard her personal rights—fetter the powers of her immortal soul by denying her the right and privilege of learning to read and write—feed her coarsely—clothe her scantily, and whip her on the naked back occasionally; more, and still more horrible, leave her unprotected—a degraded victim to the brutal lust of fiendish overseers, who would pollute, blight, and blast her fair soul—rob her of all dignity—destroy her virtue, and annihilate in her person all the graces that adorn the character of virtuous womanhood? I ask, how would you regard me, if such were my conduct? Oh! the vocabulary of the damned would not afford a word sufficiently infernal to express your idea of my God-provoking wickedness. Yet, sir, your treatment of my beloved sisters is in all essential points precisely like the case I have now supposed. Damning as would be such a deed on my part, it would be no more so than that which you have committed against me and my sisters.

I will now bring this letter to a close; you shall hear from me again unless you let me hear from you. I intend to make use of you as a weapon with which to assail the system of slavery—as a means of concentrating public attention on the system, and deepening the horror of trafficking in the souls and bodies of men. I shall make use of you as a means of exposing the character of the American church and clergy—and as a means of bringing this guilty nation, with yourself, to repentance. In doing this, I entertain no malice toward you personally. There is no roof under which you would be more safe than mine, and there is nothing in my house which you might need for your comfort, which I would not readily grant. Indeed, I should esteem it a privilege to set you an example as to how mankind ought to treat each other.

I am your fellow-man, but not your slave.

FREDERICK DOUGLASS

THE NATURE OF SLAVERY

Extract from a Lecture on Slavery, at Rochester,
December 1, 1850

MORE THAN TWENTY YEARS OF MY LIFE WERE CONSUMED IN A STATE
of slavery. My childhood was environed by the baneful peculiarities of
the slave system. I grew up to manhood in the presence of this hydra-
headed monster—not as a master—not as an idle spectator—not as the
guest of the slaveholder—but as A SLAVE, eating the bread and drinking the cup of slavery with the most degraded of my brother-bondmen,
and sharing with them all the painful conditions of their wretched lot.
In consideration of these facts, I feel that I have a right to speak, and
to speak *strongly*. Yet, my friends, I feel bound to speak truly.

Goading as have been the cruelties to which I have been subjected—
bitter as have been the trials through which I have passed—exasperating
as have been, and still are, the indignities offered to my manhood—
I find in them no excuse for the slightest departure from truth in
dealing with any branch of this subject.

First of all, I will state, as well as I can, the legal and social relation of master and slave. A master is one—to speak in the vocabulary
of the southern states—who claims and exercises a right of property
in the person of a fellow-man. This he does with the force of the law
and the sanction of southern religion. The law gives the master absolute power over the slave.

He may work him, flog him, hire him out, sell him, and, in certain
contingencies, *kill* him, with perfect impunity. The slave is a human

being, divested of all rights—reduced to the level of a brute—a mere "chattel" in the eye of the law—placed beyond the circle of human brotherhood—cut off from his kind—his name, which the "recording angel" may have enrolled in heaven, among the blest, is impiously inserted in a *master's ledger*, with horses, sheep, and swine. In law, the slave has no wife, no children, no country, and no home. He can own nothing, possess nothing, acquire nothing, but what must belong to another. To eat the fruit of his own toil, to clothe his person with the work of his own hands, is considered stealing. He toils that another may reap the fruit; he is industrious that another may live in idleness; he eats unbolted meal that another may eat the bread of fine flour; he labors in chains at home, under a burning sun and biting lash, that another may ride in ease and splendor abroad; he lives in ignorance that another may be educated; he is abused that another may be exalted; he rests his toil-worn limbs on the cold, damp ground that another may repose on the softest pillow; he is clad in coarse and tattered raiment that another may be arrayed in purple and fine linen; he is sheltered only by the wretched hovel that a master may dwell in a magnificent mansion; and to this condition he is bound down as by an arm of iron.

From this monstrous relation there springs an unceasing stream of most revolting cruelties. The very accompaniments of the slave system stamp it as the offspring of hell itself. To ensure good behavior, the slaveholder relies on the whip; to induce proper humility, he relies on the whip; to rebuke what he is pleased to term insolence, he relies on the whip; to supply the place of wages as an incentive to toil, he relies on the whip; to bind down the spirit of the slave, to imbrute and destroy his manhood, he relies on the whip, the chain, the gag, the thumb-screw, the pillory, the bowie knife, the pistol, and the bloodhound. These are the necessary and unvarying accompaniments of the system. Wherever slavery is found, these horrid instruments are also found. Whether on the coast of Africa, among the savage tribes, or in South Carolina, among the refined and civilized, slavery is the same, and its accompaniments one and the same. It makes no difference whether the slaveholder worships the God of the Christians, or is a follower of Mahomet, he is the minister of the same cruelty, and the author of the same misery. *Slavery* is always *slavery;* always the same foul, haggard, and damning scourge, whether found in the eastern or in the western hemisphere.

There is a still deeper shade to be given to this picture. The physical cruelties are indeed sufficiently harassing and revolting; but they are as a few grains of sand on the sea shore, or a few drops of water in the great ocean, compared with the stupendous wrongs which it inflicts upon the mental, moral, and religious nature of its hapless victims. It is only when we contemplate the slave as a moral and intellectual being, that we can adequately comprehend the unparalleled enormity of slavery, and the intense criminality of the slaveholder. I have said that the slave was a man. "What a piece of work is man! How noble in reason! How infinite in faculties! In form and moving how express and admirable! In action how like an angel! In apprehension how like a God! The beauty of the world! The paragon of animals!"

The slave is a man, "the image of God," but "a little lower than the angels"; possessing a soul, eternal and indestructible; capable of endless happiness, or immeasurable woe; a creature of hopes and fears, of affections and passions, of joys and sorrows, and he is endowed with those mysterious powers by which man soars above the things of time and sense, and grasps, with undying tenacity, the elevating and sublimely glorious idea of a God. It is *such* a being that is smitten and blasted. The first work of slavery is to mar and deface those characteristics of its victims which distinguish *men* from *things*, and *persons* from *property*. Its first aim is to destroy all sense of high moral and religious responsibility. It reduces man to a mere machine. It cuts him off from his Maker, it hides from him the laws of God, and leaves him to grope his way from time to eternity in the dark, under the arbitrary and despotic control of a frail, depraved, and sinful fellow-man. As the serpent-charmer of India is compelled to extract the deadly teeth of his venomous prey before he is able to handle him with impunity, so the slaveholder must strike down the conscience of the slave before he can obtain the entire mastery over his victim.

It is, then, the first business of the enslaver of men to blunt, deaden, and destroy the central principle of human responsibility. Conscience is, to the individual soul, and to society, what the law of gravitation is to the universe. It holds society together; it is the basis of all trust and confidence; it is the pillar of all moral rectitude. Without it, suspicion would take the place of trust; vice would be more than a match for virtue; men would prey upon each other, like the wild beasts of the desert; and earth would become a *hell.*

Nor is slavery more adverse to the conscience than it is to the mind. This is shown by the fact, that in every state of the American Union, where slavery exists, except the state of Kentucky, there are laws absolutely prohibitory of education among the slaves. The crime of teaching a slave to read is punishable with severe fines and imprisonment, and, in some instances, with *death itself.*

Nor are the laws respecting this matter a dead letter. Cases may occur in which they are disregarded, and a few instances may be found where slaves may have learned to read; but such are isolated cases, and only prove the rule. The great mass of slaveholders look upon education among the slaves as utterly subversive of the slave system. I well remember when my mistress first announced to my master that she had discovered that I could read. His face colored at once with surprise and chagrin. He said that "I was ruined, and my value as a slave destroyed; that a slave should know nothing but to obey his master; that to give a negro an inch would lead him to take an ell; that having learned how to read, I would soon want to know how to write; and that by-and-by I would be running away." I think my audience will bear witness to the correctness of this philosophy, and to the literal fulfillment of this prophecy.

It is perfectly well understood at the South, that to educate a slave is to make him discontented with slavery, and to invest him with a power which shall open to him the treasures of freedom; and since the object of the slaveholder is to maintain complete authority over his slave, his constant vigilance is exercised to prevent everything which militates against, or endangers, the stability of his authority. Education being among the menacing influences, and, perhaps, the most dangerous, is, therefore, the most cautiously guarded against.

It is true that we do not often hear of the enforcement of the law, punishing as a crime the teaching of slaves to read, but this is not because of a want of disposition to enforce it. The true reason or explanation of the matter is this: there is the greatest unanimity of opinion among the white population in the South in favor of the policy of keeping the slave in ignorance. There is, perhaps, another reason why the law against education is so seldom violated. The slave is too poor to be able to offer a temptation sufficiently strong to induce a white man to violate it; and it is not to be supposed that in a community where the moral and religious sentiment is in favor of slavery, many martyrs will be found sacrificing their liberty and lives by violating those prohibitory enactments.

As a general rule, then, darkness reigns over the abodes of the enslaved, and "how great is that darkness!"

We are sometimes told of the contentment of the slaves, and are entertained with vivid pictures of their happiness. We are told that they often dance and sing; that their masters frequently give them wherewith to make merry; in fine, that they have little of which to complain. I admit that the slave does sometimes sing, dance, and appear to be merry. But what does this prove? It only proves to my mind, that though slavery is armed with a thousand stings, it is not able entirely to kill the elastic spirit of the bondman. That spirit will rise and walk abroad, despite of whips and chains, and extract from the cup of nature occasional drops of joy and gladness. No thanks to the slaveholder, nor to slavery, that the vivacious captive may sometimes dance in his chains; his very mirth in such circumstances stands before God as an accusing angel against his enslaver.

It is often said, by the opponents of the anti-slavery cause, that the condition of the people of Ireland is more deplorable than that of the American slaves. Far be it from me to underrate the sufferings of the Irish people. They have been long oppressed; and the same heart that prompts me to plead the cause of the American bondman, makes it impossible for me not to sympathize with the oppressed of all lands. Yet I must say that there is no analogy between the two cases. The Irishman is poor, but he is not a slave. He may be in rags, but he is not a slave. He is still the master of his own body, and can say with the poet, "The hand of Douglass is his own." "The world is all before him, where to choose;" and poor as may be my opinion of the British parliament, I cannot believe that it will ever sink to such a depth of infamy as to pass a law for the recapture of fugitive Irishmen! The shame and scandal of kidnapping will long remain wholly monopolized by the American congress. The Irishman has not only the liberty to emigrate from his country, but he has liberty at home. He can write, and speak, and cooperate for the attainment of his rights and the redress of his wrongs.

The multitude can assemble upon all the green hills and fertile plains of the Emerald Isle; they can pour out their grievances, and proclaim their wants without molestation; and the press, that "swift-winged messenger," can bear the tidings of their doings to the extreme bounds of the civilized world. They have their "Conciliation Hall," on the banks of the Liffey, their reform clubs, and their newspapers; they pass resolutions, send forth addresses, and enjoy the right of petition. But how is it with the American slave? Where may he assemble? Where is his Conciliation Hall? Where are his newspapers? Where is his right of petition? Where is his freedom of speech? his liberty of the press? and his right of locomotion? He is said to be happy; happy men can speak. But ask the slave what is his condition—what his state of mind—what he thinks of enslavement? and you had as well address your inquiries to the *silent dead*. There comes no *voice* from the enslaved. We are left to gather his feelings by imagining what ours would be, were our souls in his soul's stead.

If there were no other fact descriptive of slavery, than that the slave is dumb, this alone would be sufficient to mark the slave system as a grand aggregation of human horrors.

Most who are present, will have observed that leading men in this country have been putting forth their skill to secure quiet to the nation. A system of measures to promote this object was adopted a few months ago in congress. The result of those measures is known. Instead of quiet, they have produced alarm; instead of peace, they have brought us war; and so it must ever be.

While this nation is guilty of the enslavement of three millions of innocent men and women, it is as idle to think of having a sound and lasting peace, as it is to think there is no God to take cognizance of the affairs of men. There can be no peace to the wicked while slavery continues in the land. It will be condemned; and while it is condemned there will be agitation. Nature must cease to be nature; men must become monsters; humanity must be transformed; Christianity must be exterminated; all ideas of justice and the laws of eternal goodness must be utterly blotted out from the human soul—ere a system so foul and infernal can escape condemnation, or this guilty republic can have a sound, enduring peace.

Inhumanity of Slavery

Extract from a Lecture on Slavery, at Rochester,
December 8, 1850

THE RELATION OF MASTER AND SLAVE HAS BEEN CALLED PATRIARCHAL, and only second in benignity and tenderness to that of the parent and child. This representation is doubtless believed by many northern people; and this may account, in part, for the lack of interest which we find among persons whom we are bound to believe to be honest and humane. What, then, are the facts? Here I will not quote my own experience in slavery; for this you might call one-sided testimony. I will not cite the declarations of abolitionists; for these you might pronounce exaggerations. I will not rely upon advertisements cut from newspapers; for these you might call isolated cases. But I will refer you to the laws adopted by the legislatures of the slave states. I give you such evidence, because it cannot be invalidated nor denied. I hold in my hand sundry extracts from the slave codes of our country, from which I will quote. . . .

Now, if the foregoing be an indication of kindness, *what is cruelty?* If this be parental affection, *what is bitter malignity?* A more atrocious and blood-thirsty string of laws could not well be conceived of. And yet I am bound to say that they fall short of indicating the horrible cruelties constantly practiced in the slave states.

I admit that there are individual slaveholders less cruel and barbarous than is allowed by law; but these form the exception. The majority of slaveholders find it necessary, to insure obedience, at times, to avail themselves of the utmost extent of the law, and many go beyond it. If kindness were the rule, we should not see advertisements filling the columns of almost every southern newspaper, offering large rewards for fugitive slaves, and describing them as being branded with irons, loaded with chains, and scarred by the whip. One of the most telling testimonies against the pretended kindness of slaveholders, is the fact that uncounted numbers of fugitives are now inhabiting the Dismal Swamp, preferring the untamed wilderness to their cultivated homes—choosing rather to encounter hunger and thirst, and to roam with the wild beasts of the forest, running the hazard of being hunted and shot down, than to submit to the authority of *kind* masters.

I tell you, my friends, humanity is never driven to such an unnatural course of life, without great wrong. The slave finds more of the milk of human kindness in the bosom of the savage Indian, than in the heart of his *Christian* master. He leaves the man of the *Bible,* and takes refuge with the man of the *tomahawk.* He rushes from the praying slaveholder into the paws of the bear. He quits the homes of men for the haunts of wolves. He prefers to encounter a life of trial, however bitter, or death, however terrible, to dragging out his existence under the dominion of these *kind* masters.

The apologists for slavery often speak of the abuses of slavery; and they tell us that they are as much opposed to those abuses as we are; and that they would go as far to correct those abuses and to ameliorate the condition of the slave as anybody. The answer to that view is, that slavery is *itself* an abuse; that it lives by abuse; and dies by the absence of abuse. Grant that slavery is right; grant that the relations of master and slave may innocently exist; and there is not a single outrage which was ever committed against the slave but what finds an apology in the very necessity of the case. As was said by a slaveholder (the Rev. A. G. Few) to the Methodist conference, "If the relation be right, the means to maintain it are also right"; for without those means slavery could not exist. Remove the dreadful scourge—the plaited thong—the galling fetter—the accursed chain—and let the slaveholder rely solely upon moral and religious power, by which to secure obedience to his orders, and how long do you suppose a slave would remain on his plantation? The case only needs to be stated; it carries its own refutation with it.

Absolute and arbitrary power can never be maintained by one man over the body and soul of another man, without brutal chastisement and enormous cruelty.

To talk of *kindness* entering into a relation in which one party is robbed of wife, of children, of his hard earnings, of home, of friends, of society, of knowledge, and of all that makes this life desirable, is most absurd, wicked, and preposterous.

I have shown that slavery is wicked—wicked, in that it violates the great law of liberty, written on every human heart—wicked, in that it violates the first command of the decalogue—wicked, in that it fosters the most disgusting licentiousness—wicked, in that it mars and defaces the image of God by cruel and barbarous inflictions—wicked, in that it contravenes the laws of eternal justice, and tramples in the dust all the humane and heavenly precepts of the New Testament.

The evils resulting from this huge system of iniquity are not confined to the states south of Mason and Dixon's line. Its noxious influence can easily be traced throughout our northern borders. It comes even as far north as the state of New York. Traces of it may be seen even in Rochester; and travelers have told me it casts its gloomy shadows across the lake, approaching the very shores of Queen Victoria's dominions.

The presence of slavery may be explained by—as it is the explanation of—the mobocratic violence which lately disgraced New York, and which still more recently disgraced the city of Boston. These violent demonstrations, these outrageous invasions of human rights, faintly indicate the presence and power of slavery here. It is a significant fact, that while meetings for almost any purpose under heaven may be held unmolested in the city of Boston, that in the same city, a meeting cannot be peaceably held for the purpose of preaching the doctrine of the American Declaration of Independence, "that all men are created equal." The pestiferous breath of slavery taints the whole moral atmosphere of the North, and enervates the moral energies of the whole people.

The moment a foreigner ventures upon our soil, and utters a natural repugnance to oppression, that moment he is made to feel that there is little sympathy in this land for him. If he were greeted with smiles before, he meets with frowns now; and it shall go well with him if he be not subjected to that peculiarly fining method of showing fealty to slavery, the assaults of a mob.

Now, will any man tell me that such a state of things is natural, and that such conduct on the part of the people of the North, springs from a consciousness of rectitude? No! every fibre of the human heart unites in detestation of tyranny, and it is only when the human mind has become familiarized with slavery, is accustomed to its injustice, and corrupted by its selfishness, that it fails to record its abhorrence of slavery, and does not exult in the triumphs of liberty.

The northern people have been long connected with slavery; they have been linked to a decaying corpse, which has destroyed the moral health. The union of the government; the union of the North and South, in the political parties; the union in the religious organizations of the land, have all served to deaden the moral sense of the northern people, and to impregnate them with sentiments and ideas forever in conflict with what as a nation we call *genius of American institutions.* Rightly viewed, this is an alarming fact, and ought to rally all that is pure, just, and holy in one determined effort to crush the monster of corruption, and to scatter "its guilty profits" to the winds. In a high moral sense, as well as in a national sense, the whole American people are responsible for slavery, and must share, in its guilt and shame, with the most obdurate men-stealers of the South.

While slavery exists, and the union of these states endures, every American citizen must bear the chagrin of hearing his country branded before the world as a nation of liars and hypocrites; and behold his cherished flag pointed at with the utmost scorn and derision. Even now an American *abroad* is pointed out in the crowd, as coming from a land where men gain their fortunes by "the blood of souls," from a land of slave markets, of blood-hounds, and slave-hunters; and, in some circles, such a man is shunned altogether, as a moral pest. Is it not time, then, for every American to awake, and inquire into his duty with respect to this subject?

Wendell Phillips—the eloquent New England orator—on his return from Europe, in 1842, said, "As I stood upon the shores of Genoa, and saw floating on the placid waters of the Mediterranean, the beautiful American war ship Ohio, with her masts tapering proportionately aloft, and an eastern sun reflecting her noble form upon the sparkling waters, attracting the gaze of the multitude, my first impulse was of pride, to think myself an American; but when I thought that the first time that gallant ship would gird on her gorgeous apparel, and wake from beneath her sides her dormant thunders, it would be in defense of the African slave trade, I blushed in utter *shame* for my country."

Let me say again, *slavery is alike the sin and the shame of the American people*; it is a blot upon the American name, and the only national reproach which need make an American hang his head in shame, in the presence of monarchical governments.

With this gigantic evil in the land, we are constantly told to look *at home*; if we say ought against crowned heads, we are pointed to our enslaved millions; if we talk of sending missionaries and Bibles abroad, we are pointed to three millions now lying in worse than heathen darkness; if we express a word of sympathy for Kossuth and his Hungarian fugitive brethren, we are pointed to that horrible and hell-black enactment, "the fugitive slave bill."

Slavery blunts the edge of all our rebukes of tyranny abroad—the criticisms that we make upon other nations, only call forth ridicule, contempt, and scorn. In a word, we are made a reproach and a by-word to a mocking earth, and we must continue to be so made, so long as slavery continues to pollute our soil.

We have heard much of late of the virtue of patriotism, the love of country, &c., and this sentiment, so natural and so strong, has been impiously appealed to, by all the powers of human selfishness, to cherish the viper which is stinging our national life away. In its name, we have been called upon to deepen our infamy before the world, to rivet the fetter more firmly on the limbs of the enslaved, and to become utterly insensible to the voice of human woe that is wafted to us on every southern gale. We have been called upon, in its name, to desecrate our whole land by the footprints of slave-hunters, and even to engage ourselves in the horrible business of kidnapping.

I, too, would invoke the spirit of patriotism; not in a narrow and restricted sense, but, I trust, with a broad and manly signification; not to cover up our national sins, but to inspire us with sincere repentance; not to hide our shame from the world's gaze, but utterly to abolish the cause of that shame; not to explain away our gross inconsistencies as a nation, but to remove the hateful, jarring, and incongruous elements from the land; not to sustain an egregious wrong, but to unite all our energies in the grand effort to remedy that wrong.

I would invoke the spirit of patriotism, in the name of the law of the living God, natural and revealed, and in the full belief that "righteousness exalteth a nation, while sin is a reproach to any people." "He that walketh righteously, and speaketh uprightly; he that despiseth the gain of oppressions, that shaketh his hands from the holding of bribes, he shall dwell on high, his place of defense shall be the munitions of rocks, bread shall be given him, his water shall be sure."

We have not only heard much lately of patriotism, and of its aid being invoked on the side of slavery and injustice, but the very prosperity of this people has been called in to deafen them to the voice of duty, and to lead them onward in the pathway of sin. Thus has the blessing of God been converted into a curse. In the spirit of genuine patriotism, I warn the American people, by all that is just and honorable, to BEWARE!

I warn them that, strong, proud, and prosperous though we be, there is a power above us that can "bring down high looks; at the breath of whose mouth our wealth may take wings; and before whom every knee shall bow"; and who can tell how soon the avenging angel may pass over our land, and the sable bondmen now in chains, may become the instruments of our nation's chastisement! Without appealing to any higher feeling, I would warn the American people, and the American government, to be wise in their day and generation. I exhort them to remember the history of other nations; and I remind them that America cannot always sit "as a queen," in peace and repose; that prouder and stronger governments than this have been shattered by the bolts of a just God; that the time *may* come when those they now despise and hate, may be needed; when those whom they now compel by oppression to be enemies, may be wanted as friends. What has been, may be again. There is a point beyond which human endurance cannot go. The crushed worm may yet turn under the heel of the oppressor. I warn them, then, with all solemnity, and in the name of retributive justice, *to look to their ways*; for in an evil hour, those sable arms that have, for the last two centuries, been engaged in cultivating and adorning the fair fields of our country, may yet become the instruments of terror, desolation, and death, throughout our borders.

It was the sage of the Old Dominion that said—while speaking of the possibility of a conflict between the slaves and the slaveholders—"God has no attribute that could take sides with the oppressor in such a contest. I tremble for my country when I reflect that God *is just*, and that his justice cannot sleep forever." Such is the warning voice of Thomas Jefferson; and every day's experience since its utterance until now, confirms its wisdom, and commends its truth.

What to the Slave is the Fourth of July?

Extract from an Oration, at Rochester,
July 5, 1852

Fellow-Citizens—Pardon me, and allow me to ask, why am I called upon to speak here today? What have I, or those I represent, to do with your national independence? Are the great principles of political freedom and of natural justice, embodied in that Declaration of Independence, extended to us? and am I, therefore, called upon to bring our humble offering to the national altar, and to confess the benefits, and express devout gratitude for the blessings, resulting from your independence to us?

Would to God, both for your sakes and ours, that an affirmative answer could be truthfully returned to these questions! Then would my task be light, and my burden easy and delightful. For who is there so cold that a nation's sympathy could not warm him? Who so obdurate and dead to the claims of gratitude, that would not thankfully acknowledge such priceless benefits? Who so stolid and selfish, that would not give his voice to swell the hallelujahs of a nation's jubilee, when the chains of servitude had been torn from his limbs? I am not that man. In a case like that, the dumb might eloquently speak, and the "lame man leap as an hart."

But, such is not the state of the case. I say it with a sad sense of the disparity between us. I am not included within the pale of this glorious anniversary! Your high independence only reveals the immeasurable distance between us. The blessings in which you this day rejoice, are not enjoyed in common. The rich inheritance of justice, liberty, prosperity, and independence, bequeathed by your fathers, is shared by you, not by me. The sunlight that brought life and healing to you, has brought stripes and death to me. This Fourth of July is *yours*, not *mine*. *You* may rejoice, *I* must mourn. To drag a man in fetters into the grand illuminated temple of liberty, and call upon him to join you in joyous anthems, were inhuman mockery and sacrilegious irony. Do you mean, citizens, to mock me, by asking me to speak today? If so, there is a parallel to your conduct. And let me warn you that it is dangerous to copy the example of a nation whose crimes, towering up to heaven, were thrown down by the breath of the Almighty, burying that nation in irrecoverable ruin! I can today take up the plaintive lament of a peeled and woe-smitten people.

"By the rivers of Babylon, there we sat down. Yea! we wept when we remembered Zion. We hanged our harps upon the willows in the midst thereof. For there, they that carried us away captive, required of us a song; and they who wasted us required of us mirth, saying, Sing us one of the songs of Zion. How can we sing the Lord's song in a strange land? If I forget thee, O Jerusalem, let my right hand forget her cunning. If I do not remember thee, let my tongue cleave to the roof of my mouth."

Fellow-citizens, above your national, tumultous joy, I hear the mournful wail of millions, whose chains, heavy and grievous yesterday, are today rendered more intolerable by the jubilant shouts that reach them. If I do forget, if I do not faithfully remember those bleeding children of sorrow this day, "may my right hand forget her cunning, and may my tongue cleave to the roof of my mouth!" To forget them, to pass lightly over their wrongs, and to chime in with the popular theme, would be treason most scandalous and shocking, and would make me a reproach before God and the world. My subject, then, fellow-citizens, is AMERICAN SLAVERY. I shall see this day and its popular characteristics from the slave's point of view. Standing there, identified with the American bondman, making his wrongs mine, I do not hesitate to declare, with all my soul, that the character and conduct of this nation never looked blacker to me than on this Fourth of July. Whether we turn to the declarations of the past, or to the professions of the present, the conduct of the nation seems equally hideous and revolting. America is false to the past, false to the present, and solemnly binds herself to be false to the future. Standing with God and the crushed and bleeding slave on this occasion, I will, in the name of humanity which is outraged, in the name of liberty which is fettered, in the name of the constitution and the Bible, which are disregarded and trampled upon, dare to call in question and to denounce, with all the emphasis I can command, everything that serves to perpetuate slavery—the great sin and shame of America! "I will not equivocate; I will not excuse"; I will use the severest language I can command; and yet not one word shall escape me that any man, whose judgment is not blinded by prejudice, or who is not at heart a slaveholder, shall not confess to be right and just.

But I fancy I hear some one of my audience say, it is just in this circumstance that you and your brother abolitionists fail to make a favorable impression on the public mind. Would you argue more, and denounce less, would you persuade more and rebuke less, your cause would be much more likely to succeed. But, I submit, where all is plain there is nothing to be argued. What point in the anti-slavery creed would you have me argue? On what branch of the subject do the people of this country need light? Must I undertake to prove that the slave is a man? That point is conceded already. Nobody doubts it. The slaveholders themselves acknowledge it in the enactment of laws for their government. They acknowledge it when they punish disobedience on the part of the slave. There are seventy-two crimes in the state of Virginia, which, if committed by a black man (no matter how ignorant he be), subject him to the punishment of death; while only two of these same crimes will subject a white man to the like punishment. What is this but the acknowledgement that the slave is a moral, intellectual, and responsible being. The manhood of the slave is conceded. It is admitted in the fact that southern statute books are covered with enactments forbidding, under severe fines and penalties, the teaching of the slave to read or write. When you can point to any such laws, in reference to the beasts of the field, then I may consent to argue the manhood of the slave. When the dogs in your streets, when the fowls of the air, when the cattle on your hills, when the fish of the sea, and the reptiles that crawl, shall be unable to distinguish the slave from a brute, then will I argue with you that the slave is a man!

For the present, it is enough to affirm the equal manhood of the Negro race. Is it not astonishing that, while we are plowing, planting, and reaping, using all kinds of mechanical tools, erecting houses, constructing bridges, building ships, working in metals of brass, iron, copper, silver, and gold; that, while we are reading, writing, and cyphering, acting as clerks, merchants, and secretaries, having among us lawyers, doctors, ministers, poets, authors, editors, orators, and teachers; that, while we are engaged in all manner of enterprises common to other men—digging gold in California, capturing the whale in the Pacific, feeding sheep and cattle on the hillside, living, moving, acting, thinking, planning, living in families as husbands, wives, and children, and, above all, confessing and worshiping the Christian's God, and looking hopefully for life and immortality beyond the grave—we are called upon to prove that we are men!

Would you have me argue that man is entitled to liberty? that he is the rightful owner of his own body? You have already declared it. Must I argue the wrongfulness of slavery? Is that a question for republicans? Is it to be settled by the rules of logic and argumentation, as a matter beset with great difficulty, involving a doubtful application of the principle of justice, hard to be understood? How should I look today in the presence of Americans, dividing and subdividing a discourse, to show that men have a natural right to freedom, speaking of it relatively and positively, negatively and affirmatively? To do so, would be to make myself ridiculous, and to offer an insult to your understanding. There is not a man beneath the canopy of heaven that does not know that slavery is wrong *for him.*

What! am I to argue that it is wrong to make men brutes, to rob them of their liberty, to work them without wages, to keep them ignorant of their relations to their fellow-men, to beat them with sticks, to flay their flesh with the lash, to load their limbs with irons, to hunt them with dogs, to sell them at auction, to sunder their families, to knock out their teeth, to burn their flesh, to starve them into obedience and submission to their masters? Must I argue that a system, thus marked with blood and stained with pollution, is wrong? No; I will not. I have better employment for my time and strength than such arguments would imply.

What, then, remains to be argued? Is it that slavery is not divine; that God did not establish it; that our doctors of divinity are mistaken? There is blasphemy in the thought. That which is inhuman cannot be divine. Who can reason on such a proposition! They that can, may! I cannot. The time for such argument is past.

At a time like this, scorching irony, not convincing argument, is needed. Oh! had I the ability, and could I reach the nation's ear, I would today pour out a fiery stream of biting ridicule, blasting reproach, withering sarcasm, and stern rebuke. For it is not light that is needed, but fire; it is not the gentle shower, but thunder. We need the storm, the whirlwind, and the earthquake. The feeling of the nation must be quickened; the conscience of the nation must be roused; the propriety of the nation must be startled; the hypocrisy of the nation must be exposed; and its crimes against God and man must be proclaimed and denounced.

What to the American slave is your Fourth of July? I answer, a day that reveals to him, more than all other days in the year, the gross injustice and cruelty to which he is the constant victim. To him, your celebration is a sham; your boasted liberty, an unholy license; your national greatness, swelling vanity; your sounds of rejoicing are empty and heartless; your denunciations of tyrants, brass-fronted impudence; your shouts of liberty and equality, hollow mockery; your prayers and hymns, your sermons and thanksgivings, with all your religious parade and solemnity, are to him mere bombast, fraud, deception, impiety, and hypocrisy—a thin veil to cover up crimes which would disgrace a nation of savages. There is not a nation on the earth guilty of practices more shocking and bloody, than are the people of these United States, at this very hour.

Go where you may, search where you will, roam through all the monarchies and despotisms of the old world, travel through South America, search out every abuse, and when you have found the last, lay your facts by the side of the every-day practices of this nation, and you will say with me, that, for revolting barbarity and shameless hypocrisy, America reigns without a rival.

The Internal Slave Trade

Extract from an Oration, at Rochester,
July 5, 1852

Take the American slave trade, which, we are told by the papers, is especially prosperous just now. Ex-senator Benton tells us that the price of men was never higher than now. He mentions the fact to show that slavery is in no danger. This trade is one of the peculiarities of American institutions. It is carried on in all the large towns and cities in one-half of this confederacy; and millions are pocketed every year by dealers in this horrid traffic. In several states this trade is a chief source of wealth. It is called (in contradistinction to the foreign slave trade) "*the internal slave trade.*" It is, probably, called so, too, in order to divert from it the horror with which the foreign slave trade is contemplated. That trade has long since been denounced by this government as piracy. It has been denounced with burning words, from the high places of the nation, as an execrable traffic. To arrest it, to put an end to it, this nation keeps a squadron, at immense cost, on the coast of Africa. Everywhere in this country, it is safe to speak of this foreign slave trade as a most inhuman traffic, opposed alike to the laws of God and of man. The duty to extirpate and destroy it is admitted even by our *doctors of divinity*. In order to put an end to it, some of these last have consented that their colored brethren (nominally free) should leave this country, and establish themselves on the western coast of Africa. It is, however, a notable fact, that, while so much execration is poured out by Americans, upon those engaged in the foreign slave trade, the men engaged in the slave trade between the states pass without condemnation, and their business is deemed honorable.

Behold the practical operation of this internal slave trade—the American slave trade sustained by American politics and American religion! Here you will see men and women reared like swine for the market. You know what is a swine-drover? I will show you a man-drover. They inhabit all our southern states. They perambulate the country, and crowd the highways of the nation with droves of human stock. You will see one of these human-flesh-jobbers, armed with pistol, whip, and bowie-knife, driving a company of a hundred men, women, and children, from the Potomac to the slave market at New Orleans. These wretched people are to be sold singly, or in lots, to suit purchasers. They are food for the cotton-field and the deadly sugar-mill. Mark the sad procession as it moves wearily along, and the inhuman wretch who drives them. Hear his savage yells and his blood-chilling oaths, as he hurries on his affrighted captives. There, see the old man, with locks thinned and gray. Cast one glance, if you please, upon that young mother, whose shoulders are bare to the scorching sun, her briny tears falling on the brow of the babe in her arms. See, too, that girl of thirteen, weeping, yes, weeping, as she thinks of the mother from whom she has been torn. The drove moves tardily. Heat and sorrow have nearly consumed their strength. Suddenly you hear a quick snap, like the discharge of a rifle; the fetters clank, and the chain rattles simultaneously; your ears are saluted with a scream that seems to have torn its way to the center of your soul. The crack you heard was the sound of the slave whip; the scream you heard was from the woman you saw with the babe. Her speed had faltered under the weight of her child and her chains; that gash on her shoulder tells her to move on. Follow this drove to New Orleans. Attend the auction; see men examined like horses; see the forms of women rudely and brutally exposed to the shocking gaze of American slave-buyers. See this drove sold and separated forever; and never forget the deep, sad sobs that arose from that scattered multitude. Tell me, citizens, where, under the sun, can you witness a spectacle more fiendish and shocking.

Yet this is but a glance at the American slave trade, as it exists at this moment, in the ruling part of the United States.

I was born amid such sights and scenes. To me the American slave trade is a terrible reality. When a child, my soul was often pierced with a sense of its horrors. I lived on Philpot Street, Fell's Point, Baltimore, and have watched from the wharves the slave ships in the basin, anchored from the shore, with their cargoes of human flesh, waiting for favorable winds to waft them down the Chesapeake. There was, at that time, a grand slave mart kept at the head of Pratt Street, by Austin Woldfolk. His agents were sent into every town and county in Maryland, announcing their arrival through the papers, and on flaming hand-bills, headed, "cash for negroes." These men were generally well dressed, and very captivating in their manners; ever ready to drink, to treat, and to gamble. The fate of many a slave has depended upon the turn of a single card; and many a child has been snatched from the arms of its mothers by bargains arranged in a state of brutal drunkenness.

The flesh-mongers gather up their victims by dozens, and drive them, chained, to the general depot at Baltimore. When a sufficient number have been collected here, a ship is chartered, for the purpose of conveying the forlorn crew to Mobile or to New Orleans. From the slave-prison to the ship, they are usually driven in the darkness of night; for since the anti-slavery agitation a certain caution is observed.

In the deep, still darkness of midnight, I have been often aroused by the dead, heavy footsteps and the piteous cries of the chained gangs that passed our door. The anguish of my boyish heart was intense; and I was often consoled, when speaking to my mistress in the morning, to hear her say that the custom was very wicked; that she hated to hear the rattle of the chains, and the heart-rending cries. I was glad to find one who sympathized with me in my horror.

Fellow citizens, this murderous traffic is today in active operation in this boasted republic. In the solitude of my spirit, I see clouds of dust raised on the highways of the South; I see the bleeding footsteps; I hear the doleful wail of fettered humanity, on the way to the slave markets, where the victims are to be sold like horses, sheep, and swine, knocked off to the highest bidder. There I see the tenderest ties ruthlessly broken, to gratify the lust, caprice, and rapacity of the buyers and sellers of men. My soul sickens at the sight.

> Is this the land your fathers loved?
> The freedom which they toiled to win?
> Is this the earth whereon they moved?
> Are these the graves they slumber in?

But a still more inhuman, disgraceful, and scandalous state of things remains to be presented. By an act of the American congress, not yet two years old, slavery has been nationalized in its most horrible and revolting form. By that act, Mason and Dixon's line has been obliterated; New York has become as Virginia; and the power to hold, hunt, and sell men, women, and children as slaves, remains no longer a mere state institution, but is now an institution of the whole United States. The power is co-extensive with the star-spangled banner and American Christianity. Where these go, may also go the merciless slave-hunter. Where these are, man is not sacred. He is a bird for the sportsman's gun. By that most foul and fiendish of all human decrees, the liberty and person of every man are put in peril. Your broad republican domain is a hunting-ground for *men*. Not for thieves and robbers, enemies of society, merely, but for men guilty of no crime. Your law-makers have commanded all good citizens to engage in this hellish sport. Your president, your secretary of state, your lords, nobles, and ecclesiastics, enforce as a duty you owe to your free and glorious country and to your God, that you do this accursed thing. Not fewer than forty Americans have within the past two years been hunted down, and without a moment's warning, hurried away in chains, and consigned to slavery and excruciating torture. Some of these have had wives and children dependent on them for bread; but of this no account was made. The right of the hunter to his prey, stands superior to the right of marriage, and to *all* rights in this republic, the rights of God included! For black men there are neither law, justice, humanity, nor religion. The fugitive slave law makes MERCY TO THEM A CRIME; and bribes the judge who tries them. An American judge GETS TEN DOLLARS FOR EVERY VICTIM HE CONSIGNS to slavery, and five, when he fails to do so. The oath of any two villains is sufficient, under this hell-black enactment, to send the most pious and exemplary black man into the remorseless jaws of slavery! His own testimony is nothing. He can bring no witnesses for himself. The minister of American justice is bound by the law to hear but *one side*, and that side is the side of the oppressor. Let this damning fact be perpetually told. Let it be thundered around the world, that, in tyrant-killing, king-hating, people-loving, democratic, Christian America, the seats of justice are filled with judges, who hold their office under an open and palpable *bribe*, and are bound, in deciding in the case of a man's liberty, *to hear only his accusers!*

In glaring violation of justice, in shameless disregard of the forms of administering law, in cunning arrangement to entrap the defenseless, and in diabolical intent, this fugitive slave law stands alone in the annals of tyrannical legislation. I doubt if there be another nation on the globe having the brass and the baseness to put such a law on the statute-book. If any man in this assembly thinks differently from me in this matter, and feels able to disprove my statements, I will gladly confront him at any suitable time and place he may select.

THE SLAVERY PARTY

Extract from a Speech Delivered before the A. A. S. Society,
in New York, May 1853

SIR, IT IS EVIDENT THAT THERE IS IN THIS COUNTRY A PURELY SLAVERY
party—a party which exists for no other earthly purpose but to promote the interests of slavery. The presence of this party is felt
everywhere in the republic. It is known by no particular name, and has
assumed no definite shape; but its branches reach far and wide in the
church and in the state. This shapeless and nameless party is not intan-
gible in other and more important respects. That party, sir, has
determined upon a fixed, definite, and comprehensive policy toward
the whole colored population of the United States. What that policy
is, it becomes us as abolitionists, and especially does it become the
colored people themselves, to consider and to understand fully. We
ought to know who our enemies are, where they are, and what are
their objects and measures. Well, sir, here is my version of it—not
original with me—but mine because I hold it to be true.

I understand this policy to comprehend five cardinal objects. They
are these: 1st. The complete suppression of all anti-slavery discussion.
2d. The expatriation of the entire free people of color from the United
States. 3d. The unending perpetuation of slavery in this republic. 4th.
The nationalization of slavery to the extent of making slavery respected
in every state of the Union. 5th. The extension of slavery over Mexico
and the entire South American states.

Sir, these objects are forcibly presented to us in the stern logic of passing events; in the facts which are and have been passing around us during the last three years. The country has been and is now dividing on these grand issues. In their magnitude, these issues cast all others into the shade, depriving them of all life and vitality. Old party ties are broken. Like is finding its like on either side of these great issues, and the great battle is at hand. For the present, the best representative of the slavery party in politics is the democratic party. Its great head for the present is President Pierce, whose boast it was, before his election, that his whole life had been consistent with the interests of slavery, that he is above reproach on that score. In his inaugural address, he reassures the South on this point. Well, the head of the slave power being in power, it is natural that the pro slavery elements should cluster around the administration, and this is rapidly being done. A fraternization is going on. The stringent protectionists and the free-traders strike hands. The supporters of Fillmore are becoming the supporters of Pierce. The silver-gray whig shakes hands with the hunker democrat; the former only differing from the latter in name. They are of one heart, one mind, and the union is natural and perhaps inevitable. Both hate Negroes; both hate progress; both hate the "higher law;" both hate William H. Seward; both hate the free democratic party; and upon this hateful basis they are forming a union of hatred. "Pilate and Herod are thus made friends." Even the central organ of the whig party is extending its beggar hand for a morsel from the table of slavery democracy, and when spurned from the feast by the more deserving, it pockets the insult; when kicked on one side it turns the other, and perseveres in its importunities. The fact is, that paper comprehends the demands of the times; it understands the age and its issues; it wisely sees that slavery and freedom are the great antagonistic forces in the country, and it goes to its own side. Silver grays and hunkers all understand this. They are, therefore, rapidly sinking all other questions to nothing, compared with the increasing demands of slavery. They are collecting, arranging, and consolidating their forces for the accomplishment of their appointed work.

The keystone to the arch of this grand union of the slavery party of the United States, is the compromise of 1850. In that compromise we have all the objects of our slaveholding policy specified. It is, sir, favorable to this view of the designs of the slave power, that both the whig and the democratic party bent lower, sunk deeper, and strained harder, in their conventions, preparatory to the late presidential election, to meet the demands of the slavery party than at any previous time in their history. Never did parties come before the northern people with propositions of such undisguised contempt for the moral sentiment and the religious ideas of that people. They virtually asked them to unite in a war upon free speech, and upon conscience, and to drive the Almighty presence from the councils of the nation. Resting their platforms upon the fugitive slave bill, they boldly asked the people for political power to execute the horrible and hell-black provisions of that bill. The history of that election reveals, with great clearness, the extent to which slavery has shot its leprous distillment through the lifeblood of the nation. The party most thoroughly opposed to the cause of justice and humanity, triumphed; while the party suspected of a leaning toward liberty, was overwhelmingly defeated, some say annihilated.

But here is a still more important fact, illustrating the designs of the slave power. It is a fact full of meaning, that no sooner did the democratic slavery party come into power, than a system of legislation was presented to the legislatures of the northern states, designed to put the states in harmony with the fugitive slave law, and the malignant bearing of the national government toward the colored inhabitants of the country. This whole movement on the part of the states, bears the evidence of having one origin, emanating from one head, and urged forward by one power. It was simultaneous, uniform, and general, and looked to one end. It was intended to put thorns under feet already bleeding; to crush a people already bowed down; to enslave a people already but half free; in a word, it was intended to discourage, dishearten, and drive the free colored people out of the country. In looking at the recent black law of Illinois, one is struck dumb with its enormity. It would seem that the men who enacted that law, had not only banished from their minds all sense of justice, but all sense of shame. It coolly proposes to sell the bodies and souls of the blacks to increase the intelligence and refinement of the whites; to rob every black stranger who ventures among them, to increase their literary fund.

While this is going on in the states, a pro-slavery, political board of health is established at Washington. Senators Hale, Chase, and Sumner are robbed of a part of their senatorial dignity and consequence as representing sovereign states, because they have refused to be inoculated with the slavery virus. Among the services which a senator is expected by his state to perform, are many that can only be done efficiently on committees; and, in saying to these honorable senators, you shall not serve on the committees of this body, the slavery party took the responsibility of robbing and insulting the states that sent them. It is an attempt at Washington to decide for the states who shall be sent to the senate. Sir, it strikes me that this aggression on the part of the slave power did not meet at the hands of the proscribed senators the rebuke which we had a right to expect would be administered. It seems to me that an opportunity was lost, that the great principle of senatorial equality was left undefended, at a time when its vindication was sternly demanded. But it is not to the purpose of my present statement to criticise the conduct of our friends. I am persuaded that much ought to be left to the discretion of anti-slavery men in congress, and charges of recreancy should never be made but on the most sufficient grounds. For, of all the places in the world where an anti-slavery man needs the confidence and encouragement of friends, I take Washington to be that place.

Let me now call attention to the social influences which are operating and coöperating with the slavery party of the country, designed to contribute to one or all of the grand objects aimed at by that party. We see here the black man attacked in his vital interests; prejudice and hate are excited against him; enmity is stirred up between him and other laborers. The Irish people, warm-hearted, generous, and sympathizing with the oppressed everywhere, when they stand upon their own green island, are instantly taught, on arriving in this Christian country, to hate and despise the colored people. They are taught to believe that we eat the bread which of right belongs to them. The cruel lie is told the Irish, that our adversity is essential to their prosperity. Sir, the Irish-American will find out his mistake one day. He will find that in assuming our avocation he also has assumed our degradation. But for the present we are sufferers. The old employments by which we have heretofore gained our livelihood, are gradually, and it may be inevitably, passing into other hands. Every hour sees us elbowed out of some employment to make room perhaps for some newly arrived emigrants, whose hunger and color are thought to give them a title to especial favor. White men are becoming house-servants, cooks, and stewards, common laborers, and flunkeys to our gentry, and, for aught I see, they adjust themselves to their stations with all becoming obsequiousness. This fact proves that if we cannot rise to the whites, the whites can fall to us. Now, sir, look once more. While the colored people are thus elbowed out of employment; while the enmity of emigrants is being excited against us; while state after state enacts laws against us; while we are hunted down, like wild game, and oppressed with a general feeling of insecurity—the American colonization society—that old offender against the best interests and slanderer of the colored people—awakens to new life, and vigorously presses its scheme upon the consideration of the people and the government. New papers are started—some for the North and some for the South—and each in its tone adapting itself to its latitude. Government, state and national, is called upon for appropriations to enable the society to send us out of the country by steam! They want steamers to carry letters and Negroes to Africa. Evidently, this society looks upon our "extremity as its opportunity," and we may expect that it will use the occasion well. They do not deplore, but glory, in our misfortunes.

But, sir, I must hasten. I have thus briefly given my view of one aspect of the present condition and future prospects of the colored people of the United States. And what I have said is far from encouraging to my afflicted people. I have seen the cloud gather upon the sable brows of some who hear me. I confess the case looks black enough. Sir, I am not a hopeful man. I think I am apt even to undercalculate the benefits of the future. Yet, sir, in this seemingly desperate case, I do not despair for my people. There is a bright side to almost every picture of this kind; and ours is no exception to the general rule. If the influences against us are strong, those for us are also strong. To the inquiry, will our enemies prevail in the execution of their designs, in my God and in my soul, I believe they will not. Let us look at the first object sought for by the slavery party of the country, viz: the suppression of anti-slavery discussion. They desire to suppress discussion on this subject, with a view to the peace of the slaveholder and the security of slavery. Now, sir, neither the principle nor the subordinate objects here declared, can be at all gained by the slave power, and for this reason: It involves the proposition to padlock the lips of the whites, in order to secure the fetters on the limbs of the blacks. The right of speech, precious and priceless, cannot, will not, be surrendered to slavery. Its suppression is asked for, as I have said, to give peace and security to slaveholders. Sir, that thing cannot be done. God has interposed an insuperable obstacle to any such result. "There can be no peace, saith my God, to the wicked." Suppose it were possible to put down this discussion, what would it avail the guilty slaveholder, pillowed as he is upon heaving bosoms of ruined souls? He could not have a peaceful spirit. If every anti-slavery tongue in the nation were silent—every anti-slavery organization dissolved—every anti-slavery press demolished—every anti-slavery periodical, paper, book, pamphlet, or what not, were searched out, gathered, deliberately burned to ashes, and their ashes given to the four winds of heaven, still, still the slaveholder could have "*no peace.*" In every pulsation of his heart, in every throb of his life, in every glance of his eye, in the breeze that soothes, and in the thunder that startles, would be waked up an accuser, whose cause is, "Thou art, verily, guilty concerning thy brother."

THE ANTI-SLAVERY MOVEMENT

Extracts from a Lecture before Various Anti-Slavery Bodies,
in the Winter of 1855

A GRAND MOVEMENT ON THE PART OF MANKIND, IN ANY DIRECTION, or for any purpose, moral or political, is an interesting fact, fit and proper to be studied. It is such, not only for those who eagerly participate in it, but also for those who stand aloof from it—even for those by whom it is opposed. I take the anti-slavery movement to be such an one, and a movement as sublime and glorious in its character, as it is holy and beneficent in the ends it aims to accomplish. At this moment, I deem it safe to say, it is properly engrossing more minds in this country than any other subject now before the American people. The late John C. Calhoun—one of the mightiest men that ever stood up in the American senate—did not deem it beneath him; and he probably studied it as deeply, though not as honestly, as Gerrit Smith, or William Lloyd Garrison. He evinced the greatest familiarity with the subject; and the greatest efforts of his last years in the senate had direct reference to this movement. His eagle eye watched every new development connected with it; and he was ever prompt to inform the South of every important step in its progress. He never allowed himself to make light of it; but always spoke of it and treated it as a matter of grave import; and in this he showed himself a master of the mental, moral, and religious constitution of human society. Daniel Webster, too, in the better days of his life, before he gave his assent to the fugitive slave bill, and trampled upon all his earlier and better convictions—when his eye was yet single—he clearly comprehended the nature of the elements involved in this movement; and in his own majestic eloquence, warned the South, and the country, to have a care how they attempted to put it down. He is an illustration that it is easier to give, than to take, good advice. To these two men—the greatest men to whom the nation has yet given birth—may be traced the two great facts of the present—the South triumphant, and the North humbled. Their names may stand thus, Calhoun and domination—Webster and degradation. Yet again. If to the enemies of liberty this subject is one of engrossing interest, vastly more so should it be such to freedom's friends. The latter, it leads to the gates of all valuable knowledge—philanthropic, ethical, and religious; for it brings them to the study of man, wonderfully and fearfully made—the proper study of man through all time—the open book, in which are the records of time and eternity.

Of the existence and power of the anti-slavery movement, as a fact, you need no evidence. The nation has seen its face, and felt the controlling pressure of its hand. You have seen it moving in all directions, and in all weathers, and in all places, appearing most where desired least, and pressing hardest where most resisted. No place is exempt. The quiet prayer meeting, and the stormy halls of national debate, share its presence alike. It is a common intruder, and of course has the name of being ungentlemanly. Brethren who had long sung, in the most affectionate fervor, and with the greatest sense of security,

Together let us sweetly live—together let us die,

have been suddenly and violently separated by it, and ranged in hostile attitude toward each other. The Methodist, one of the most powerful religious organizations of this country, has been rent asunder, and its strongest bolts of denominational brotherhood started at a single surge. It has changed the tone of the northern pulpit, and modified that of the press. A celebrated divine, who, four years ago, was for flinging his own mother, or brother, into the remorseless jaws of the monster slavery, lest he should swallow up the Union, now recognizes anti-slavery as a characteristic of future civilization. Signs and wonders follow this movement; and the fact just stated is one of them. Party ties are loosened by it; and men are compelled to take sides for or against it, whether they will or not. Come from where he may, or come for what he may, he is compelled to show his hand. What is this mighty force? What is its history? and what is its destiny? Is it ancient or modern, transient or permanent? Has it turned aside, like a stranger and a sojourner, to tarry for a night? or has it come to rest with us forever? Excellent chances are here for speculation; and some of them are quite profound. We might, for instance, proceed to inquire not only into the philosophy of the anti-slavery movement, but into the philosophy of the law, in obedience to which that movement started into existence. We might demand to know what is that law or power, which, at different times, disposes the minds of men to this or that particular object—now for peace, and now for war—now for freedom, and now for slavery; but this profound question I leave to the abolitionists of the superior class to answer. The speculations which must precede such answer, would afford, perhaps, about the same satisfaction as the learned theories which have rained down upon the world, from time to time, as to the origin of evil. I shall, therefore, avoid water in which I cannot swim, and deal with anti-slavery as a fact, like any other fact in the history of mankind, capable of being described and understood, both as to its internal forces, and its external phases and relations.

[After an eloquent, a full, and highly interesting exposition of the nature, character, and history of the anti-slavery movement, from the insertion of which want of space precludes us, he concluded in the following happy manner.]

Present organizations may perish, but the cause will go on. That cause has a life, distinct and independent of the organizations patched up from time to time to carry it forward. Looked at, apart from the bones and sinews and body, it is a thing immortal. It is the very essence of justice, liberty, and love. The moral life of human society, it cannot die while conscience, honor, and humanity remain. If but one be filled with it, the cause lives. Its incarnation in any one individual man, leaves the whole world a priesthood, occupying the highest moral eminence even that of disinterested benevolence. Whoso has ascended his height, and has the grace to stand there, has the world at his feet, and is the world's teacher, as of divine right. He may set in judgment on the age, upon the civilization of the age, and upon the religion of the age; for he has a test, a sure and certain test, by which to try all institutions, and to measure all men. I say, he may do this, but this is not the chief business for which he is qualified. The great work to which he is called is not that of judgment. Like the Prince of Peace, he may say, if I judge, I judge righteous judgment; still mainly, like him, he may say, this is not his work. The man who has thoroughly embraced the principles of justice, love, and liberty, like the true preacher of Christianity, is less anxious to reproach the world of its sins, than to win it to repentance. His great work on earth is to exemplify, and to illustrate, and to ingraft those principles upon the living and practical understandings of all men within the reach of his influence. This is his work; long or short his years, many or few his adherents, powerful or weak his instrumentalities, through good report, or through bad report, this is his work. It is to snatch from the bosom of nature the latent facts of each individual man's experience, and with steady hand to hold them up fresh and glowing, enforcing, with all his power, their acknowledgment and practical adoption. If there be but *one* such man in the land, no matter what becomes of abolition societies and parties, there will be an anti-slavery cause, and an anti-slavery movement. Fortunately for that cause, and fortunately for him by whom it is espoused, it requires no extraordinary amount of talent to preach it or to receive it when preached. The grand secret of its power is, that each of its principles is easily rendered appreciable to the faculty of reason in man, and that the most unenlightened conscience has no difficulty in deciding on which side to register its testimony. It can call its preachers from among the fishermen, and raise them to power. In every human breast, it has an advocate which can be silent only when the heart is dead. It comes home to every man's understanding, and appeals directly to every man's conscience. A man that does not recognize and approve for himself the rights and privileges contended for, in behalf of the American slave, has not yet been found. In whatever else men may differ, they are alike in the apprehension of their natural and personal rights. The difference between abolitionists and those by whom they are opposed, is not as to principles. All are agreed in respect to these. The manner of applying them is the point of difference.

The slaveholder himself, the daily robber of his equal brother, discourses eloquently as to the excellency of justice, and the man who employs a brutal driver to flay the flesh of his negroes, is not offended when kindness and humanity are commended. Every time the abolitionist speaks of justice, the anti-abolitionist assents says, yes, I wish the world were filled with a disposition to render to every man what is rightfully due him; I should then get what is due me. That's right; let us have justice. By all means, let us have justice. Every time the abolitionist speaks in honor of human liberty, he touches a chord in the heart of the anti-abolitionist, which responds in harmonious vibrations. Liberty—yes, that is evidently my right, and let him beware who attempts to invade or abridge that right. Every time he speaks of love, of human brotherhood, and the reciprocal duties of man and man, the anti-abolitionist assents—says, yes, all right—all true—we cannot have such ideas too often, or too fully expressed. So he says, and so he feels, and only shows thereby that he is a man as well as an anti-abolitionist. You have only to keep out of sight the manner of applying your principles, to get them endorsed every time. Contemplating himself, he sees truth with absolute clearness and distinctness. He only blunders when asked to lose sight of himself. In his own cause he can beat a Boston lawyer, but he is dumb when asked to plead the cause of others. He knows very well whatsoever he would have done unto himself, but is quite in doubt as to having the same thing done unto others. It is just here, that lions spring up in the path of duty, and the battle once fought in heaven is refought on the earth. So it is, so hath it ever been, and so must it ever be, when the claims of justice and mercy make their demand at the door of human selfishness. Nevertheless, there is that within which ever pleads for the right and the just.

In conclusion, I have taken a sober view of the present anti-slavery movement. I am sober, but not hopeless. There is no denying, for it is everywhere admitted, that the anti-slavery question is the great moral and social question now before the American people. A state of things has gradually been developed, by which that question has become the first thing in order. It must be met. Herein is my hope. The great idea of impartial liberty is now fairly before the American people. Anti-slavery is no longer a thing to be prevented. The time for prevention is past. This is great gain. When the movement was younger and weaker—when it wrought in a Boston garret to human apprehension, it might have been silently put out of the way. Things are different now. It has grown too large—its friends are too numerous—its facilities too abundant—its ramifications too extended—its power too omnipotent, to be snuffed out by the contingencies of infancy. A thousand strong men might be struck down, and its ranks still be invincible. One flash from the heart-supplied intellect of Harriet Beecher Stowe could light a million camp fires in front of the embattled host of slavery, which not all the waters of the Mississippi, mingled as they are with blood, could extinguish. The present will be looked to by after-coming generations, as the age of anti-slavery literature—when supply on the gallop could not keep pace with the ever growing demand—when a picture of a Negro on the cover was a help to the sale of a book—when conservative lyceums and other American literary associations began first to select their orators for distinguished occasions from the ranks of the previously despised abolitionists. If the anti-slavery movement shall fail now, it will not be from outward opposition, but from inward decay. Its auxiliaries are everywhere. Scholars, authors, orators, poets, and statesmen give it their aid. The most brilliant of American poets volunteer in its service. Whittier speaks in burning verse to more than thirty thousand, in the *National Era*. Your own Longfellow whispers, in every hour of trial and disappointment, "labor and wait." James Russell Lowell is reminding us that "men are more than institutions." Pierpont cheers the heart of the pilgrim in search of liberty, by singing the praises of "the North Star." Bryant, too, is with us; and though chained to the car of party, and dragged on amidst a whirl of political excitement, he snatches a moment for letting drop a smiling verse of sympathy for the man in chains. The poets are with us. It would seem almost absurd to say it, considering the use that has been made of them, that we have allies in the Ethiopian songs; those songs that constitute our national music, and without which we have no national music. They are heart songs, and the finest feelings of human nature are expressed in them. "Lucy Neal," "Old Kentucky Home," and "Uncle Ned," can make the heart sad as well as merry, and can call forth a tear as well as a smile. They awaken the sympathies for the slave, in which anti-slavery principles take root, grow, and flourish. In addition to authors, poets, and scholars at home, the moral sense of the civilized world is with us. England, France, and Germany, the three great lights of modern civilization, are with us, and every American traveler learns to regret the existence of slavery in his country. The growth of intelligence, the influence of commerce, steam, wind, and lightning are our allies. It would be easy to amplify this summary, and to swell the vast conglomeration of our material forces; but there is a deeper and truer method of measuring the power of our cause, and of comprehending its vitality. This is to be found in its accordance with the best elements of human nature. It is beyond the power of slavery to annihilate affinities recognized and established by the Almighty. The slave is bound to mankind by the powerful and inextricable net-work of human brotherhood. His voice is the voice of a man, and his cry is the cry of a man in distress, and man must cease to be man before he can become insensible to that cry. It is the righteous of the cause—the humanity of the cause—which constitutes its potency. As one genuine bank-bill is worth more than a thousand counterfeits, so is one man, with right on his side, worth more than a thousand in the wrong. "One may chase a thousand, and put ten thousand to flight." It is, therefore, upon the goodness of our cause, more than upon all other auxiliaries, that we depend for its final triumph.

Another source of congratulation is the fact that, amid all the efforts made by the church, the government, and the people at large, to stay the onward progress of this movement, its course has been onward, steady, straight, unshaken, and unchecked from the beginning. Slavery has gained victories large and numerous; but never as against this movement—against a temporizing policy, and against northern timidity, the slave power has been victorious; but against the spread and prevalence in the country, of a spirit of resistance to its aggression, and of sentiments favorable to its entire overthrow, it has yet accomplished nothing. Every measure, yet devised and executed, having for its object the suppression of anti-slavery, has been as idle and fruitless as pouring oil to extinguish fire. A general rejoicing took place on the passage of "the compromise measures" of 1850. Those measures were called peace measures, and were afterward termed by both the great parties of the country, as well as by leading statesmen, a final settlement of the whole question of slavery; but experience has laughed to scorn the wisdom of pro-slavery statesmen; and their final settlement of agitation seems to be the final revival, on a broader and grander scale than ever before, of the question which they vainly attempted to suppress forever. The fugitive slave bill has especially been of positive service to the anti-slavery movement. It has illustrated before all the people the horrible character of slavery toward the slave, in hunting him down in a free state, and tearing him away from wife and children, thus setting its claims higher than marriage or parental claims. It has revealed the arrogant and overbearing spirit of the slave states toward the free states; despising their principles—shocking their feelings of humanity, not only by bringing before them the abominations of slavery, but by attempting to make them parties to the crime. It has called into exercise among the colored people, the hunted ones, a spirit of manly resistance well calculated to surround them with a bulwark of sympathy and respect hitherto unknown. For men are always disposed to respect and defend rights, when the victims of oppression stand up manfully for themselves.

There is another element of power added to the anti-slavery movement, of great importance; it is the conviction, becoming every day more general and universal, that slavery must be abolished at the South, or it will demoralize and destroy liberty at the North. It is the nature of slavery to beget a state of things all around it favorable to its own continuance. This fact, connected with the system of bondage, is beginning to be more fully realized. The slave-holder is not satisfied to associate with men in the church or in the state, unless he can thereby stain them with the blood of his slaves. To be a slave-holder is to be a propagandist from necessity; for slavery can only live by keeping down the under-growth morality which nature supplies. Every new-born white babe comes armed from the Eternal presence, to make war on slavery. The heart of pity, which would melt in due time over the brutal chastisements it sees inflicted on the helpless, must be hardened. And this work goes on every day in the year, and every hour in the day.

What is done at home is being done also abroad here in the North. And even now the question may be asked, have we at this moment a single free state in the Union? The alarm at this point will become more general. The slave power must go on in its career of exactions. Give, give, will be its cry, till the timidity which concedes shall give place to courage, which shall resist. Such is the voice of experience, such has been the past, such is the present, and such will be that future, which, so sure as man is man, will come. Here I leave the subject; and I leave off where I began, consoling myself and congratulating the friends of freedom upon the fact that the anti-slavery cause is not a new thing under the sun; not some moral delusion which a few years' experience may dispel. It has appeared among men in all ages, and summoned its advocates from all ranks. Its foundations are laid in the deepest and holiest convictions, and from whatever soul the demon, selfishness, is expelled, there will this cause take up its abode. Old as the everlasting hills; immovable as the throne of God; and certain as the purposes of eternal power, against all hinderances, and against all delays, and despite all the mutations of human instrumentalities, it is the faith of my soul, that this anti-slavery cause will triumph.

ORATION DELIVERED ON THE OCCASION OF THE UNVEILING OF THE FREEDMEN'S MONUMENT

In Memory of Abraham Lincoln, in Lincoln Park
Washington, D.C., April 14, 1876

FRIENDS AND FELLOW-CITIZENS:

I warmly congratulate you upon the highly interesting object which has caused you to assemble in such numbers and spirit as you have today. This occasion is, in some respects, remarkable. Wise and thoughtful men of our race, who shall come after us, and study the lesson of our history in the United States, who shall survey the long and dreary spaces over which we have traveled and who shall count the links in the great chain of events by which we have reached our present position, will make a note of this occasion. They will think of it and speak of it with a sense of manly pride and complacency.

I congratulate you, also, upon the very favorable circumstances in which we meet today. They are high, inspiring, and uncommon. They lend grace, glory, and significance to the object for which we have met. Nowhere else in this great country, with its uncounted towns and cities, unlimited wealth, and immeasurable territory extending from sea to sea, could conditions be found more favorable to the success of this occasion than here.

We stand today at the national center to perform something like a national act—an act which is to go into history; and we are here where every pulsation of the national heart can be heard, felt, and reciprocated A thousand wires, fed with thought and winged with lightning, put us in instantaneous communication with the loyal and true men all over this country.

Few facts could better illustrate the vast and wonderful change which has taken place in our condition as a people than the fact of our assembling here today for the purpose which has called us together. Harmless, beautiful, proper and praiseworthy as this demonstration is, I cannot forget that no such demonstration would have been tolerated here twenty years ago. The spirit of slavery and barbarism, which in some dark and distant parts of our country, still lingers to blight and destroy, would have made our assembling here the signal and excuse for opening upon us all the floodgates of wrath and violence. That we are here in peace today is a compliment and a credit to American civilization, and a prophecy of still greater national enlightenment and progress in the future. I refer to the past, not in malice, for this is no day for malice, but simply to place more distinctly in front the gratifying and glorious change which has come both to our white fellow-citizens and ourselves, and to congratulate all upon the contrast between now and then—between the new dispensation of freedom with its thousand blessings to both races, and the old dispensation of slavery with its ten thousand evils to both races, white and black. In view, then, of the past, the present, and the future, with the long and dark history of our bondage behind us. and with liberty, progress, and enlightenment before us, I again congratulate you upon this auspicious day and hour.

Friends and fellow-citizens, the story of our presence here is soon and easily told. We are here in the District of Columbia, here in the city of Washington, the most luminous point of American territory, a city recently transformed and made beautiful in its body and in its spirit. We are here in the place where the ablest and best men of the country are sent to devise the policy, enact the laws, and shape the destiny of the Republic. We are here, with the stately pillars and majestic dome of the Capitol of the nation looking down upon us; we are here, with the broad earth freshly adorned with the foliage and flowers of spring for our church, and all races, colors, and conditions of men for our congregation—in a word, we are here to express, as best we may, by appropriate forms and ceremonies, our grateful sense of the vast, high, and preëminent services rendered to ourselves, to our race, to our country, and to the whole world by Abraham Lincoln.

The sentiment that brings us here today is one of the noblest that can stir and thrill the human heart. It has crowned and made glorious the high places of all civilized nations with the grandest and most enduring works of art, designed to illustrate the characters and perpetuate the memories of great public men. It is the sentiment which from year to year adorns with fragrant and beautiful flowers the graves of our loyal, brave, and patriotic soldiers who fell in defence of the Union and liberty. It is the sentiment of gratitude and appreciation, which often, in presence of many who hear me, has filled yonder heights of Arlington with the eloquence of eulogy and the sublime enthusiasm of poetry and song; a sentiment which can never die while the Republic lives.

For the first time in the history of our people, and in the history of the whole American people, we join in this high worship, and march conspicuously in the line of this time-honored custom. First things are always interesting, and this is one of our first things. It is the first time that, in this form and manner, we have sought to do honor to an American great man, however deserving and illustrious. I commend the fact to notice; let it be told in every part of the Republic. Let men of all parties and opinions hear it. Let those who despise us, not less than those who respect us, know that now and here, in the spirit of liberty, loyalty and gratitude, we unite in this act of reverent homage. Let it be known everywhere, and by everybody who takes an interest in human progress and in the amelioration of the condition of mankind, that, in the presence and with the approval of the members of the American House of Representatives, reflecting the general sentiment of the country; that in the presence of that august body, the American Senate, representing the highest intelligence and the calmest judgment of the country; in presence of the Supreme Court and Chief-Justice of the United States, to whose decisions we all patriotically bow; in the presence and under the steady eye of the honored and trusted President of the United States, with the members of his wise and patriotic Cabinet, we, the colored people, newly emancipated and rejoicing in our blood-bought freedom, near the first of the first century in the life of this Republic, have now and here unveiled, set apart, and dedicated a monument of enduring granite and bronze, in every line, feature, and figure of which the men of this generation may read, and those of after-coming generations may read, something of the exalted character and great works of Abraham Lincoln, the first martyr President of the United States.

Fellow-citizens, in what we have said and done today, and in what we may say and do hereafter, we disclaim everything like arrogance and assumption. We claim for ourselves no superior devotion to the character, history, and memory of the illustrious name whose monument we have here this day dedicated. We fully comprehend the relation of Abraham Lincoln both to ourselves and to the white people of the United States. Truth is proper and beautiful at all times and in all places, and it is never in any case more proper and beautiful in any case than when speaking of a great public man whose example is likely to be commended for honor and imitation long after his departure to the solemn shades, the silent continents of eternity. It must be admitted, truth compels me to admit, even here in the presence of the monument we have erected to his memory, Abraham Lincoln was not, in the fullest sense of the word, either our man or our model. In his interests, in his associations, in his habits of thought, and in his prejudices, he was a white man.

He was preëminently the white man's President, entirely devoted to the welfare of white men. He was ready and willing at any time during the first years of his administration to deny, postpone and sacrifice the rights of humanity in the colored people to promote the welfare of the white people of this country. In all his education and feeling he was an American of the Americans. He came into the Presidential chair upon one principle alone, namely, opposition to the extension of slavery. His arguments in furtherance of this policy had their motive and mainspring in his patriotic devotion to the interests of his own race. To protect, defend, and perpetuate slavery in the States where it existed Abraham Lincoln was not less ready than any other President to draw the sword of the nation. He was ready to execute all the supposed constitutional guarantees of the United States Constitution in favor of the slave system anywhere inside the slave States. He was willing to pursue, recapture, and send back the fugitive slave to his master, and to suppress a slave rising for liberty, though his guilty master were already in arms against the Government. The race to which we belong were not the special objects of his consideration. Knowing this, I concede to you, my white fellow-citizens, a preëminence in this worship at once full and supreme. First, midst, and last, you and yours were the objects of his deepest affection and his most earnest solicitude. You are the children of Abraham Lincoln. We are at best only his step-children: children by adoption, children by force of circumstances and necessity. To you it especially belongs to sound his praises, to preserve and perpetuate his memory, to multiply his statues, to hang his pictures high upon your walls, and commend his example, for to you he was a great and glorious friend and benefactor. Instead of supplanting you at this altar, we would exhort you to build high his monuments; let them be the most costly material, of the most cunning workmanship. Let their forms be symmetrical, beautiful and perfect. Let their bases be upon solid rocks and their summits lean against the unchanging blue, overhanging sky, and let them endure forever! But while in the abundance of your wealth, and in the fullness of your just and patriotic devotion, you do all this, we entreat you to despise not the humble offering we this day unveil to view; for while Abraham Lincoln saved for you a country, he delivered us from a bondage, according to Jefferson, one hour of which was worse than ages of the oppression your fathers rose in rebellion to oppose.

Fellow-citizens, ours is no new-born zeal and devotion—merely a thing of this moment. The name of Abraham Lincoln was near and dear to our hearts in the darkest and most perilous hours of the Republic. We were no more ashamed of him when shrouded in clouds of darkness, of doubt, and defeat than when we saw him crowned with victory, honor, and glory. Our faith in him was often taxed and strained to the uttermost, but it never failed. When he tarried long in the mountain; when he strangely told us that we were the cause of the war; when he still more strangely told us to leave the land in which we were born; when he refused to employ our arms in defence of the Union; when, after accepting our services as colored soldiers, he refused to retaliate our murder and torture as colored prisoners; when he told us he would save the Union if he could with slavery; when he revoked the Proclamation of Emancipation of General Frémont; when he refused, in the days of its inaction and defeat of the Army of the Potomac, to remove its popular commander, who was more zealous in his efforts to protect slavery than to suppress rebellion; when we saw all this, and more, we were at times grieved, stunned, and greatly bewildered; but our hearts believed while they ached and bled. Nor was this, even at that time, a blind and unreasoning superstition. Despite the mist and haze that surround him; despite the tumult, the hurry, and confusion of the hour, we were able to take a comprehensive view of Abraham Lincoln, and to make reasonable allowance for the circumstances of his position. We saw him, measured him, and estimated him; not by stray utterances to injudicious and tedious delegations, who often tried his patience; not by isolated facts torn from their connection; not by any partial and imperfect glimpses, caught at inopportune moments; but by a broad survey, in the light of the stern logic of great events, and in view of that "divinity which shapes our ends, rough hew them how we will." We came to the conclusion that the hour and the man of our redemption had somehow met in the person of Abraham Lincoln. It mattered little to us what language he might employ on special occasions; it mattered little to us, when we fully knew him, whether he was swift or slow in his movements; it was enough for us that Abraham Lincoln was at the head of a great movement, and was in living and earnest sympathy with that movement, which, in the nature of things, must go on until slavery should be utterly and forever abolished in the United States.

When, therefore, it shall be asked what we have to do with the memory of Abraham Lincoln, or what Abraham Lincoln had to do with us, the answer is ready, full, and complete. Though he loved Cæsar less than Rome, though the Union was more to him than our freedom or our future, under his wise and beneficent rule we saw ourselves gradually lifted from the depths of slavery to the heights of liberty and manhood; under his wise and beneficent rule, and by measures approved and vigorously pressed by him, we saw that the handwriting of ages, in the form of prejudice and proscription, was rapidly fading from the face of our whole country; under his rule, and in due time about as soon after all as the country could tolerate the strange spectacle, we saw our brave sons and brothers laying off the rags of bondage, and being clothed all over in the blue uniforms of the soldiers of the United States; under his rule we saw two hundred thousand of our dark and dusky people responding to the call of Abraham Lincoln, and with muskets on their shoulders, and eagles on their buttons, timing their high footsteps to liberty and union under the national flag; under his rule we saw the independence of the black republic of Haiti, the special object of slave-holding aversion and horror, fully recognized, and her minister, a colored gentleman, duly received here in the city of Washington; under his rule we saw the internal slave-trade, which so long disgraced the nation, abolished, and slavery abolished in the District of Columbia; under his rule we saw for the first time the law enforced against the foreign slave-trade, and the first slave-trader hanged like any other pirate or murderer; under his ride, assisted by the greatest captain of our age, and his inspiration, we saw the Confederate States, based upon the idea that our race must be slaves, and slaves forever, battered to pieces and scattered to the four winds; under his rule, and in the full-ness of time, we saw Abraham Lincoln, after giving the slaveholders three months' grace in which to save their hateful slave system, penning the immortal paper, which, though special in its language, was general in its principles and effect, making slavery forever impossible in the United States. Though we waited long, we saw all this and more.

Can any colored man, or any white man friendly to the freedom of all men, ever forget the night which followed the first day of January, 1863, when the world was to see if Abraham Lincoln would prove to be as good as his word? I shall never forget that memorable night, when in a distant city I waited and watched at a public meeting, with three thousand others not less anxious than myself, I waited and watched for the word of deliverance which we have heard read today. Nor shall I ever forget the outburst of joy and thanks giving that rent the air when the lightning brought to us the emancipation proclama-tion. In that happy hour we forgot all delay, and forgot all tardiness, forgot that the President, by a promise to withhold the bolt which would smite the slave system with destruction, had bribed the rebels to lay down their arms; and we were thenceforward willing to allow the

President all the latitude of time, phraseology, and every honorable device that statesmanship might require for the achievement of a great and beneficent measure of liberty and progress.

Fellow-citizens, there is little necessity on this occasion to speak at length and critically of this great and good man and of his high mission in the world. That ground has been fully occupied and completely covered both here and elsewhere. The whole field of fact and fancy has been gleaned and garnered. Any man can say things that are true of Abraham Lincoln, but no man can say anything that is new of Abraham Lincoln. His personal traits and public acts are better known to the American people than are those of any other man of his age. He was a mystery to no man who saw him and heard him. Though high in position, the humblest could approach him and feel at home in his presence. Though deep, he was transparent; though strong, he was gentle; though decided and pronounced in his convictions, he was tolerant towards those who differed from him, and patient under reproaches. Even those who only knew him through his public utterances obtained a tolerably clear idea of his character and his personality. The image of the man went out with his words, and those who read them, knew him.

I have said that President Lincoln was a white man, and shared the prejudices common to his countrymen towards the colored race. Looking back to his times and to the condition of his country, we are compelled to admit that this unfriendly feeling on his part may be safely set down as one element of his wonderful success in organizing the loyal American people for the tremendous conflict before them, and bringing them safely through that conflict. His great mission was to accomplish two things: first, to save his country from dismemberment and ruin; and second, to free his country from the great crime of slavery. To do one or the other, or both, he must have the earnest sympathy and the powerful coöperation of his loyal fellow countrymen. Without this primary and essential condition to success his efforts must have been vain and utterly fruitless. Had he put the abolition of slavery before the salvation of the Union, he would have inevitably driven from him a powerful class of the American people and rendered resistance to rebellion impossible. Viewed from the genuine abolition ground, Mr. Lincoln seemed tardy, cold, dull, and indifferent; but measuring him by the sentiment of his country, a sentiment he was bound as a statesman to consult, he was swift, zealous, radical, and determined.

Though Mr. Lincoln shared the prejudices of his white fellow countrymen against the negro, it is hardly necessary to say that in his heart of hearts he loathed and hated slavery.* The man who could say, "Fondly do we hope, fervently do we pray, that this mighty scourge of war shall soon pass away, yet if God wills it continue till all the wealth piled by two hundred years of bondage shall have been wasted, and each drop of blood drawn by the lash shall have been paid for by one drawn by the sword, the judgments of the Lord are true and righteous altogether," gives all needed proof of his feeling on the subject of slavery. He was willing, while the South was loyal, that it should have its pound of flesh, because he thought that it was so nominated in the bond; but farther than this no earthly power could make him go.

Fellow-citizens, whatever else in this world may be partial, unjust, and uncertain, time, time! is impartial, just, and certain in its action. In the realm of mind, as well as in the realm of matter, it is a great worker, and often works wonders. The honest and comprehensive statesman, clearly discerning the needs of his country, and earnestly endeavoring to do his whole duty, though covered and blistered with reproaches, may safely leave his course to the silent judgment of time. Few great public men have ever been the victims of fiercer denunciation than Abraham Lincoln was during his administration. He was often wounded in the house of his friends. Reproaches came thick and fast upon him from within and from without, and from opposite quarters. He was assailed by abolitionists; he was assailed by slaveholders; he was assailed by the men who were for peace at any price; he was assailed by those who were for a more vigorous prosecution of the war; he was assailed for not making the war an abolition war: and he was most bitterly assailed for making the war an abolition war.

But now behold the change: the judgment of the present hour is, that taking him for all in all; measuring the tremendous magnitude of

---

* "I am naturally anti-slavery. If slavery is not wrong, nothing is wrong. I cannot remember when I did not so think and feel." *Letter of Mr. Lincoln to Mr. Hodges, of Kentucky, April 4, 1864.*

the work before him; considering the necessary means to ends, and surveying the end from the beginning, infinite wisdom has seldom sent any man into the world better fitted for his mission than Abraham Lincoln. His birth, his training, and his natural endowments, both mental and physical, were strongly in his favor. Born and reared among the lowly; a stranger to wealth and luxury; compelled from tender youth to sturdy manhood to grapple single-handed with the flintiest hardships of life, from tender youth to sturdy manhood, he grew strong in the manly and heroic qualities demanded by the great mission to which he was called by the votes of his countrymen. The hard condition of his early life, which would have depressed and broken down weaker men, only gave greater life, vigor, and buoyancy to the heroic spirit of Abraham Lincoln. He was ready for any kind and any quality of work. What other young men dreaded in the shape of toil, he took hold of with the utmost cheerfulness.

> A spade, a rake, a hoe,
>   A pick-axe, or a bill;
> A hook to reap, a scythe to mow,
>   A flail, or what you will.

All day long he could split heavy rails in the woods, and half the night long he could study his English grammar by the uncertain flare and glare of the light made by a pine knot. He was at home on the land with his axe, with his maul, with gluts, and his wedges; and he was equally at home on water, with his oars, with his poles, with his planks, and with his boathooks. And whether in his flat-boat on the Mississippi river, or at the fireside of his frontier cabin, he was a man of work. A son of toil himself, he was linked in brotherly sympathy with the sons of toil in every loyal part of the republic. This very fact gave him tremendous power with the American people, and materially contributed not only to selecting him to the presidency, but in sustaining his administration of the government.

Upon his inauguration as President of the United States, an office fitted to tax and strain the largest abilities, even where assumed under the most favorable conditions, Abraham Lincoln was met by a tremendous crisis. He was called upon not merely to administer the government, but to decide in the face of terrible odds, the fate of the republic.

A formidable rebellion rose in his path before him. The Union was already practically dissolved. His country was torn and rent asunder at the center. Hostile armies, armed with the munitions of war which the republic had provided for its own defense, were already organized against the republic. The tremendous question for him to decide was whether his country should survive the crisis and flourish, or be dismembered and perish. His predecessor in office had already decided the question in favor of national dismemberment by denying to it the right of self-defense and self-preservation—a right which belongs to the meanest insect.

Happily for the country, happily for you and for me, the judgment of James Buchanan, the patrician, was not the judgment of Abraham Lincoln, the plebeian. He brought his strong common sense, sharpened in the school of adversity, to bear upon the question. He did not hesitate, he did not doubt, he did not falter; but at once resolved that at whatever peril, at whatever cost, the union of the States should be preserved. A patriot himself, his faith was strong and unwavering in the patriotism of his countrymen. Timid men said before Mr. Lincoln's inauguration, that we had seen the last President of the United States. A voice in influential quarters said "Let the Union slide." Some said that a Union maintained by the sword was worthless. Others said a rebellion of eight millions cannot be suppressed. But in the midst of all this tumult and timidity, and against all this, Abraham Lincoln was clear in his duty, and had an oath in heaven. He calmly and bravely heard the voice of doubt and fear all around him, but he had an oath in heaven, and there was not power enough on the earth to make this honest boatman, backwoodsman, and broad-handed splitter of rails evade or violate that sacred oath. He had not been schooled in the ethics of slavery; his plain life had favored his love of truth. He had not been taught that treason and perjury were the proof of honor and honesty. His moral training was against his saying one thing when he meant another. The trust which Abraham Lincoln had in himself and in the people was surprising and grand, but it was also enlightened and well founded. He knew the American people better than they knew themselves and his truth was based upon this knowledge.

Fellow-citizens, the fourteenth day of April, 1865, of which this is the eleventh anniversary, is now and will ever remain a memorable day in the annals of this republic. It was on the evening of this day, while a fierce and sanguinary rebellion was in the last stages of its desolating power, while its armies were broken and scattered before the invincible armies of Grant and Sherman, while a great nation, torn and rent by war, was already beginning to raise to the skies loud anthems of joy at the dawn of peace, it was startled, amazed, and overwhelmed by the crowning crime of slavery—the assassination of Abraham Lincoln. It was a new crime—a pure act of malice. No purpose of the rebellion was to be served by it. It was the simple gratification of a hell-black spirit of revenge. But it has done good after all. It has filled the country with a deeper abhorrence of slavery and a deeper love for the great liberator.

Had Abraham Lincoln died from any of the numerous ills to which flesh is heir; had he reached that good old age of which his vigorous constitution and his temperate habits gave promise; had he been permitted to see the end of his great work; had the solemn curtain of death come down but gradually, we should still have been smitten with a heavy grief, and treasured his name lovingly. But, dying as he did die, by the red hand of violence, killed, assassinated, taken off without warning, not because of personal hate—for no man who knew Abraham Lincoln could hate him—but because of his fidelity to union and liberty, he is doubly dear to us, and his memory will be precious forever.

Fellow-citizens, I end as I began, with congratulations. We have done a good work for our race today. In doing honor to the memory of our friend and liberator we have been doing highest honors to ourselves and to those who come after us. We have been attaching ourselves to a name and fame imperishable and immortal; we have also been defending ourselves from a blighting scandal. When now it shall be said that the colored man is soulless, that he has no appreciation of benefits or benefactors; when the foul reproach of ingratitude is hurled at us, and it is attempted to scourge us beyond the range of human brotherhood, we may calmly point to the monument we have this day erected to the memory of Abraham Lincoln.

RECONSTRUCTION

THE ASSEMBLING OF THE SECOND SESSION OF THE THIRTY-NINTH
Congress may very properly be made the occasion of a few earnest
words on the already much-worn topic of reconstruction.

Seldom has any legislative body been the subject of a solicitude
more intense, or of aspirations more sincere and ardent. There are the
best of reasons for this profound interest. Questions of vast moment,
left undecided by the last session of Congress, must be manfully grap-
pled with by this. No political skirmishing will avail. The occasion
demands statesmanship.

Whether the tremendous war so heroically fought and so victori-
ously ended shall pass into history a miserable failure, barren of
permanent results, a scandalous and shocking waste of blood and trea-
sure, a strife for empire, as Earl Russell characterized it, of no value to
liberty or civilization, an attempt to re-establish a Union by force,
which must be the merest mockery of a Union, an effort to bring under
Federal authority States into which no loyal man from the North may
safely enter, and to bring men into the national councils who deliberate with daggers and vote with revolvers, and who do not even conceal
their deadly hate of the country that conquered them; or whether, on
the other hand, we shall, as the rightful reward of victory over treason,
have a solid nation, entirely delivered from all contradictions and
social antagonisms, based upon loyalty, liberty, and equality, must be
determined one way or the other by the present session of Congress.
The last session really did nothing which can be considered final as to

these questions. The Civil Rights Bill and the Freedmen's Bureau Bill and the proposed constitutional amendments, with the amendment already adopted and recognized as the law of the land, do not reach the difficulty, and cannot, unless the whole structure of the government is changed from a government by States to something like a despotic central government, with power to control even the municipal regulations of States, and to make them conform to its own despotic will. While there remains such an idea as the right of each State to control its own local affairs, an idea, by the way, more deeply rooted in the minds of men of all sections of the country than perhaps any one other political idea, no general assertion of human rights can be of any practical value. To change the character of the government at this point is neither possible nor desirable. All that is necessary to be done is to make the government consistent with itself, and render the rights of the States compatible with the sacred rights of human nature.

The arm of the Federal government is long, but it is far too short to protect the rights of individuals in the interior of distant States. They must have the power to protect themselves, or they will go unprotected, spite of all the laws the Federal government can put upon the national statute-book.

Slavery, like all other great systems of wrong, founded in the depths of human selfishness, and existing for ages, has not neglected its own conservation. It has steadily exerted an influence upon all around it favorable to its own continuance. And today it is so strong that it could exist, not only without law, but even against law. Custom, manners, morals, religion, are all on its side everywhere in the South; and when you add the ignorance and servility of the ex-slave to the intelligence and accustomed authority of the master, you have the conditions, not out of which slavery will again grow, but under which it is impossible for the Federal government to wholly destroy it, unless the Federal government be armed with despotic power, to blot out State authority, and to station a Federal officer at every cross-road. This, of course, cannot be done, and ought not even if it could. The true way and the easiest way is to make our government entirely consistent with itself, and give to every loyal citizen the elective franchise, a right and power which will be ever present, and will form a wall of fire for his protection.

One of the invaluable compensations of the late Rebellion is the highly instructive disclosure it made of the true source of danger to republican government. Whatever may be tolerated in monarchical and despotic governments, no republic is safe that tolerates a privileged class, or denies to any of its citizens equal rights and equal means to maintain them. What was theory before the war has been made fact by the war.

There is cause to be thankful even for rebellion. It is an impressive teacher, though a stern and terrible one. In both characters it has come to us, and it was perhaps needed in both. It is an instructor never a day before its time, for it comes only when all other means of progress and enlightenment have failed. Whether the oppressed and despairing bondman, no longer able to repress his deep yearnings for manhood, or the tyrant, in his pride and impatience, takes the initiative, and strikes the blow for a firmer hold and a longer lease of oppression, the result is the same, society is instructed, or may be.

Such are the limitations of the common mind, and so thoroughly engrossing are the cares of common life, that only the few among men can discern through the glitter and dazzle of present prosperity the dark outlines of approaching disasters, even though they may have come up to our very gates, and are already within striking distance. The yawning seam and corroded bolt conceal their defects from the mariner until the storm calls all hands to the pumps. Prophets, indeed, were abundant before the war; but who cares for prophets while their predictions remain unfulfilled, and the calamities of which they tell are masked behind a blinding blaze of national prosperity?

It is asked, said Henry Clay, on a memorable occasion, Will slavery never come to an end? That question, said he, was asked fifty years ago, and it has been answered by fifty years of unprecedented prosperity. Spite of the eloquence of the earnest Abolitionists, poured out against slavery during thirty years, even they must confess, that, in all the probabilities of the case, that system of barbarism would have continued its horrors far beyond the limits of the nineteenth century but for the Rebellion, and perhaps only have disappeared at last in a fiery conflict, even more fierce and bloody than that which has now been suppressed.

It is no disparagement to truth, that it can only prevail where reason prevails. War begins where reason ends. The thing worse than rebellion is the thing that causes rebellion. What that thing is, we have been taught to our cost. It remains now to be seen whether we have the needed courage to have that cause entirely removed from the Republic. At any rate, to this grand work of national regeneration and entire purification Congress must now address itself, with full purpose that the work shall this time be thoroughly done. The deadly upas, root and branch, leaf and fibre, body and sap, must be utterly destroyed. The country is evidently not in a condition to listen patiently to pleas for postponement, however plausible, nor will it permit the responsibility to be shifted to other shoulders. Authority and power are here commensurate with the duty imposed. There are no cloud-flung shadows to obscure the way. Truth shines with brighter light and intenser heat at every moment, and a country torn and rent and bleeding implores relief from its distress and agony.

If time was at first needed, Congress has now had time. All the requisite materials from which to form an intelligent judgment are now before it. Whether its members look at the origin, the progress, the termination of the war, or at the mockery of a peace now existing, they will find only one unbroken chain of argument in favor of a radical policy of reconstruction. For the omissions of the last session, some excuses may be allowed. A treacherous President stood in the way; and it can be easily seen how reluctant good men might be to admit an apostasy which involved so much of baseness and ingratitude. It was natural that they should seek to save him by bending to him even when he leaned to the side of error. But all is changed now. Congress knows now that it must go on without his aid, and even against his machinations. The advantage of the present session over the last is immense. Where that investigated, this has the facts. Where that walked by faith, this may walk by sight. Where that halted, this must go forward, and where that failed, this must succeed, giving the country whole measures where that gave us half-measures, merely as a means of saving the elections in a few doubtful districts. That Congress saw what was right, but distrusted the enlightenment of the loyal masses; but what was forborne in distrust of the people must now be done with a full knowledge that the people expect and require it. The members go to Washington fresh from the inspiring presence of the people. In every considerable public meeting, and in almost every conceivable way, whether at courthouse, school-house, or cross-roads, in doors and out, the subject has been discussed, and the people have emphatically pronounced in favor of a radical policy. Listening to the doctrines of expediency and compromise with pity, impatience, and disgust, they have everywhere broken into demonstrations of the wildest enthusiasm when a brave word has been spoken in favor of equal rights and impartial suffrage. Radicalism, so far from being odious, is now the popular passport to power. The men most bitterly charged with it go to Congress with the largest majorities, while the timid and doubtful are sent by lean majorities, or else left at home. The strange controversy between the President and the Congress, at one time so threatening, is disposed of by the people. The high reconstructive powers which he so confidently, ostentatiously, and haughtily claimed, have been disallowed, denounced, and utterly repudiated; while those claimed by Congress have been confirmed.

Of the spirit and magnitude of the canvass nothing need be said. The appeal was to the people, and the verdict was worthy of the tribunal. Upon an occasion of his own selection, with the advice and approval of his astute Secretary, soon after the members of the Congress had returned to their constituents, the President quitted the executive mansion, sandwiched himself between two recognized heroes, men whom the whole country delighted to honor, and, with all the advantage which such company could give him, stumped the country from the Atlantic to the Mississippi, advocating everywhere his policy as against that of Congress. It was a strange sight, and perhaps the most disgraceful exhibition ever made by any President; but, as no evil is entirely unmixed, good has come of this, as from many others. Ambitious, unscrupulous, energetic, indefatigable, voluble, and plausible, a political gladiator, ready for a "set-to" in any crowd, he is beaten in his own chosen field, and stands today before the country as a convicted usurper, a political criminal, guilty of a bold and persistent attempt to possess himself of the legislative powers solemnly secured to Congress by the Constitution. No vindication could be more complete, no condemnation could be more absolute and humiliating. Unless reopened by the sword, as recklessly threatened in some circles, this question is now closed for all time.

Without attempting to settle here the metaphysical and somewhat theological question (about which so much has already been said and written), whether once in the Union means always in the Union, agreeably to the formula, Once in grace always in grace, it is obvious to common sense that the rebellious States stand today, in point of law, precisely where they stood when, exhausted, beaten, conquered, they fell powerless at the feet of Federal authority. Their State governments were overthrown, and the lives and property of the leaders of the Rebellion were forfeited. In reconstructing the institutions of these shattered and overthrown States, Congress should begin with a clean slate, and make clean work of it. Let there be no hesitation. It would be a cowardly deference to a defeated and treacherous President, if any account were made of the illegitimate, one-sided, sham governments hurried into existence for a malign purpose in the absence of Congress. These pretended governments, which were never submitted to the people, and from participation in which four millions of the loyal people were excluded by Presidential order, should now be treated according to their true character, as shams and impositions, and supplanted by true and legitimate governments, in the formation of which loyal men, black and white, shall participate.

It is not, however, within the scope of this paper to point out the precise steps to be taken, and the means to be employed. The people are less concerned about these than the grand end to be attained. They demand such a reconstruction as shall put an end to the present anarchical state of things in the late rebellious States, where frightful murders and wholesale massacres are perpetrated in the very presence of Federal soldiers. This horrible business they require shall cease. They want a reconstruction such as will protect loyal men, black and white, in their persons and property; such a one as will cause Northern industry, Northern capital, and Northern civilization to flow into the South, and make a man from New England as much at home in Carolina as elsewhere in the Republic. No Chinese wall can now be tolerated. The South must be opened to the light of law and liberty, and this session of Congress is relied upon to accomplish this important work.

The plain, common-sense way of doing this work, as intimated at the beginning, is simply to establish in the South one law, one government, one administration of justice, one condition to the exercise of the elective franchise, for men of all races and colors alike. This great measure is sought as earnestly by loyal white men as by loyal blacks, and is needed alike by both. Let sound political prescience but take the place of an unreasoning prejudice, and this will be done.

Men denounce the negro for his prominence in this discussion; but it is no fault of his that in peace as in war, that in conquering Rebel armies as in reconstructing the rebellious States, the right of the negro is the true solution of our national troubles. The stern logic of events, which goes directly to the point, disdaining all concern for the color or features of men, has determined the interests of the country as identical with and inseparable from those of the negro.

The policy that emancipated and armed the negro—now seen to have been wise and proper by the dullest—was not certainly more sternly demanded than is now the policy of enfranchisement. If with the negro was success in war, and without him failure, so in peace it will be found that the nation must fall or flourish with the negro.

Fortunately, the Constitution of the United States knows no distinction between citizens on account of color. Neither does it know any difference between a citizen of a State and a citizen of the United States. Citizenship evidently includes all the rights of citizens, whether State or national. If the Constitution knows none, it is clearly no part of the duty of a Republican Congress now to institute one. The mistake of the last session was the attempt to do this very thing, by a renunciation of its power to secure political rights to any class of citizens, with the obvious purpose to allow the rebellious States to disfranchise, if they should see fit, their colored citizens. This unfortunate blunder must now be retrieved, and the emasculated citizenship given to the negro supplanted by that contemplated in the Constitution of the United States, which declares that the citizens of each State shall enjoy all the rights and immunities of citizens of the several States, so that a legal voter in any State shall be a legal voter in all the States.

ENDNOTES

INTRODUCTION

1. William L. Andrews, introduction, *The Oxford Frederick Douglass Reader,* ed. William L. Andrews (New York: Oxford University Press, 1996), 3.
2. Anna Murray became Frederick Douglass' first wife. Born of free black parents in Maryland about 1813, she moved to Baltimore to find work when she was about seventeen years old; historians suspect Murray met the man who would become known as Frederick Douglass at a church social, although at that time, he was still Frederick Bailey, a young slave working on the Baltimore docks. Douglass may have omitted specific information about his wife in the *Narrative* because she might have helped him in his escape plans and he did not want to incriminate her or, despite his apparent support of gender equality, because he did not consider specific information about her important to his story. See Darlene Clark Hine, Elsa Barkley Brown, Rosalyn Terborg-Penn, eds., *Black Women in America: An Historical Encyclopedia,* vol. 2, *M-Z,* (Bloomington: Indiana University Press, 1993), 347–348.
3. Nathan Irvin Huggins, *Slave and Citizen: The Life of Frederick Douglass* (New York: Longman, 1980), 1.
4. Manning Marable and Leith Mullings, eds., *Let Nobody Turn Us Around: Voices of Resistance, Reform, and Renewal* (New York: Rowman and Littlefield, 2000); Andrews, 8.
5. Frederick Douglass, *My Bondage and My Freedom, The Oxford Frederick Douglass Reader,* 214.
6. Douglass, 217.
7. Angela Y. Davis, introduction to *Narrative of the Life of Frederick Douglass, An American Slave* by Frederick Douglass (San Francisco: City Lights Books, 2010), 22.
8. Andrews, 3.

PREFACE

1. (p. xxi) *Narrative:* The slave narrative became a popular form of American and African-American self-definition in the antebellum period; most such

works were written by black men who had successfully escaped southern slavery to become free members of US society in the north. The narratives illustrated the possibility of mounting a successful fight against the institution of slavery and were therefore also popular with anti-slavery and abolitionist activists.

2. (p. xxviii) *WM LLOYD GARRISON:* William Lloyd Garrison, author of the Preface to the *Narrative,* was a white abolitionist, who supported an immediate end to slavery with no compensation of any kind to slaveholders. Garrison saw the US Constitution as a "pro-slavery" document that protected rather than undercut the institution of slavery.

CHAPTER I

1. (p. 3) *I have no accurate knowledge of my age:* By law, slaves were "chattel"— property like any other owned "thing," and therefore, the exact date of a slave's birth often was not recorded. Likewise, slave children were routinely separated from and, therefore, sometimes only possessed minimal knowledge of their mothers or fathers, who might even have been sold away from them and moved to other locations. In fact, slaves sometimes had more detailed biographical information about white owners' families, although this was likely considered a necessary strategy for survival (for example, to be aware of individual whites' temperaments, likes, or dislikes).

2. (p. 5) *the children of slave women shall in all cases follow the condition of their mothers:* Although Douglass' father was reputed to have been white, individuals born of slave women were slaves by law.

3. (p. 6) *overseer:* An overseer was a supervisor of slave workers on a plantation; typically, this individual was a local white man who did not own property himself; in many ways, the white overseer was only slightly more elevated in the social hierarchy than a black slave, but as overseer, he possessed the power to order and chastise slaves.

CHAPTER VI

1. (p. 27) *city slave:* The mythical or stereotypical view of slavery places it in a rural plantation setting, but slaves were also utilized in a variety of tasks in cities; for example, Douglass was specifically trained to work as a ship's caulker on the docks in Baltimore. One of the uniquely beneficial aspects of urban slavery from the perspective of the slave was the relative "freedom" slaves enjoyed in cities; for Douglass, residence in a city made it possible for him to learn to read, an invaluable key to free identity.

CHAPTER VIII

1. (p. 35) *he left no will as to the disposal of his property:* As property, slaves were "distributed" according to the desires expressed in a will or according to

county or state law. In some cases, slaves were manumitted (freed) in a deceased owner's will, but often they were sold to pay taxes or debts with the remaining distributed among family members.

2. (p. 37) *slave for life:* Slaves were also slaves for life: from birth to death.

CHAPTER IX

1. (p. 44) *breaking young slaves:* A discontented or recalcitrant slave was considered to have a negative impact on other slaves and therefore on productivity and order; every effort was made to "break" a slave considered to have potential value before selling such a slave to avoid the spread of discontent and rebellion among other slaves.

CHAPTER X

1. (p. 56) *holidays:* Slaves worked long days and typically worked at least six days a week, but certain holidays were lavishly celebrated with the expectation that slaves would demonstrate gratitude by working hard and not attempting to run away or, worse, provoke widespread rebellion.

2. (p. 70) *freemen:* Another myth is that in the antebellum period all blacks were slaves. In fact, by the time of the Civil War, although four million blacks were slaves in the South, there was also a population of five hundred thousand free blacks, the vast majority of whom lived in the North. Douglass met his wife, a free black woman, in Baltimore. He also worked with free black men on the docks.

CHAPTER XI

1. (p. 76) *hiring my time:* On occasion, slave owners permitted slaves to "hire out" to a free employer; the slave typically received a small percentage of the salary, with the lion's share going to the slave's owner. Douglass used the experience to prepare himself for life as a free man, but in some instances, owners permitted slaves to use their earnings to purchase themselves and thereby pay their way out of slavery.

BASED ON THE BOOK

OTHER WRITINGS IN THE SAME GENRE

DOUGLASS PUBLISHED THREE AUTOBIOGRAPHIES IN ALL; IN ADDITION TO the *Narrative*, he also published *My Bondage and My Freedom* (1855) and two versions of *Life and Times of Frederick Douglass* (1881 and 1892). Why three autobiographies? The second was written to fill in some of the deliberately oblique references in the *Narrative* to specific individuals and places, especially those connected to Douglass' successful escape from slavery; in the *Narrative*, Douglass omitted these specifics to protect the identities of those who had helped him and to avoid creating unnecessary obstacles to those who sought freedom after him. In the final autobiography, Douglass also included details of his life in the decades subsequent to his escape and the beginning of his involvement in the abolition movement.

OTHER WRITINGS IN OTHER GENRES

A prolific writer, Douglass wrote countless speeches, as well as editorials in a variety of newspapers (the *North Star, Frederick Douglass' Paper, Douglass' Monthly,* and the *New National Era*), pamphlets (including the anti-lynching *The Lessons of the Hour*), and fiction (*The Heroic Slave*). *The Heroic Slave* was Douglass' only known work of fiction and was written for the collection *Autographs for Freedom* published by the

Rochester Ladies' Anti-Slavery Society. The short work was loosely based on an actual shipboard slave rebellion and sought, as indicated by the title, to portray the slave seeking his freedom as someone involved in an honorable fight for individual liberty.

OTHER SLAVE NARRATIVES

The slave narrative is foundational to both African-American literature and history, as well as to American literature and history, more generally. Douglass' *Narrative* is often compared to the iconic *Autobiography of Benjamin Franklin* in terms of the slave narrative's practical illustration of how exactly a person defined as property under the law could take matters into most typically his, but also her, hands and construct free identity under the law, and sometimes achieve spectacular success besides. The most well-known of the slave narratives besides Douglass' is William Wells Brown's *Narrative of William W. Brown, A Slave, Written by Himself* (1847), which describes Brown's disparate "jobs" as a slave, the most striking of which is certainly Brown's time spent working for a Missouri slave trader. Of the narratives written by women, Sojourner Truth's vies with her own speech "Ar'n't I A Woman?" (1851, 1863) as the most often cited; perhaps the notable aspect of Truth's "autobiography" is that it was written by Truth's amanuensis, Olive Gilbert, because Truth herself was illiterate. Although typically thought of as antebellum literature, *Interesting Narrative of the Life of Olaudah Equiano,* published in 1798, is crucial because it links the experiences of a slave kidnapped from Africa as a child, who was nevertheless able to gain liberty and personhood, to Douglass' narrative of his experiences as an American slave.

TELEVISION

Part of A&E's Biography series, "Frederick Douglass: Biography of a Slave" is a fifty-minute DVD providing an overview of Douglass' life from slavery to freedom. Produced in 2005, the documentary is based on the *Narrative* and includes commentary by scholars and biographers. "Presenting Mr. Frederick Douglass: The Lesson of the Hour" (1994), which was produced as part of the PBS series *Bill Moyers Journal*, re-creates Douglass' abolitionist orations in a theatrical setting. PBS' *When the Lion Wrote History* (1998) is a ninety-minute depiction of Douglass' life from slavery to abolitionist orator.

MUSIC AND ART

In 2010 noted jazz bassist Tyrone Brown composed *A Sky with More Stars—Suite for Frederick Douglass*. Performed and recorded by the Tyrone Brown Ensemble, pieces are set to speeches originally made by Douglass. The chamber jazz ensemble interprets events from Douglass' life through music, including songs titled "North Star," "Independence Day," "The Last Time I Saw Lincoln," and "The Race Problem."

Artist Jacob Lawrence's The Frederick Douglass and Harriet Tubman Series of 1938–1941 contains thirty-two paintings of Douglass, completed in 1938 and 1939, and thirty-one of Tubman, completed in 1939 and 1940, with captions by Lawrence describing his interpretation of emancipation, the relevance of Douglass and Tubman to his own era, and the continuing inspirational impact of these two historical figures.

In 2010, a bronze statue of Douglass by Gabriel Koren and a memorial designed by Algernon Miller were unveiled in the midst of the Frederick Douglass Circle, located at the northwest corner of Central Park (110th Street and Eighth Avenue) in Manhattan.

FURTHER READING

ANDREWS, WILLIAM L. *Critical Essays on Frederick Douglass.* Boston: G.K. Hall, 1991.

BLASSINGAME, JOHN, ED. *The Frederick Douglass Papers.* New Haven: Yale University Press, 1979.

CHESNUTT, CHARLES WADDELL. *Frederick Douglass: A Biography.* Lexington, KY: Pentleton House Publishing, 2011.

CURRY, LEONARD P. *The Free Black in Urban America, 1800–1850.* Chicago: University of Chicago Press, 1986.

DOUGLASS, FREDERICK. *Life and Times.* New York: Crowell-Collier, 1962.

———. *My Bondage and My Freedom.* Barnes & Noble Classics. New York: Barnes & Noble, 2005.

GARFIELD, DEBORAH, AND RAFIA ZAFAR, EDS. *Harriet Jacobs and Incidents in the Life of A Slave Girl: New Critical Essays.* Cambridge: Cambridge University Press, 1996.

GREENBERG, KENNETH S. *Nat Turner: A Slave Rebellion in History and Memory.* New York: Oxford University Press, 2003.

HUGGINS, NATHAN. *Slave and Citizen: The Life of Frederick Douglass.* New York: Harper-Collins, 1980.

KING, WILMA. *Stolen Childhood: Slave Youth in Nineteenth-Century America.* Bloomington: Indiana University Press, 1995.

LEE, MAURICE S., ED. *The Cambridge Companion to Frederick Douglass.* Cambridge: Cambridge University Press, 2009.

MARTIN, WALDO E. *The Mind of Frederick Douglass.* Chapel Hill: University of North Carolina Press, 1982.

MCFEELY, WILLIAM S. *Frederick Douglass.* New York: W. W. Norton, 1991.

MEIER, AUGUST. *Negro Thought in America, 1880–1915.* Ann Arbor: University of Michigan Press, 1966.

NORTHUP, SOLOMON. *Twelve Years a Slave.* Barnes & Noble Library of Essential Reading. New York: Barnes & Noble, Inc., 2009.

OAKES, JAMES. *The Radical and the Republican: Frederick Douglass, Abraham Lincoln, and the Triumph of Antislavery Politics.* New York: W. W. Norton, 2008.

OSOFSKY, GILBERT, ED. *Puttin' on Ole Massa: The Slave Narratives of Henry Bibb, William Wells Brown, and Solomon Northup.* New York: Harper, 1969.

SUNDQUIST, ERIC, ED. *Frederick Douglass: New Literary and Historical Essays.* Cambridge: Cambridge University Press, 1990.

TRUTH, SOJOURNER. *Narrative of Sojourner Truth.* Barnes & Noble Classics. New York: Barnes & Noble, 1998.

YETMAN, NORMAN, ED. *Voices From Slavery: 100 Authentic Slave Narratives.* New York: Dover, 1999.